CP   lot 22⁵⁰

Dawn and the Darkest Hour

A Study of Aldous Huxley

DAWN AND
THE DARKEST HOUR

A Study of Aldous Huxley

by
GEORGE WOODCOCK

FABER AND FABER
3 Queen Square
London

*First published in 1972
by Faber and Faber Limited
3 Queen Square London WC1
Printed in Great Britain by
Western Printing Services Limited
Bristol*

ISBN 0 571 08939 9

Acknowledgements

For permission to quote from the works and letters of Aldous Huxley and from *Aldous Huxley – A Memorial Volume*, I am grateful to Chatto & Windus and to Mrs. Laura Huxley.

The books from which I have quoted with this permission are *Letters of Aldous Huxley*, ed. Grover Smith, *Literature and Science, Point Counter Point, Antic Hay, Eyeless in Gaza, Heaven and Hell, Themes and Variations, The Doors of Perception, The Art of Seeing, Along the Road, Verses and a Comedy, Crome Yellow, Limbo, Little Mexican, Mortal Coils, Those Barren Leaves, Two or Three Graces, Jesting Pilate, Proper Studies, Do What You Will, Music at Night, Brief Candles, Brave New World, Beyond the Mexique Bay, The Olive Tree, Texts and Pretexts, Ends and Means, What Are You Going to Do About It?, After Many a Summer, Grey Eminence, Time Must Have a Stop, The Perennial Philosophy, Science, Liberty and Peace, Ape and Essence, Adonis and the Alphabet, The Devils of Loudun, The Genius and the Goddess, Island* and *Brave New World Revisited*.

I would like further to express my appreciation to Mrs. Mary Anne Anderson for her assistance in the preparation and typing of this book.

Contents

PART I

CHAPTER ONE

Introduction

To read Aldous Huxley forty years ago in his prime as a novelist, was to become aware immediately of a mind divided and searching. And at no time did this aspect of Huxley's writing become more evident than when his search led him in a direction unfamiliar and even repugnant to those who had admired him as a personification of the critical spirit in the decades between the great wars. I remember, when *Eyeless in Gaza* was published thirty-four years ago, reading it with bewilderment and a sense of betrayal.

I was twenty-four, emerging from that provincial innocence which the long sleep of rural England still preserved into my adolescent years in the Twenties. Huxley's early novels, from *Crome Yellow* to *Point Counter Point*, had accelerated the mental liberation which began for me with the belated reading of Wells and Shaw. 'He seemed to represent the kind of freedom which might be termed *freedom from*,' said Stephen Spender of one's youthful impressions of Huxley: 'freedom from all sorts of things such as conventional orthodoxies, officious humbug, sexual taboos, respect for establishments.'

I had felt also, without completely understanding it, the characteristic ambivalence of novels like *Crome Yellow* and *Antic Hay*, the sense of delicious treason in the knowledge that Huxley was fascinated as well as repelled by the life of meretricious intellectuality and futile moneyed gaiety which he portrayed so sardonically and yet, at times, so seductively. I was dazzled–how could one be less?–to encounter the mind of one of the great polymaths of our age as it played over an encyclopaedic variety of subjects; I was stirred to endless speculation by the discussions and pontifications on novel, daring themes with which Huxley's characters perpetually bored and entertained each other, and which spilled over into the brilliant essays in collections like *Proper Studies* and *Do What You Will*. I doubt if I have since read any writer who has offered such manifold stimulation as one found in Huxley when one began to read him at the age of eighteen.

Even *Brave New World* on its appearance in 1932 I admired mainly for its intellectual agility, as a brilliant feat of futurist fantasy, combined perhaps with a little cautionary fun at the scientific world with which Huxley had such close links through his grandfather and his brother Julian. I gave as little thought as most other readers then to the seriousness of its criticism of the scientific method, or, for that matter, to the prospect–which became alarmingly evident only ten years later in the 1940's–that what one read as a fantasy might actually be a prophecy, and that if politicians and scientists did not combine for more positive ends than had moved them up to the present, an intellectual and spiritual wilderness of the kind Huxley portrayed might be not six centuries away, but in the immediate future.

My attitude to Huxley was complicated by the fact that in my own way–as a libertarian pacifist–I accepted the political militancy of the Thirties. I applauded Huxley's abandonment in 1935 of his political agnosticism, and his willingness to advocate not only militant resistance to war, but also a policy of general social reorganization aimed at replacing the institution of the State, with its built-in tendency to coercion and bellicosity, by a libertarian society in which–as he later said in prefacing the 1946 edition of *Brave New World*–'economics would be decentralist and Henry-Georgian, politics Kropotkinesque and cooperative.' When war came I even took part at some temperamental cost in experimental communities of pacifists which followed the same lines as the co-operative community planned by Mr. Propter in Huxley's war's-eve novel, *After Many a Summer*. In these communities we aimed to oppose the negation of the war by building the nuclei of an alternative society in what we called–using a phrase invented by Huxley's quondam friend John Middleton Murry–'the interstices of the totalitarian order'. We failed, but the point I would make is that at the end of the Thirties, despite the rival attractions of fashionable Marxism, a great many young people regarded Huxley not only as one of the finest novelists of the time, but also as a prophet who in many ways spoke on their behalf.

He expressed with admirable skill the disillusionment with war and with the society that produced it which characterized the Twenties and ripened through the Depression. Up to *Brave New World*, his novels seemed inspired by that liberal scepticism which survived as a heritage from the Enlightenment and from the great evolutionary controversy to which, by descent from Darwin's great champion, he was peculiarly related. At the same time, his belated conversion to active war resistance seemed to place him within the parallel tradition of radical political dissent that stemmed in England from Godwin, the Chartists and the largely pacifist British socialist movement.

Then, in the summer of 1936, on the eve of the Spanish Civil War, *Eyeless in Gaza* was published. The man who had seemed the most gleamingly rational of all the writers to emerge into prominence during the 1920's (only compare the intellectual clarity of any of his earlier novels with the manifold obscurities of Virginia Woolf, James Joyce and even D. H. Lawrence!) had written a novel describing a conversion to mystical religion. He had also suggested–with obvious didactic intent–that such a spiritual evolution was not merely compatible with the pacifist and decentralist politics which he had recently been preaching in print and on public platforms, but was perhaps the only condition under which they could become effective.

In the atmosphere of the later Thirties, as the Spanish War heightened in intensity and became the focus of a passionate mental agony among European intellectuals, the radical young became what Huxley later called 'nothing-but' men. Whether we termed ourselves Communists, Socialists, Anarchists or Militant Pacifists, we not only believed in the ultimate power of scientific progress to lead us to Utopia; we also saw no problem that the reasonable application of social planning could not solve. Perhaps we did not hold with Rousseau that man was naturally good, but we did hold that he was naturally social; where he gave the appearance of being antisocial, we believed, the fault lay not in him but in the perverting effect of artificial and coercive institutions, puritanical rules of behaviour and unjust economic systems. Remove the institutions, clean up the economics, expel the puritans; then the naturally co-operative qualities of man could produce a society that would work without coercion and merely from its inherent tendency to mutual aid. We did not pause to consider how it was that man– if he were so naturally inclined to live peacefully and helpfully with his fellows–had contrived to build up such a remarkable variety of social and political institutions based on power, domination and violence, and had so rarely, in the great sweep of history, achieved a society that operated by mutual aid alone. We were not–I realize in looking back– very different in our attitudes from the radical youth of today. It was because of this naïve confidence in human reason and idealism that swept over us in the Thirties (in spite of the hysterical evil that was transforming Germany, in spite of the corruption of the Russian revolution displayed by the Moscow Trials) that we were disturbed and disappointed at what seemed a retreat into obscurantism on the part of one of the writers we most admired.

It seemed another case of the Lost Leader. But Huxley was too independent ever to have posed as a leader, and too speculative ever to become a Lost Leader, as we might have recognized if we had interpreted correctly the ambivalence of his early novels. His great virtue–the kind of virtue that did not shine brightly in such a period–was the combination of honesty and courage with which he moved from stage to stage in a highly personal intellectual progress. He never feared to reverse an opinion, to appear in opposition to his own past; he had that willingness to accept the appearance of self-contradiction which has always been the mark of an independent and creative thinker.

Long before the fate of Republican Spain had led quasi-Communist writers like W. H. Auden and Stephen Spender to agonizing reappraisals of their philosophical positions, Huxley had recognized that there is more to the human condition than bread alone, or bread and political freedom, or even bread and art. The cult of the body he had always mistrusted; there are few modern books so permeated with a sense of the vulnerability and corruptibility of the flesh as Huxley's novels. The cult of the mind he had begun to mistrust–largely because his own mental agility made every intellectual trick seem so easy–by the time he became friendly with D. H. Lawrence in 1926. For a few years Lawrence's influence drew him to a kind of vitalist limbo where, still declaring his faith in reason, he sketched out in *Do What You Will* and in the speeches of the Lawrencian Rampion in *Point Counter Point* a philosophy of balanced living that went as far in constructing a moral system as was possible without a religious foundation. It did not go far enough for Huxley, who reasoned himself eventually into two drastic conclusions. First, he abandoned a cherished tradition of the Huxley clan by recognizing that the process of abstraction implicit in the scientific method actually diverted men from perceiving the realities of existence. This he derived largely from Lawrence. He also reached, as independently as a man of omnivorous reading ever reaches a mental goal, the conclusion that man's miseries were due to the lack of a spiritual dimension to his existence.

In reasoning thus, Huxley did not feel that he was escaping into the mental isolation of which others accused him. Far from it, he saw himself joining the great invisible church of men and women from all races, religions and times, who have embraced what he termed the Perennial Philosophy. Often during his later life he was to expound that philosophy: its essential doctrines were stated with the succinctness of maxims in the introduction he wrote in 1947 to a translation of the *Bhagavad Gita* by Swami Prabhavananda and Christopher Isherwood (another defector from the political orthodoxies of the Thirties).

First: the phenomenal world of matter and of individualized consciousness—the world of things and animals and men and even gods—is the manifestation of a Divine Ground within which all partial realities have their being, and apart from which they would be nonexistent.

Second: human beings are capable not merely of knowing *about* the Divine Ground by inference; they can also realize its existence by a direct intuition, superior to discursive reasoning. This immediate knowledge unites the knower with that which is known.

Third: man possesses a double nature, a phenomenal ego and an eternal Self, which is the inner man, the spirit, the spark of divinity within the soul. It is possible for a man, if he so desires, to identify himself with the spirit and therefore with the Divine Ground, which is of the same or like nature with the spirit.

Fourth: man's life on earth has only one end and purpose, to identify himself with his eternal Self and so to come to unitive knowledge of the Divine Ground.

In hindsight, away from the literary ambiance and the political passions of the Thirties, one can follow more clearly the path that brought Huxley to this destination. His exploration of the apparent meaninglessness of man's fate and his universe had been as thorough as that of any French absurdist. From the early brightness of *Crome Yellow*—which had struck one as a *jeu d'esprit* as gratuitous as *The Importance of Being Earnest*—his vision darkened, with only a faint light gleaming from Calamy's private Thebaid in *Those Barren Leaves*; *Point Counter Point*, the terminal novel of this first period, projected a sardonic pessimism which made John Atkins describe it justly as Huxley's 'descent into Hell'. It was indeed a parallel to the classic journey into the underworld that in heroic myths precedes victory and in religious myths precedes enlightenment; it was in many ways a novel of no return.

As Huxley surveyed the impasse into which even Lawrencian vitalism had led him, he must have seen three possible paths before him. He could lapse into silence: but he was by nature, vocation and habit a writer, and, as he said long afterwards to Atkins, he did not 'think that

writing is in any way incompatible with understanding'. He could
continue with diminishing vigour to repeat himself as a chronicler of
futility; there is always a market for cynicism. But Huxley never wrote
merely for the sake of writing or the sake of fame, and even when,
without false shame, he worked for money, he wrote only of what
interested him. He had to go where his thoughts led him, and at the
beginning of the Thirties they led him along a path quite different from
any he had followed before.

The change in direction was marked–though none at the time read
the sign correctly–by the appearance of *Brave New World*. *Brave New
World*, expressing the neo-Lawrencian rejection of science as the basis
of moral values, stood on the borderline between the Peacockian novels,
which examined the negations of the educated and moneyed strata of
contemporary western society (for Huxley knew and wrote little of
the submerged nine-tenths of his world), and the later novels in which
the materialistic existence typical of our times was always balanced by
the search for positive moral existence. The latter tendency may not be
immediately evident in *Brave New World* itself, for the society which
the novel portrays has abandoned even the inadequate spiritual and
intellectual goals of the twentieth century for a mess of synthetic
happiness, while John, the savage from the Indian reservation in New
Mexico who embodies the contrary attitude, presents a strange,
ineffectual combination of the better values of the past (screened through
his solitary readings of Shakespeare) and the mindless primitivism he
has absorbed from an unchanging and artificially preserved Indian
tradition. It is the form more than the content of *Brave New World* that
is important in the light of Huxley's later development. The book is a
Utopia, even if a negative one, and Huxley will return constantly to
the genre as a convenient fictional frame for portraying sometimes the
search for a positive society and sometimes its diametrical opposite. In
positive form it will be represented by Mr. Propter and his co-operative
commune in *After Many a Summer*. It will swing back into negation in
Ape and Essence when the realm of Belial is established as a savage
anti-Utopia among the survivors of nuclear holocaust in post-World
War III California. And then, in *Island*, Huxley's last novel and almost
his final book, all the evils he has been warning against since the late
Thirties–over-population and coercive politics, militarism and mechan-
ization, the destruction of the environment and the slavish worship of
science–will find their opposites in the gentle and doomed Utopia of
the insular realm of Pala.

There is of course another way in which *Brave New World* sets a pattern for Huxley's later novels. It is the first among his imaginative works to be avowedly didactic, to teach a lesson we are invited to follow. In his earlier novels Huxley had been at great pains to construct works that were artistically pleasing, and he found in his patterns of ideas developed in conversation, and of behaviour observed in emotional detachment, the means of creating–if not novels in the orthodox sense–at least a kind of fiction that had its appealing forms. *Point Counter Point* in particular was a work of impressive literary artifice, though, as Huxley's forgotten contemporary Humbert Wolfe once said less accurately of Spring, it has 'all of beauty Save the heart'. But in *Brave New World* the form is less emphatic because it is deliberately less elaborated. Huxley has a lesson he is anxious to teach, and he is willing to sacrifice something of elegance, something of pattern, to make sure that his homily does not go unheard. He is facing, as he will face with growing acuteness, the dilemma of the writer, possessed with religious and moral convictions to which he must give expression, yet aware that in such matters the teacher is always the enemy of the artist. He will solve the question by changing his views on the necessity of artistic perfection.

Even before he explicitly changed his views he had changed his practice, for all the novels that follow *Brave New World* are homiletic rather than artistic in intent, and if, as I now believe, *Eyeless in Gaza* is Huxley's best novel even in purely literary terms, this must be regarded as accidental, for his prime intention was to tell the tale of a conversion in a way that would leave no doubt of its implications in terms of what the Buddhist would call Right Actions proceeding from Right Understanding.

Though the novel is written in only obliquely autobiographical terms, the conversion that *Eyeless in Gaza* portrays is obviously a reflection of Huxley's own, of that extraordinary inversion of his view of existence which took place after the death of Lawrence. Huxley's actual interest in mystical religion was nothing new. As an undergraduate at Balliol twenty years before the writing of *Eyeless in Gaza* he had read many western and oriental religious texts. Later he was to use these books as material for constructing *The Perennial Philosophy*, but in his youth he read them with a quizzical eye; mystical experiences, like the amorous habits of the cuttlefish in which he displayed an equal knowledgeability, were among the oddities of life that provoked his curiosity and satisfied his sense of the grotesque. He read them in order to criticize, to debunk, to mock. But ten years later, by the time he wrote *Those Barren Leaves*, the way of the mystic began to appear to him in a much more positive light. He was not yet converted, but at least he was willing to accept that some kind of undogmatic religious life might be as good a way of dealing with one's sense of the meaninglessness of existence as—say—the lucky but haphazard insights that emerge from the life of art. In his 'Uncle Spencer', Huxley even foreshadowed his own achievement in *Eyeless in Gaza* by half-prophesying: 'Some day, it may be, the successful novelist will write about man's relation to God.'

The real conversion came later, and Huxley was obviously still undergoing its agonies while he tried to give them expression in *Eyeless in Gaza*. He started to write that book in 1932, and there is evidence to suggest that it was originally planned as something very different from the novel that emerged out of four years of creative agony of a kind Huxley had never experienced before. He did not finish it until towards the end of 1935, after long interruptions due to mental depressions and disturbances of a kind he had never experienced before. This agony of the early Thirties was no merely personal grief; it was, rather, a spiritual climacteric not unlike that which accompanied the conversion of Leo Tolstoy, so vividly represented as the dark night of mental and spiritual agony through which Levin in *Anna Karenina* passed before he came ultimately to a sense of inner peace and certainty. The result was the most complexly constructed and the most psychologically convincing novel Huxley ever wrote.

I shall return to a closer consideration of *Eyeless in Gaza*, but the point I wish to make now is that the novel can be seen as the Great Divide in Huxley's creative life. Geological divides have two aspects, of course, according to whether one crosses or follows them. Crossing, one rises on one side and descends on the other, and this is the way the literary critic is likely to approach the Huxleian Divide. For his novels grow in complexity and quality—with the special exception of *Brave New World*—as they proceed from *Crome Yellow* to *Eyeless in Gaza*, and decline just as steadily from that novel through *After Many a Summer* and *Time Must Have a Stop* to the splendidly intentioned bathos of *Island*.

The reason, of course, is that in the latter thirty years of his life Huxley quite deliberately turned from the role of writer as artist to that of writer as teacher. One can even present the change statistically. Among the *first* ten books Huxley published, between 1916 and 1924, nine could be classed as imaginative (fiction or verse) and only one as expository (and that merely a collection of light occasional pieces written while Huxley was assistant editor of the *Athenaeum*). Huxley's last ten books, appearing between 1948 and 1963, included only three examples of imaginative writing (all fiction); the rest were essays of varying lengths devoted to the social and philosophical questions which Huxley now found so important. Even this count is deceptive, for all the three novels Huxley completed in his last period—*Ape and Essence*, *The Genius and the Goddess* and *Island*—were *romans à thèse*, didactic to a degree beyond anything he wrote in his earlier period.

By this time, in fact, Huxley had abandoned the life of art. He had never been an aesthete—such a stance would hardly have been compatible with the fiction of ideas to which he always aspired—but, as he told two enquirers in 1942, he cared, as a young man, 'supremely for knowledge for its own sake, for the play of ideas, for the arts of literature, painting and music', whereas by the time of writing this letter his attitude had changed. He could no longer pursue such things disinterestedly.

> For some years now [he continued] I have felt a certain dissatisfaction with these things, have felt that even the great masterpieces were somehow inadequate. Recently I have begun to know something about the reality in relation to which such things as art and general knowledge can be appraised. Inadequate in and for themselves, these activities of the mind can be seen in their true perspective when looked at from the vantage point of mysticism. 'Those barren leaves of science and of art' are barren only when regarded as ultimate ends.

Later on Huxley was not content merely to give art a subsidiary place in his philosophic scheme. Like Tolstoy, he began to question its moral justification. True, he never committed the kind of aberrations of fanaticism into which Tolstoy was led. He never demanded a literature that would lower its standards or debase its language to give moral lessons to hypothetically simple people (though he was always willing to write on his own terms for popular magazines). And his inbred sense of proportion saved him from such a philistinism as Tolstoy displayed in his condemnation of Shakespeare. Instead, in his last essay, completed the week before his death, 'Shakespeare and Religion', he attempted to place Shakespeare securely within the pattern of the Perennial Philosophy.

Yet, as he grew older, there were times when Huxley had his doubts about even the best works of art. Partly, he felt, they were inadequate instruments in the search for enlightenment. He expressed this thought a few years after his 'conversion' by means of an image which showed no diminution in his power of artifice.

> The more I think of art [he said at the founding of Gerald Heard's Trabuco College in 1942] I realize that, though artists do establish contact with spiritual reality, they establish it unconsciously. Beauty is imprisoned, as it were, within the white spaces between the lines of a poem, between the notes of music, in the apertures between groups of sculpture. This function or talent is unconscious. They throw a net and catch something, though the net is trivial. . . . But one wants to go further. One wants to have a conscious taste of those holes between the strings of the net.

More than that, Huxley realized that art flourishes on human misery and folly; if we are to accept the beauty of its flowers, we must accept the corruption from which they spring, and this he was increasingly unwilling to do. He would rather live in some Switzerland of the spirit, where artists flourished rarely but wars never came, than inhabit the Frances and Germanies of the intellect with their splendour built on human wretchedness. The logical consequence of such a view was necessarily a literature in which the aesthetic element is always sub-ordinated to the moral message, and this is the case in all of Huxley's books after *Eyeless in Gaza*.

Such a renunciation would be impossible to imagine in the case of a Compleat Artist like James or Joyce. But Huxley, while to the end he took a pride in the craft of writing, had never considered himself exclusively the artist. The fact that he was as enamoured of knowledge for its own sake as of any of the arts suggested already a polygamous relationship with the muses, an insecure loyalty. There were times when he was as much aware as his strictest critics that—as he put it himself—'I am not a born novelist, but some other kind of man of letters possessing enough ingenuity to be able to simulate a novelist's behaviour not too convincingly.' Perhaps, indeed, he was too harsh to himself in such a judgement, made after he had reached the Divide, for, whatever kind of fiction writer one may class him, there is no doubt that *Eyeless in Gaza* and his earlier novels in the Peacockian vein are the best English examples of a kind of intellectual-moralist fiction more widely practised on the continent of Europe. Indeed, it is in a continental tradition, that of the *homme de lettres* (his own 'some kind of man of letters') that he really belongs, the writer who is proud first of all of his sheer ability to write, and is willing to apply that ability to any task which seems at the time important, without feeling in any way demeaned if–instead of a novel or a poem–he happens to write a political tract or a newspaper article, provided always he is saying something that seems worth recording.

Given his desire to apprehend the truths that art finds only unconsciously, Huxley would not have shared the idea that once he had reached the Divide of his career, the journey was downward. Rejecting the aesthetic criteria that would make inevitable such an admission, he chose to see himself travelling along the ridge, with the chance of climbing more than one peak of insight before he reached the end of his journey. He had not entered these mountains of speculation to become a hermit, like Calamy in *Those Barren Leaves*. On the contrary, he found the views stupendous and revealing, and because of the greater understanding of the world and its problems which his new path gave him, he felt he could reveal more clearly the dangers that beset mankind through the retention of moral and political errors and through the destruction of an environment in which man had his proper place and no more.

Huxley perceived no real division between his views of the life of the spirit and his ideas of what should be done by sensible beings in the phenomenal world. He saw both as projections of man's dual nature; it seemed to him that the intuition leading to the knowledge of divinity was no less rational than the intelligence that sought to reshape existence so as to reach the limit of human happiness.

Certainly, though a perceptible decline in Huxley's powers as an imaginative writer cannot be denied, there appeared little loss, to the end of his life, in his power of argument and exposition. His remarkable intelligence, differently deployed than in his youth, remained acute as ever; his knowledge as broad, though otherwise channelled; his power of fertile generalization even more impressive than in the past. The retreat into a religio-political conservatism resembling that of his friend T. S. Eliot which was expected by those who were troubled by *Eyeless in Gaza*, did not materialize. Indeed, on many issues Huxley worked ahead of his time. Long before the Civil Disobedience movement changed American society in the 1960s, he had accepted the transforming power of non-violent rebellion. World problems like population growth, the exhaustion of resources, the destruction of the environment, now subjects of urgent public discussion, might have been solved if men had listened to Huxley's warnings twenty years ago.

The decentralist society which fashionable anarchists like Paul Good-
man and perpetual student rebels like Tom Hayden now advocate he
had already sketched out before the end of the Thirties. Partly from
scientific curiosity and partly from a desire to open any door that might
lead to a mystical experience matching his rational understanding of the
contemplative path, Huxley was one of the pioneer experimenters with
psychedelic drugs and certainly the first writer of distinction to describe
his experiences with them. If the young rebels of today have spiritual
ancestors, among them – in all but their acceptance of violence – Huxley
has a usually unacknowledged place.

Distant as this later Huxley may appear from the young student who
in 1916 hoped that the 'nightmarish interruption of reality' produced
by World War I might be followed by 'a race of golden young men
and crystal young women', and remoter still from the novelist who in
the Twenties watched the gold tarnishing and the crystal cracking in a
new nightmare of disillusionment, he was in reality the same man.
Rebirth is the metaphor we use to describe the process of conversion,
but the seed of new birth germinates in the unregenerate past. Conversion is never a break; it is merely a redirection. Many of Tolstoy's
critics mistakenly assumed that a great gulf divided the converted Leo
from the unconverted Count, but the continuity is unbroken, and the
two aspects of the man fit together like the dark and light sides of a
face seen in lamplight. Some attitudes were inverted, some modified;
few were entirely new. The same applies to Huxley. To understand him
completely we must see his life and work as a unity. In that way, not
only do his later teachings acquire the background that places them in
perspective, but his earlier works deepen as their half-conscious anticipations open into the future.

That unity is the more striking since both parts of Huxley's career
can be seen as a movement out of darkness towards light, a movement
that begins in the events of his early life. These events not only affected
his physical existence; they also became transformed into metaphors
that were powerful in shaping the thoughts and directing the spiritual
pilgrimage of a lifetime.

In the chapters that follow I shall begin by discussing those vital
aspects of Huxley's youth. I shall then turn to his writings and trace in
them not merely the arc of artistic achievement and decline, but also
the progress of a dedicated generalist seeking to bring all knowledge –
in so far as it lies within one man's compass – into a synthesis that will
give total meaning to existence. In the earlier chapters of criticism, up

to 1936, the expository works will tend to cluster round and illuminate the dominant novels. In the later chapters the situation will be reversed; if it is obvious that in the Twenties *Point Counter Point* was more important than *Do What You Will*, it is equally evident that in the Sixties *Island* derived its slight importance almost entirely from the fact that it brought into a convenient synthesis all the ideas on problems of human living and dying that had been scattered in a whole series of expository books from *Ends and Means* in 1937 to *Brave New World Revisited* in 1958.

Any book on an author whose influence one has felt strongly becomes inevitably something of a personal testament, though the criticism it contains may be all the sharper for having emerged from the undulations of passionate reaction. Having admitted to the alternation of admiration and rejection that shaped my view of Huxley in the Thirties, I feel an obligation at least to sketch out the philosophic standpoint from which I now take my view of him; my acceptance of *Eyeless in Gaza* as his best novel will, I hope, have removed the suspicion of surviving artistic bias.

I am still as strongly a pacifist, a social decentralist and a political libertarian as I was in 1936 and as Huxley remained to the end of his days; I have never disputed his warnings of the science-bred perils that threaten mankind and the earth even more darkly today than when he was alive. Yet I am convinced that the views of art and the artist's function which Huxley developed after 1936 were not only false in themselves, but also unfortunate in their effect on his work.

I am no longer, as I was in 1936, a militant agnostic who halted before atheism only because it seemed another dogmatic position. I believe now that God exists; the universe, in all its complexity and order, is not accidental. I have reached this conclusion not through any agonizing spiritual crisis, nor by any flash of revelation, but by rational inference, and mainly because, if I have found the acceptance of a shaping and inspiring intelligence difficult, I have found it impossible in any other terms to explain the patterns in which nature and existence arrange themselves. I recognize no personal God, I see no function in organized worship beyond the assertion of human fellowship, and if I recognize an efficacy in prayer I cannot dissociate this from my recognition of the existence of telepathic communication, and I cannot see either as more than unexplained aspects of the phenomenal world. If I see no reason to deny the occurrence of what we call mystical experiences, or to doubt the sincerity of those who describe such experiences as best they can, I equally see no reason to believe that they are more than psychological episodes or that the world they reveal is other than that of the human mind, which of course reflects, as all else does, the universal intelligence. Thus there are many ways in which I disagree with Huxley's view of the religious life. Yet I find his development of great psychological interest, and I admire above all the courage with which he embarked on a quest of dubious outcome that aroused first the mockery and afterwards no more than the grudging tolerance of the intellectual and literary world.

PART II

CHAPTER TWO

Twilight in a Golden Age

I

An ageing man in California, Huxley looked back with nostalgia to childhood in the twilight of Victorian England. He remembered it, seen from the brutal chaos of the 1940s, as 'the end of one of history's rare Golden Ages'. He was born in 1894, at Godalming in Surrey, near Charterhouse School, where his father Leonard Huxley was a teacher. But it was his mother Julia, daughter of Thomas Arnold the younger, who felt the pedagogic urge more strongly; at the turn of the century, when Aldous was seven years old, Leonard retired from teaching to take up the life of a man of letters, and Julia, who had been one of the first women to graduate from Oxford, founded the school that was to dominate the rest of her brief life and to remain as her monument. Prior's School, which she started, is still in operation.

In these careers of his parents, the future of Aldous Huxley was foreshadowed. In childhood, remembering his grandfather, and seeking to emulate his brother Julian, seven years older, he wished to become a biologist or a doctor, but the onset of near-blindness, when he was a little over sixteen, made both careers impossible, and he was to become, on a grander scale than either, a man of letters like his father Leonard and a teacher–though rarely with a classroom–like his mother Julia.

The world into which Aldous Huxley was born seemed delusively kind to people of his class. Perhaps, had he spent his childhood in a back-to-back terrace house in a north-country milltown or an insanitary tied cottage on a midland farm, he might not have looked back upon the 1890's and the Edwardian decade as a Golden Age. But for the middle class to which he belonged it was in many ways better than any succeeding age. Nearing the height of its prestige as an imperial power, England had not been involved in a major war–if one discounts the costly farce of the Crimean–for eighty years since Waterloo, and there seemed no reason why the Pax Britannica should not last even longer than the Pax Romana. Taxes were low, prices cheap, frontiers open, and servants easy to find. For those with money life had an ease, a grace, and a racy glamour that made the Edwardian age a Belle Époque, not only for France but for the whole of Europe. Later on, after the Great War, Huxley was to describe his caste–by then considerably impoverished–in terms of almost Orwellian contempt as 'that impecunious but dignified section of the upper-middle class which is in the habit of putting on dress clothes to eat–with the most studied decorum and out of porcelain and burnished silver–a dinner of dishwater and codfish, mock duck and cabbage'. But there is no evidence that life in the house of Leonard and Julia Huxley was ever so bleak, and what physical lacks and Victorian Spartanisms did exist were more than counterbalanced by the intellectual abundance of a resolutely literary household where many influences fertilely intertwined.

On one side there was the evolutionary tradition embodied in Thomas Henry Huxley, who died when Aldous was less than a year old, but whose memory was kept green through Aldous's childhood by the fact that Leonard was working for years on a biography of his father which he followed by a Life of the great botanist, Joseph Hooker, companion and friend of Thomas Henry and of the other paladins of the evolutionary controversy, Darwin and Tyndall, Wallace and Bates.

From the Arnold side the threads that wove into the ambiance of Aldous's childhood were more numerous and perhaps, in the end, more influential. In early-Victorian distance loomed the passionate shadow of great-grandfather Thomas–Arnold of Rugby–dead half a century by the time Aldous was born. As the formidable reformer of the English public schools, he not only left a direct mark on Aldous's childhood by shaping the system of education he endured; he also, like his son Thomas, recognized the necessity for the religious life, and, long before Aldous followed the same path, he decided that in education and in life the intellectual and the moral must not be divided, and that it is only within a field of spiritual awareness that they can be united.

The younger Thomas Arnold, Aldous's grandfather, was impelled to teaching more by paternal example than by vocation. The search for fulfilment led him to a vain quest as a pioneer in New Zealand and Tasmania; tempests of faith and doubt swept him into the Roman Church, and out of it, and in again, before he ended his life teaching in an Irish Catholic university as a colleague of Gerard Manley Hopkins.

Julia Sorell, daughter of the Governor of Tasmania, who had married Thomas Arnold in the Antipodes, refused to accompany his religious peregrinations, and when he left for Dublin she remained behind with her children in Oxford. Her three daughters were among the little girls whom Lewis Carroll loved to photograph; for the Arnold children he wrote one of his lesser works, *Sylvie and Bruno*. The oldest of the three, Mary Augusta, became Mrs. Humphry Ward, the celebrated late-Victorian novelist. As a child, Aldous was much attached to Aunt Mary, and lived with her for long periods, particularly after his mother's death in 1908. There is no reason to suggest that his aunt's example led Aldous to take up fiction, but there are curious affinities between these two apparently so different novelists. Aldous was to adopt his aunt's habit of incorporating thinly disguised living people into her novels and including incidents based on episodes in real life that would be known to at least some of her readers, so that, like hers, his books acquired the special interest of the *roman à clef*. It is significant of similar frames of mind, that Mrs. Humphry Ward's *Robert Elsmere* and Huxley's *Eyeless in Gaza* should both have turned on accounts of religious crises.

The most formidable of all the Arnolds, and perhaps intellectually the nearest to Aldous Huxley, was not a direct ancestor, but a great-uncle, the poet Matthew Arnold. Though he had died six years before Aldous was born, Matthew had attended the wedding of Leonard and Julia. There was an ironic aspect to this union of the Huxley and Arnold clans, a joining together of intellectual Montagus and Capulets, for Matthew Arnold and Thomas Henry Huxley had been the combatants in one of the classic confrontations of the Victorian age. Ostensibly it concerned the relative merits of the classical and scientific systems of education, but, as they disputed in the 1880s, Arnold and Huxley were basically concerned with that question which became so urgent to Aldous Huxley in the middle of the twentieth century–the possibility, as Thomas Henry expressed it in describing the fears of his opponents, that 'man's moral nature be debased by the increase of his wisdom'. The controversy between Huxley and Arnold, embodied in the former's *Science and Education* (1883) and in the latter's *Discourses in America* (1885), was so central to the preoccupations of the late Victorians that it acquired a special place in literary history and still remains a standard item in many North American college survey courses in English Literature.

Obviously the famous controversy had a personal relevance for both

Aldous and Julian Huxley, who throughout their careers were concerned with reconciling the sciences and the humanities in the academic sense, and with saving mankind from the perils induced by the amorality of the disinterested search for physical truth where it is not allied to an equally disinterested search for spiritual truth. Indeed, Aldous Huxley's last book, *Science and Literature*, which appeared hardly two months before his death in 1963, opened with a reference to the Arnold-Huxley debate, now almost eighty years in the past, and proceeded to review the whole question of the rivalry between literature and science, which had been revived by the dispute between C. P. Snow and F. R. Leavis.

By the end of his life Aldous Huxley had gone far beyond both his great forebears in his criticism of scientific presumptions. It is true that in 1932 he delivered a lecture on 'T. H. Huxley as a Man of Letters', in which he cautiously evaded all reference to the debate with Arnold, and concentrated on praising the stylistic virtues of his grandfather's works. Yet the same year, in *Brave New World*, he had castigated the presumptions of those who put their faith in science alone, and later, in *Ends and Means*, he declared that modern men saw the world as void of meaning because of the 'intellectual error . . . of identifying the world of science, a world from which all meaning and value has been deliberately excluded, with ultimate reality'. Thomas Henry Huxley certainly sensed this danger, but, archetypal agnostic that he was, could never provide any basis for meaning or value beyond the limited physical truths of nineteenth-century scientific materialism. Aldous never denied agnosticism. It suited the continued distrust of dogma which he attributed to his rationalistic upbringing. But he went beyond his grandfather when he described himself at the end of his life as 'an agnostic who aspired to be a gnostic – but a gnostic only on the mystical level, a gnostic without symbols, cosmologies or a pantheon'. By that aspiration towards gnosticism, he introduced an element completely alien to his grandfather's view of existence; he implicitly condemned as insufficient in the direction of wisdom, and as excessive in the direction of uncontrolled power, the pursuit of science without spiritual illumination.

There was obviously no such peril in Matthew Arnold's advocacy of the supremacy of the humanities over the sciences. And Aldous, who named his son Matthew, felt a strong affinity with his great-uncle the poet. There were occasions – and whole periods of his life – when he saw his own predicament embodied in the words of 'Stanzas from the Grande Chartreuse':

> *Wandering between two worlds, one dead,*
> *The other powerless to be born,*
> *With nowhere yet to rest my head . . .*

And in the unregenerate days when he talked of the world in quasi-absurdist terms as 'vast, beautiful and appalling' he must have appreciated the poignancy with which 'Dover Beach' drew to a close.

> *Ah, love, let us be true*
> *To one another! for the world, which seems*
> *To lie before us like a land of dreams,*
> *So various, so beautiful, so new,*
> *Hath really neither joy, nor love, nor light,*
> *Nor certitude, nor peace, nor help for pain;*
> *And we are here as on a darkling plain*
> *Swept by confused alarms of struggle and flight,*
> *Where ignorant armies clash by night.*

In 1961, when his house in California burned down and his library was lost, one of the first books Aldous Huxley asked his friends to get him was a volume of Arnold's poems. He had quoted freely from them in 1932 when he compiled his idiosyncratic anthology, *Texts and Pretexts*, and even then he discovered the other self to the pessimistic Arnold of 'Dover Beach': the Arnold of religious overtones, who could write:

> *Still doth the soul, from its lone fastness high,*
> *Upon our life a ruling effluence send;*
> *And when it fails, fight as we will, we die;*
> *And while it lasts, we cannot wholly end.*

And in 1938, after the travail that produced *Eyeless in Gaza*, he had talked explicitly of 'the Arnold of the mystical tradition'.

But the pattern of thought which Arnold devised in *Culture and Anarchy* to serve a world where traditional religion seemed to be losing all its relevance, Huxley in his later decades found lacking from his own mystical point of view. 'More and more'–claimed Arnold–'mankind will discover that we have to turn to poetry to interpret life for us, to console us, to sustain us.' Mankind has not in fact turned in this way to poetry, and Huxley would certainly have argued that it is because the burden is too great for poetry or any other art to bear. He would probably have agreed with Arnold's definition of culture as 'a study of perfection' and of perfection as 'a harmonious expansion of *all* the powers which make the beauty and worth of human nature', a harmony 'not consistent with the over-development of any one power at the expense of the rest'. Indeed, when he wrote *Do What You Will* in 1929, Huxley would have found this definition sufficient. By the time he wrote *Ends and Means* in 1937, however, he would have found it inadequate. His objection to any reliance on science or art, or on a culture based on both, without the deepening intuitive apprehension of 'the essential Suchness of the world', is implied in the termination of *Science and Literature*, the last statement of his viewpoint: 'Words are few and can only be arranged in certain conventionally fixed ways; the counterpoint of unique events is infinitely wide and their succession indefinitely long. That the purified language of science, or even the richer purified language of literature should ever be adequate to the givenness of the world and of our experience is, in the very nature of things, impossible.'

Matthew Arnold is never quoted in that key exposition of Huxley's post-conversion outlook, *The Perennial Philosophy*, but Matthew's father, Arnold of Rugby, does make an appearance, through a letter written to his biographer, Dean Stanley, in which he condemns fanaticism as 'idolatry' and declares that it breeds wickedness because it fails to develop freely all parts of our moral nature. Huxley criticizes what he regards as a cardinal omission on his great-grandfather's part; the ancestral Thomas, in laying a typically Arnoldian stress on the need for all-round moral development, has neglected what for the adherent of the Perennial Philosophy must be the essential consideration–that any form of self-will prevents 'recollectedness and non-attachment' and so closes the heart to 'the enlightening and liberating knowledge of Reality'. One suspects that Aldous Huxley in his final decades would have found this omission in all the Arnolds, as he certainly found it in all the Huxleys but himself.

2

All these questions were far in the future when Aldous was a child in the Surrey hills. From the *Memories* which Julian Huxley has recently written, and from the fragmentary references and oblique reflections in Aldous's novels, one gathers that, as Victorian childhoods went, theirs was a happy and relatively permissive one. Leonard Huxley retained his father's agnosticism, and Thomas Arnold's fluctuations into and out of Catholicism had turned his daughter Julia into a resolutely unsectarian Christian, intent on witnessing to her religion through direct and honest human relationships and through useful works. She was an excellent and dedicated teacher, and she transmitted her beliefs to her own children with tact and intelligence. The Victorian social pattern made a nominal deference to religious customs expedient; one of Aldous's earliest recollections was of vomiting during the sermon in the church at Godalming–'a precocious expression, no doubt, of anti-clericalism'. But at home religious teaching consisted mainly of simple prayers and a knowledge of the life of Jesus, accompanied by the inculcation of ideas of truth and unselfishness. As Julian remarked, in *Religion without Revelation:* 'I do not subscribe to Matthew Arnold's definition of religion as "morality tinged with emotion"; but that certainly formed part of the atmosphere of my upbringing.'

The Huxley interest in natural history and the Arnold interest in vigorous exercise as an aid to character building encouraged all the three boys–Julian, Trevenen and Aldous–to roam far afield through the Surrey countryside, on foot and by bicycle. There was even a religious aspect to such activities. 'Brought up as children in the Wordsworthian tradition,' Aldous remembered, 'we were taught to believe that a Sunday walk among the hills was somehow equivalent to churchgoing.' Great sweeps of unspoilt countryside stretched between places like Godalming and Farnham that were still mainly market towns with a few preparatory schools and a few houses of well-to-do city men. Mechanical transport of any kind was so rare on the roads that Aldous held in his memories of remote infancy the image of a steam roller, smelling of hot oil, as a remarkable and 'truly glorious object'. 'We knew our countryside by heart for an eight-mile radius round the house,' he recalled. 'We knew precisely where to find this flower or that bird.'

Perhaps it was because of those naturalizing expeditions of his boyhood that in later years Aldous could write with special understanding of Wordsworth at his best and his worst, criticizing in *Do What You Will* the smug and facile aspects of his cult of Nature, assessing in *Texts and Pretexts* his shams and honesties, yet acknowledging in *The Perennial Philosophy* that at times Wordsworth had gratuitous experiences of the Divine Ground, genuine theophanies of a kind granted sometimes to poets and sometimes to children, and to Wordsworth as both. When Huxley quotes approvingly in this context the opening lines of *Intimations of Immortality*, one feels, though he does not say so, that he too looks back on a childhood setting of preternatural brightness, a brightness more intense in recollection because he was to lose it when near-blindness struck him at the age of sixteen. One has to remember in reading Huxley's writings and observing their curious visual quality, that he was physically unable for the greater part of his life to see the surface of the earth except in vague forms and vague blocks of colour. All the descriptions of the English countryside one finds in his novels owe their details to the memories he carried on from boyhood days in Godalming. Read to its end, the first stanza of *Intimations* gives a movingly exact picture of the difference between the child Aldous and the young man Huxley who a few years later turned–half blind–to the profession of writing.

> *There was a time when meadow, grove, and stream,*
> *The earth, and every common sight,*
> > *To me did seem*
> > *Apparelled in celestial light,*
> *The glory and the freshness of a dream.*
> *It is not now as it hath been of yore;–*
> > *Turn wheresoe'er I may,*
> > *By night or day,*
> *The things which I have seen I now can see no more.*

Everywhere in Huxley's books the innocent eye of childhood is important. Tragedy comes when the eye is blinded; the darkest scene of that dark book, *Point Counter Point*, is perhaps that in which little Philip Quarles lies sick of meningitis, and his mother goes in one morning to find the child awake.

> ... One eyelid was wide open and the eye, all pupil, was looking straight up at the ceiling; the other was half shut in a permanent wink that imparted to the thin and shrunken face an expression of ghastly facetiousness.
> 'He can't open it,' the nurse explained. 'It's paralysed.'
> Between those long and curly lashes, which she had so often envied him, Elinor could see that the eyeball had rolled away to the exterior corner of the eye and was staring out sideways in a fixed unseeing squint.

Sight returns to little Philip, but only as a prelude to rapid death, the total darkness.

In other, less physical ways, the eye of childhood is blinded, when innocence is lost for example; that loss plays a great part in Huxley's novels, assuming dramatic form in characters who, like Spandrell in *Point Counter Point*, having lost their own innocence, are impelled to destroy it in others. But the loss of innocence comes not only from moral corruption; it can come also from the apparently gratuitous disaster which destroys happiness and makes life seem suddenly meaningless and appalling.

And if Huxley's novels have characters who are corrupted by other ruined innocents, the main force that destroys innocence, and sets man on the tortuous way that may with good fortune lead through damnation towards light, is the realization that suffering and death exist. Three times before he assumed his vocation as a writer that realization beat upon Aldous Huxley's mind: when his mother Julia died in 1908; when his eyesight failed him less than three years later; when his favourite brother Trevenen committed suicide in 1914. At Julia Huxley's death Aldous was fourteen; at Trevenen's he was twenty; the adolescence contained between these events was shadowed by physical as well as emotional darkness.

The impact of these tragedies was all the greater because Aldous had grown up more dependent and more vulnerable than his brothers. He was a delicate child, born with a weak heart that time strengthened, and with a large head; he could not walk until the age of two, and yet he was precocious in acquiring a large and idiosyncratic vocabulary and in developing his lifelong taste for indiscriminate reading. The age gap between him and his brothers Julian and Trevenen produced loneliness which he later cultivated deliberately. His cousin, Laurence Collier, remembered him at the age of nine on a Swiss holiday of the Huxley clan as 'aloof and secretly critical . . . ; he said nothing, but looked at something else or gazed abstractedly into the distance with a fixed and enigmatic smile, and I began to think that he liked neither Switzerland nor his father. . . .'

Julia Huxley died of cancer, going home from a summer holiday in France to waste rapidly away, conscious of what was killing her, and to cry out on her deathbed against the enormity of the sentence. 'Why do I have to die, and die so young!' That cry remained implanted for ever in the memory of Julian who heard it: at the funeral Aldous stood 'in stony misery'.

'I am sure', says Julian in *Memories*, 'that this meaningless catastrophe was the main cause of the protective cynical skin in which he clothed himself and his novels in the twenties.' The evidence to support this opinion is abundant. It is there in Aldous's earliest book of fiction, *Limbo*, and especially in 'The Death of Lully', his first attempt to portray a conversion and a curious anticipation of *Eyeless in Gaza*. Lully desires and courts a grave and beautiful woman, and at last she surrenders to him; he finds that another lover has been there before him, for her breast has been eaten half away by cancer. Horror and pity turn him from the life of gallantry to that of religion, and he dies in sanctity.

In novel after novel Huxley returned to Julia's death. It broke out, after the sunny interlude of *Crome Yellow*, in the very first pages of *Antic Hay*, when Gumbril, listening to the Reverend Pelvey reading the lesson in the school chapel, finds the recollections of his mother thrusting irresistibly above the voice that brays in his ears.

> . . . As for Gumbril's mother, her diligence had not been dogmatic. She had just been diligently good, that was all. . . . You felt the active radiance of her goodness when you were near her. . . .
>
> She had been good and she had died when he was still a boy; died–but he hadn't been told that till much later–of creeping and devouring pain. Malignant disease–oh, *caro nome!*
>
> 'Thou shalt fear the Lord thy God,' said Mr. Pelvey.
>
> Even when the ulcers were benign; thou shalt fear. He had travelled up from school to see her, just before she died. He hadn't known that she was going to die, but when he entered her room, when he saw her lying so weakly in the bed, he had suddenly begun to cry, uncontrollably. All the fortitude, the laughter even, had been hers. And she had spoken to him. A few words only; but they had contained all the wisdom he needed to live by. She had told him what he was, and what he should try to be, and how to be it. And crying, still crying, he had promised that he would try.

In *Antic Hay* there is the mere suggestion that the death of his mother in meaningless agony is one example of the neutral brutality of existence that produced in Gumbril a sense of futility parallel to that which envelops the whole world of Bohemian London through which he moves, a world in which those who live most nihilistically bear the deepest wounds: Myra Viveash for example, in the psychological sense is almost literally a vampire; her real self died in the war that killed her young husband, and now she carries on a semblance of life, sustained by preying emotionally on the men she attracts and whose happiness she destroys.

Julia Huxley's death even more pervasively shadows *Eyeless in Gaza*; the action of that chronologically splintered novel, once one has sorted it out, begins in Anthony Beavis's memories of his mother and her funeral, of that 'hole in Lollingdon churchyard' which haunted him into manhood as a symbol of the horror and absurdity of existence.

One of the most significant features of his treatment of the death of Anthony's mother is the way in which Huxley relates it to the vision of the world 'apparelled in celestial light' that he acknowledges as one of the occasional graces of childhood. Anthony, with his father and his uncle James, is travelling by train to his mother's funeral.

> Anthony looked out of the window again, through tears. The green and golden brightness of St. Martin's Summer swam in an obscuring iridescence. And suddenly the wheels of the train began to chant articulately. 'Dead-a-dead-a-dead,' they shouted, 'dead-a-dead. . . .' For ever. The tears overflowed, were warm for an instant on his cheek, then icy cold. He pulled out his handkerchief and wiped them away, wiped the fog out of his eyes. Luminous under the sun, the world before him was like one vast and intricate jewel. The elms had withered to a pale gold. Huge above the fields, and motionless, they seemed to be meditating in the crystal light of the morning, seemed to be remembering, seemed, from the very brink of dissolution, to be looking back and in a last ecstasy of recollection living over again, concentrated in this shining moment of autumnal time, all the long-drawn triumph of spring and summer.
> 'Dead-A-Dead,' in a sudden frenzy yelled the wheels, as the train crossed a bridge, 'A-DEAD-A-DEAD!'

That vision of the earthly scene as a 'vast and intricate jewel' is of course related to the experience of the mystics. 'Gems . . . come from the soul's visionary heaven; but they also lead the soul back to that heaven,' Huxley remarks many years later in *Heaven and Hell*. At this moment in *Eyeless in Gaza* he deliberately presents a vision of the nature of eternity that is instantaneous, intellectually uncomprehended, and terminated when the racket of the wheels breaks in with the realities of the world we inhabit in time, of which the inescapable is death. Later, at the funeral, looking into the grave, Anthony has another visionary moment when, with closed eyes, he apprehends his mother's presence, 'swooping towards him, white, like a sea-gull, and white again in the satin evening-dress when she came to say good-night before she went out to dinner, with that scent on her as she bent over him in bed, and the coolness of her bare arms'. But when the earth begins to fall into the grave, and Anthony tries to recall that vision, there comes into his mind instead the image of an absurd and vulgar Oxo advertisement he had seen from the train repeated on billboards through the Home Counties. 'Like a sea-gull she had swooped towards him, beautiful. But the ox was still there, still in its teacup, still base and detestable; and he himself yet baser, yet more hateful.' In that moment he is conscious that, as in Wordsworth's line, 'It is not now as it hath been of yore.' His mother is dead, and time and death have ended the consciousness of glory, which Anthony must spend his life seeking to recover.

It seems clear that Anthony's experience at this point reflects Huxley's own: that the death of Julia Huxley coincided with a fading of that irradiated perception of the innocent eye of childhood, a fading that actually preceded Huxley's physical quasi-blindness. But the reverberations which this event set going in Huxley's consciousness went beyond the awareness of the nature of time and corruption and death. A preoccupation of his later novels is the actual process of dying. That agonized and rebellious cry of his mother – 'Why do I have to die, and die so young?' – burnt itself into his mind as it did into Julian's, and out of his meditations on this theme arose the sense of a need to establish the distinction between the physical fact and the spiritual reality of death.

If death is the last bad joke of a meaningless universe, then we are right to cry out in defiance, since, as the existentialists suggest, it is only in denying the absurdity of death that we can give our humanity significance. 'Do not go gentle into that good night,' Dylan Thomas exhorted his dying father. 'Rage, rage against the dying of the light.'

But what if the real light is not dimmed? After his conversion Huxley became concerned with the question of survival after death. As was his wont, he examined the question from two opposing viewpoints. First, in *After Many a Summer*, he presented in grotesque form the desire for physical immortality, and, in that macabre scene when the millionaire Joe Stoyte sees the Fifth Earl of Gonister as a double centenarian reverting to the form and habits of an ape, and prefers such a survival to death, he shows the futility of any attempt to realize in time what belongs to eternity. Then, in *Time Must Have a Stop*, he treats the death of that amiable hedonist Eustace Barnack according to the accounts of the after-life contained in the Tibetan Book of the Dead. Far from death bringing a dimming of the light, he shows it bringing back in unimaginable intensity that lost 'celestial light' of the innocent vision. Spiritually unprepared, Eustace Barnack is terrified, and returns by reincarnation to the suffering gyrations of the Buddhist wheel of existence.

In later life Huxley became fascinated by the idea of the *ars moriendi*, the Art of Holy Dying of which people in earlier ages had been more conscious than modern men, who think that by ignoring it, death can somehow be evaded. How can we recognize the reality of death, and yet not rebel against its inevitability as Julia Huxley had done? It was bitter irony that Huxley should lose his first wife, Maria, to whom he was devoted, through the disease that killed his mother. He tried to help her to die in peace, and among his letters is published an amazing narrative, sent to Frieda Lawrence, in which he describes stage by stage how he prepared Maria for her death, urging her to contemplate eternal light while she was conscious, whispering his message into her ear after she passed out of consciousness, and witnessing her passing out of life with an appearance of total tranquillity. The sense that he had discovered the means of transcending rather than defying death led to the passage in his last novel *Island*, in which Dr. Robert MacPhail helps his wife Lakshmi to die in peace–also of cancer–and with full consciousness of the light into which she was advancing. At last, two years before his own death–from all external accounts an exemplary instance of the *ars moriendi*–Aldous Huxley had exorcized the consciousness of the 'Essential Horror' springing from his mother's death, that haunted all his previous novels.

3

The imagery of light and darkness that surrounds the concept of death in Huxley's novels extends into other aspects of his writing, and inspires the dialectic of opposites–nihilism-mysticism, flesh-spirit, corruption-regeneration–which dominates his thought and work. Preceding the search for light in darkness that is the grand metaphor of his life, is the physical experience of blindness and its conquest, partially and precariously so far as his actual eyesight was concerned, but triumphantly so far as he succeeded in living a life not only inwardly full and complicated but also endued amazingly with outward perception. No-one has demonstrated this aspect of Huxley with more understanding than Kenneth Clark.

Nothing could show more clearly [said Clark] the difference between two divisions of sight–if I may be excused such amateur physiology– the efficient functioning of the physical organ in carrying messages to the brain, and the reception of those messages by a prepared intelligence. As we all know, Aldous Huxley's eyes were physical organs of extreme fragility. For some years he was actually blind, and even when he could see enough for practical purposes, he was painfully far from normal vision. I remember, about thirty years ago, looking at a Seurat with him, and he scrutinized it from the distance of a few inches. I should have supposed he saw nothing but dots. And yet, the fact remains, that what he wrote about painting proves him to have been one of the most discerning lookers of our time. ... Should we say that Aldous's gift of perception was not so much a matter of eye as a part of a general sensibility to all forms of orderly or impassioned communication–what used to be called a strong aesthetic sense?

Clark's hypothesis is sustained by Huxley's remarkable essays on painting and painters. In his criticisms of works of art he combined two ways of looking; the minute examination to get the sense of texture and technique which Clark describes, and an inspired comprehension of larger forms, such as the snow landscapes of Breughel in which the dark figures stand out clearly, the boneless, ectoplasmic forms of El Greco, the 'solid geometrical qualities' so characteristic of his admired Piero della Francesca. Most significant is his interest in draperies, those flowing and half-abstract elements that carry so much of the motion of a classic painting. In his 'Variations on El Greco', this almost obsessive concern is used with extraordinary effect to dramatize both aspects of his perception–the broad and the minuscule–as he begins with a comparison of Piero and Cosimo Tura, and then, with the assurance of his great knowledge, sweeps Poussin and Watteau into an exemplary consideration of the varying uses of drapery.

> ... A painter or a sculptor can be simultaneously representational and non-representational. In their architectural backgrounds and, above all, in their draperies, many works, even of the Renaissance and the Baroque, incorporate passages of almost unadulterated abstraction. These are often expressive in the highest degree. Indeed, the whole tone of a representational work may be established, and its inner meaning expressed, by those parts of it which are most nearly abstract. Thus, the pictures of Piero della Francesca leave upon us an impression of calm, of power, of intellectual objectivity and stoical detachment. From those of Cosimo Tura there emanates a sense of disquiet, even of anguish. When we analyse the purely pictorial reasons for our perception of a profound difference in the temperaments of the two artists, we find that a very important part is played by the least representational elements in their pictures–the draperies. In Piero's draperies there are large unbroken surfaces, and the folds are designed to emphasize the elementary solid-geometrical structure of the figures. In Tura's draperies the surfaces are broken up, and there is a profusion of sharp angles, of jagged and flamelike

forms. Something analogous may be found in the work of two great painters of a later period, Poussin and Watteau. Watteau's draperies are broken into innumerable tiny folds and wrinkles, so that the colour of a mantle or a doublet is never the same for half an inch together. The impression left upon the spectator is one of extreme sensibility and the most delicate refinement. Poussin's much broader treatment of these almost non-representational accessories seems to express a more masculine temperament and a philosophy of life akin to Piero's noble stoicism.

In such a passage one sees clearly how far Huxley triumphed over his defects of sight, and how, even in triumphing, his perceptions were modified by them. Not only do we perceive the striking gap between the minute and the grand–with none of the intermediate elements of the picture recognized. We also realize that Huxley is really using his intelligence rather than his eye, abstracting from the picture not only its general lines of form, but also the temperament of the artist who created it; that what interests him as much as any purely aesthetic element is the combination of psychological and sociological clues that emerge from the kind of painting or sculpture he appreciates. Significantly, he did not like purely non-representational pictures; there had to be a theme so that the mind's eye could take over where the body's eye surrenders.

The cause of Huxley's near-blindness was an attack of *keratitis punctata*, an inflammation of the cornea, which he suffered at the age of sixteen. However, as Julian remarked in his *Memories*, 'Aldous's eyesight had ever been a mystery', and it is not certain that he did not experience difficulties with seeing even before he was afflicted with *keratitis*. After he had been using the Bates method to improve his eyesight in 1940, he reported to Julian: 'Yesterday for the first time I succeeded, for short stretches, in getting a single fixed image from both eyes together–a thing I have never had.' If we are to take the last phrase literally, it means that even in his boyhood Aldous Huxley did not enjoy normal stereoscopic vision; whether this was the case, and if it was, whether the disorder was organic or psychosomatic in origin, it is impossible now to determine for lack of any evidence dating from that period; all we know is that there may already have been a history of undiagnosed eye trouble by the time Aldous began to go blind.

It is however certain that Huxley suffered throughout his life from a different kind of defect of vision–the inability to visualize mentally. 'Words, even the pregnant words of poets, do not evoke pictures in my mind. No hypnagogic visions greet me on the verge of sleep.' He could remember scenes, but could not create a scene by invention in his mind's eye, as writers collaborating with him in dramatizations were to discover; this explains why his novels were always set in scenes that were familiar to him from memory – the south of England, France and Italy, California. One cannot assume a link between the deficiencies of Huxley's physical and of his mental vision, but one can assume that these deficiencies combined to enhance his eventual desire for a visionary life that would overleap the physical world, real or imagined.

The immediate effect of Huxley's blindness was increased vulnerability and aloofness. Already, at the age of sixteen, his physical as well as his mental peculiarities set him apart. He was six foot four in height and had acquired the characteristic stoop with which he would henceforward address the shorter majority of mankind. Seated, he remained extraordinary. 'His body is a thing of two parts,' an American interviewer recorded a quarter of a century later. 'From the waist up he is a man of average size, but his enormously long legs bend out in front of him grotesquely; and he keeps shifting them, sometimes crossing them at the knees, sometimes twining them round each other and sometimes unwinding them and resting one ankle on the knee of the other leg.' He used his hands restlessly, in expressive gestures to reinforce whatever quiet monologue he might be pronouncing, and there was an expression of questing curiosity in his face which became intensified as his sight left him.

He never went completely blind, but he was so near to it that he could not distinguish objects; at best he could tell night from day, sunlight from dark shadow. He had to stay with relatives and friends who could care for him constantly; he could not walk without a guide. It was the time of being physically 'eyeless in Gaza' that he was later to make into a metaphor for spiritual darkness; just as Anthony Beavis in the end conquered the night of the soul, so Aldous Huxley conquered the night of the body, and in the process changed permanently the course of his life.

He left Eton, which he had entered in 1908, and was thus, as he remarked, 'saved from becoming a complete public-school English gentleman', though it seems doubtful indeed that he – any more than George Orwell – would have become the typical old Etonian.

But in that realm of mere luminosity and darkness to which he was condemned, and in which aloofness from the world inevitably induced an almost solipsistic sense of mental self-sufficiency to complement his physical dependence, he set about creating the disciplines needed for a new existence. He developed into a splendid tool his already exceptional memory, and stored it with a growing multitude of facts which he acquired by learning Braille. Braille in turn taught him the virtues of economy in writing; only the least verbose of writers can be read through the finger tips. He also learnt to follow music in Braille, and taught himself to type by touch. In this way he began his literary career. He had written poems and fragments of prose, a normal activity in a household so oriented to literature as that of the Huxleys. But it was when he sat at his typewriter and composed a whole novel of eighty thousand words which he could not read that he felt he had found his vocation. The novel was lost before his sight improved; he never did read it.

After operations and eighteen months of near-darkness, the inflammation left Huxley's eyes; much of the harm it had done remained. He now had 'one eye just capable of light perception, and the other with enough vision to permit my detecting the two-hundred-foot letter on the Snellen Chart at ten feet'. He could read, but only with a powerful magnifying glass. Slowly his eyesight improved, and he was allowed to wear spectacles, which he did with humorous resignation. 'I never move without a plentiful supply of optical glass,' he remarked in his travel book of the mid Twenties, *Along the Road*. 'A pair of spectacles for reading, a pair for long range, with a couple of monocles in reserve – these go with me everywhere. . . . But when, in any month after the vernal equinox and before the autumn, my wanderings take me southwards, towards the sun, my armoury of spectacles is enlarged by the addition of three pairs of coloured glasses – two of lighter and darker shades of green, and one black.'

Yet, until he discovered the Bates method, the best Huxley could do was to 'recognize the seventy-foot line at ten feet and to read tolerably well – provided always that I kept my better pupil dilated with atropine, so that I might see round a particularly heavy patch of opacity at the centre of the cornea'. Strain and exhaustion were the inevitable consequences of excessive reading or writing; yet Huxley kept extraordinarily well read and wrote an average of one and a half full-length books a year throughout the Twenties and Thirties. In 1939, through his introduction to W. H. Bates's system of eye training, he gained a considerable improvement in his vision; it is a measure of the importance which the problem of sight had assumed for him that he devoted a great deal of time to writing a book (*The Art of Seeing*) which defended

Bates and his method–and treated it as seriously as any of his more ambitiously literary works.

Even the Bates method did not save Huxley's sight permanently. During the last decade of his life cataracts began to form, and there is a pathetically wistful passage in a letter he wrote in 1959 to the medium Eileen Garrett, a close friend of his later years. He told her that he had seen 'an interesting demonstration . . . by a man . . . who has trained his daughter and niece to see without their eyes. If the phenomenon is genuine–and there seems to be no obvious trickery (tho' one never knows, of course)–he has done something very remarkable.' To see without eyes, to live by the inner vision in the pure land of ideas and visions, Amitabha's paradise! For long periods of his life the thought haunted Huxley and helped to shape his writings.

By 1912 the fog of his first blindness had cleared enough for Aldous to spend the spring in Marburg, learning German and music; in 1913 he entered Balliol. In 1914 he achieved first publication in a student publication, *The Climbers' Club Journal*, edited by his brother Trevenen, who was an enthusiastic mountaineer; Aldous wrote on the climbing of staircases. Assiduously attending lectures, reading doggedly with magnifying glass, entertaining his friends with the newest ragtime, played (as Naomi Mitchison remembered) with 'his half-blind face reaching forward into the music', he surprised everyone but himself by gaining in 1916 a First in English Literature.

Aldous's last years at Oxford were shadowed by the death of Trevenen. Trevenen, who lives on at least partially in the character of the sensitive and over-scrupulous Brian Foxe in *Eyeless in Gaza*, was among his siblings the closest in age and disposition to Aldous, and his presence and devotion enabled his younger brother, still half sightless and walking with the deliberate lifting tread of the near-blind, to find his place in the unfamiliar world of Oxford.

Trevenen's death was a tragedy out of Gissing. He had overworked at college; had been driven into depression by a series of failures. He was devoted to poetry, but, like Aldous, he failed to win the Newdigate, which their scientifically minded brother Julian had carried off in his day. Trevenen also failed to win his expected First in Greats, and he failed in the Civil Service examination. He suffered from the Huxley tendency to psychological depression, and in 1914 he went into a nursing home at Reigate, where Julian also was recuperating at the same time from a nervous breakdown. Julian left, but Trevenen remained, alone, and other problems than his academic failures came to trouble his mind. A maid in the household Leonard Huxley had set up after his second marriage had aroused Trevenen's interest and he began secretly to take her to concerts and lectures. Both Trevenen and the girl felt themselves trapped in the rigidities of the Edwardian class structure, and neither had the courage to break free. The girl left the house; they agreed not to meet again. When Trevenen hanged himself in a Kentish wood, a letter from the girl was found in his pocket; she had written to say how unendurable she found it to be apart from him, and he had discovered no solution but suicide. Later, in creating the character of Brian Foxe, Aldous perceived and portrayed the vein of Quixotic weakness that had driven Trevenen to his death. At the time however he was stricken with grief. He had loved and admired in Trevenen an uprightness he felt he did not himself possess, and there was a bitterness in his sorrow. To his cousin Gervas Huxley, he wrote in August, 1914:

> There is—apart from the sheer grief of the loss—an added pain in the cynicism of the situation. It is just the highest and best in Trev—his ideals—which have driven him to his death—while there are thousands, who shelter their weakness from the same fate by a cynical, unidealistic outlook on life. Trev was not strong, but he had the courage to face life with ideals—and his ideals were too much for him.

That letter was written a few days before the First World War began. Trevenen's death prepared Aldous for the horrors of the years that followed, when he was to see many other idealists destroyed, and cynicism everywhere triumphant. He found his own idealism—that facile innocent idealism of the pre-1914 world—shredding away, and a despairing cynicism taking its place. He began, like so many other young men, with patriotic sentiments, and only his defective eyesight prevented him from volunteering with the others. By the end of 1914, sickened by the news from France and by the deterioration of moral standards at home, illustrated by the official persecution of aliens, he began to doubt if the war was justified. In May, 1916, he wrote to Julian, advising him not to return from the United States. 'The longer this war goes on, the more one loathes and detests it. At the beginning I shd. have liked very much to fight; but now, if I could (having seen all the results), I think I'd be a conscientious objector, or nearly so. But I shudder to think what England will be like afterwards—barely habitable.' And a few months later, after complaining in other letters of the injustices perpetrated by the tribunals for conscientious objectors, he expressed to Julian his view that the more men 'there were left in the world unconnected with this bloody affair, the better for the said world'. But he feared for the age that would follow the war, and foresaw with disillusioned insight the world he was later to portray in his early novels. 'Much more likely we shall have a generation of creatures incapable of thought or of action, victims of the incredible anarchy that others brought about.'

That month his first book appeared. It was *The Burning Wheel*, a 'tomelet' of fifty pages of verse in English and French, published by the Oxford bookseller Blackwell in a series entitled 'Adventurers All, a Series of Young Poets Unknown to Fame'.

CHAPTER THREE

A Circle in Time

I

'Cloistered darkness and sleep offer us their lotuses,' wrote Huxley in a prose poem entitled 'Beauty' which appeared in his fourth volume of verse, *Leda*, published in 1920. 'Not to perceive where all is ugly, eaten into by the syphilis of time, heart-sickening – this is beauty; not to desire where death is the only consummation – wisdom. Night is a measure-less deep silence: daybreak brings back the foetid gutters of the town. O supreme beauty of a night that knows no limitations – stars or the jagged edges of cock-crowing. Desperate, my mind has desired it; never my blood, whose pulse is a rhythm of the world.'

One makes allowances for the adolescent excesses of expression, for the surviving *fin de siècle* embellishments: 'the syphilis of time', 'the foetid gutters'. And in passages of this kind, which recur frequently in Huxley's early verse and prose, one encounters the preoccupations characteristic of his youth and his young manhood.

In part he remains the nervous youth, his aloofness enhanced by the darkness and isolation of the country of the blind. Darkness is always an ambiguous metaphor in Huxley's writing. In this early period it often had a protective quality, shielding the poet from the evils that become evident once he passes 'the jagged edges of cock-crowing', as Huxley had done when he emerged from blindness into a world in which Trevenen killed himself as a tragic prelude to the greater horror of war. Yet even as he felt the urge to withdraw into the darkness, where the failure to see is beauty and the failure to desire is wisdom, he recognized that other self 'whose pulse is a rhythm of the world'.

This duality does not leave Huxley's writing until after *Eyeless in Gaza*, and it dominates his earlier works. It projects on the one hand the idea of a microcosm of inner light protected by darkness, vividly represented at the point in *Crome Yellow* when Denis Stone comes for a moment near fulfilling his love for the wayward Anne Wimbush. Anne has fallen in the darkness of the garden at home; she calls out, and Denis finds her. He kneels beside her, lights a match. 'The light spurted and then grew steady. Magically, a little universe had been created, a world of colours and forms – Anne's face, the shimmering orange of her dress, her white, bare arms, a patch of green turf – and round about a darkness that had become solid and utterly blind.' This moment, epiphanous as the candlelit revelation in a painting by Georges de La Tour, is the only moment of real happiness Denis experiences in the duration of the novel. And the tiny luminous world he inhabits for that instant is analogous to the worlds of threatened joy which Huxley enters through his passions for learning and art, until eventually he realizes the insufficiency of both and exchanges the symbol of protecting darkness for the dominant symbol of later life, the liberating light.

In 1920, light is an equivocal gift, for it illuminates that imperfect physical world in which still exist the horrors of death and war and poverty, as well as the joys of love and friendship. In terms of recent personal experience, as his time at Oxford drew to an end, that world had been represented by the stratum of society, artistic, iconoclastic and privileged, which he entered by way of Garsington Manor.

Garsington, which lies close to Oxford, was the country home of Philip Morrell, whose wife, Lady Ottoline, claims her place in the history of English literature as the assiduous patroness of young writers over a whole generation beginning with D. H. Lawrence and ending with Auden and Spender. On long weekends, and through the benign months of summer, Garsington Manor never lacked its contingents of visiting poets, painters and radical intellectuals. Aldous from 1915, and Julian from his return from the United States in 1916, were regular visitors, and a young Swiss girl, then employed by Lady Ottoline as a governess, remembered how astonishingly different the two brothers seemed. 'Julian ebullient, forthcoming, putting himself out to entertain; Aldous reticent, gentle, often remote; but both with innate gifts of high-powered intellect and imagination.' This girl, Juliette Baillot, was in 1919 to become Julian's wife; in the same year Aldous married Maria Nys, another inhabitant of the great household at Garsington, where she was living as a refugee from the war in Belgium.

Few of the young writers Lady Ottoline gathered around her can have benefited more than Aldous Huxley, for whom Garsington Manor was in a remarkable variety of ways the starting-point of his adult life. There he found not only a wife who penetrated his aloofness more deeply than any other person, but also a place of shelter from the perplexities of war, where he could put in an appearance of working on the land until, in 1917, he began his brief and unenthusiastic period of schoolmastering at Repton and Eton. Garsington also gave him the setting for his first novel, *Crome Yellow*, and at Lady Ottoline's great house parties he met as fellow guests already established writers like the ebulliently vulgar H. G. Wells and the drily intellectual Bertrand Russell, and younger men and women who would dominate the literary scene of the Twenties, such as T. S. Eliot and Clive Bell, the three flamboyant Sitwells, John Middleton Murry, and Katherine Mansfield.

Already, at Oxford, Huxley had armoured himself with a quiet self-assurance, and had developed a monologizing manner that manifested not only a disinterested passion for knowledge, but also the curiosity about human actions and motives proper to a developing novelist.

Versed in every modern theory of science, politics, paintings, literature and psychology [Osbert Sitwell remembered long after-wards], he was qualified by his disposition to deal in ideas and play with them. Nor would gossip or any matter of the day be beneath his notice; though even these lesser things would be treated as by a philosopher, with detachment and an utter want of prejudice. But he preferred to discourse on more erudite and impersonal scandals, such as the incestuous mating of melons, the elaborate love-making of lepidoptera, or the curious amorous habits of cuttlefish. He would speak with obvious enjoyment, in a voice of great charm, unhurried, clear, without being loud, and utterly indifferent to any sensation he was making.

It was the poised and mannered conversational style of the deliberate writer, and it won Aldous Huxley, even before he had published more than a few verses in *Oxford Poetry*, the regard of writers tempera-mentally and artistically remote from him, such as D. H. Lawrence. Lawrence did not meet Huxley at Garsington, but, in December 1915, invited him at the suggestion of Lady Ottoline to tea at Hampstead. He found his visitor so congenial that he urged him to join the expedition he was organizing to establish the community of Rananim in the wilds of Florida. Huxley, impressed in his turn by Lawrence's plebeian vitality, accepted, but the community was never founded, and it would be a decade before Huxley and Lawrence met again and became close friends for the last four years of Lawrence's life.

In the event it was Lawrence's beloved enemy, John Middleton

Murry, who played the most important part in Huxley's life at this period, providing him—after an offer from Roger Fry to edit the *Burlington Magazine* had turned out to be too penurious—with a post as assistant editor of the *Athenaeum* which gave Huxley not only a modest income on which he could marry, but also a place in the London literary world. Until he had grown tired of working with a man so devious and emotionally unstable as Murry, Huxley found the *Athenaeum*, 'delightfully remote, in its purely literary preoccupations, from the horrors of the present'. Much of his work was literary drudgery, and a generation later he remembered 'the asininity of doing "shorter notices" of bad books' which was part of his regular routine. But he lacked completely the vanity which makes so many Anglo-Saxon writers despise the humbler tasks of the man of letters; like Francis Chelifer in *Those Barren Leaves*, he was willing to put his typewriter to any journeyman task and to give it of his best ability. He wrote articles on subjects like 'Decorating walls with maps' (*House and Garden*, 1924) and compiled advertisements for *Vogue*. He also worked for a period as dramatic critic to the *Westminster Gazette*. During that year he claimed to have seen as many as two hundred and fifty performances ('three theatres per diem during Christmas week' he recorded), yet the viewing of so many bad plays did not destroy a lifelong desire, like that of Henry James, to shine as a dramatist, any more than reviewing three books a week at another period of his early career made him less dedicated to the general vocation of writing.

I mention these aspects of Huxley's early career, not because the majority of his journalistic writings at this time have had any lasting significance, but because they demonstrate that he was a literary craftsman who, like the traditional French man of letters, took pride in everything he wrote. When he had to write a piece on house decoration he would make it as good of its kind as he was able. Throughout his life Huxley had to write for a living, for he had no other marketable ability, and in his later years, when he had lost much of his early faith in the art of writing, he still retained a sense of the necessity of craftsmanship; good writing obviously transmitted ideas more effectively than bad writing.

2

The versatility that appeared in the ephemerae of journalism was equally evident in the more serious work Huxley produced before the publication of his first novel, *Crome Yellow*, in 1921. It included four books of verse (*The Burning Wheel, Jonah, The Defeat of Youth* and *Leda*), the essays he wrote for the *Athenaeum* under the *nom de plume* 'Autolycus' (later collected in *On the Margin*), and, gathered in *Limbo*, two novelle, four short stories, and a closet play, 'Happy Families'.

Huxley's poems have rarely been highly regarded by other poets. 'My prestige', said T. S. Eliot with a touch of smugness as he remembered their early friendship, 'was such that Aldous submitted for my opinion his own book of verse, *Leda*: I am afraid that I was unable to show any enthusiasm for his verse.' Eliot's reaction is understandable; they admired the same masters, Laforgue and Malarmé, but while Eliot developed by experiment far beyond his models, Huxley, as a poet, was unassailably conventional. His earliest critical writings, long neglected and perhaps best forgotten except for the hints they give of his poetic inclinations, were three brief essays on *fin de siècle* poets–Ernest Dowson, John Davidson and Richard Middleton–which he wrote for his uncle Humphry Ward's *English Poets*. And to the versifiers of the Nineties and their Edwardian successors Huxley had in fact much closer affinities than to any of the poets–like Eliot, Pound and Read–who at that time were engaged in founding the movement we now call 'modern' poetry. The most important poetical phenomenon of the time–Imagism–left little evident mark on Huxley's early verse, whose general tone was that mixture of the Romantic and the neo-Augustan, with a pinch of gutter realism, which was characteristic of the Yellow Book poets. (The best men of the Nineties were in fact better than Huxley in his early poems, for they had more sense of the concrete, more power to put every word to a use, more feel of what to do with an image.) His most ambitious poem of this period, 'Leda', would have lent itself admirably to illustration by Aubrey Beardsley.

> . . . *Closer he nestled, mingling with the slim*
> *Austerity of virginal flank and limb*
> *His curved and florid beauty, till she felt*
> *That downy warmth strike through her flesh and melt*
> *The bones and marrow of her strength away.*
> *One lifted arm bent o'er her brow, she lay*
> *With limbs relaxed, scarce breathing, deathly still;*
> *Save when a quick, involuntary thrill*
> *Shook her sometimes with passing shudderings,*
> *As though some hand had plucked the aching strings.*

There is a mingling of elegance and perversity in such lines that reminds one of Huxley's admiration for the libidinous periphrases of the eighteenth-century French writer Crébillon fils, whom he was to celebrate in an essay written not long after the composition of *Leda*. Like many essentially moral men, Huxley was fascinated by the decadent, and *Leda* is on one level a notably decadent poem.

Given Huxley's mentality and his vast knowledge of the curious and the arcane, one might have imagined that he would have been most successful in a kind of Byronic satire, and Virginia Woolf, reviewing his *Defeat of Youth* in 1918, perceptively suggested that he should 'cease to use poetry in the serious, traditional manner, and . . . use it instead to explore those fantastic, amusing or ironical aspects of life which can only be expressed by people of high technical skill and great sensibility'. Huxley followed her advice, but mainly in prose; his poetry remained skilful but conventional, hence insignificant. By the end of the Twenties the urge to express himself in verse had died away. After his last collection, *The Cicadas*, in 1931, he published only two isolated short poems. While he evolved a highly characteristic way of expressing himself in prose, he never did so in verse, and his lack of interest in experiment, his adherence to conservative metrical forms and poetic diction, suggest that for him poetry as such never became a major interest, and that the most he gained from it was harmonious practice in the use of words. In a letter to Julian written as early as 1916 when his first book of verse, *The Burning Wheel*, appeared, he remarked:

> But what we want is men who write prose. And we don't get them. Alas, alas, it is very difficult and discouraging work looking for prose. No young men write anything but journalism or verse. A sad fact. And that pure verbal beauty, that conscientiousness so necessary in the maker of a good style, is nowhere to be got. . . . Well, well, when we have done crying havoc and letting slip the hogs of war, I dare say there will be a few young men who will be found able to write prose.

Yet even if Huxley never became a poet of importance, his verse retains a great documentary interest. One draws meanings out of the papers relating to Chaucer's lawsuits, just because he was Chaucer, and it is this kind of interest that Huxley's poems retain. They often anticipate what is later developed in prose, and for this reason they can frequently be read with effect as glosses on his novels. For example, there are two poems in *Leda*—'Verrey's' and 'Frascati's'—which look beyond *Crome Yellow* and project the spirit of aimless pleasure-hunting that permeates *Antic Hay*.

> *What negroid holiday makes free*
> *With such priapic revelry?*
> *What songs? What gongs? What nameless rites?*
> *What gods like wooden stalagmites?*
> *What steams of blood or kidney pie?*
> *What blasts of Bantu melody?*
> *Ragtime . . . But when the wearied Band*
> *Swoons to a waltz, I take her hand*
> *And there we sit in blissful calm,*
> *Quietly sweating palm to palm.*

And if love is here reduced to the physiology of perspiration, the whole carousel which is the shape of *Antic Hay* is epitomized in the grim image that ends a prose poem, 'The Merry-go-Round', also in *Leda*.

> But I happened to look inwards among the machinery of our roundabout, and there I saw a slobbering cretin grinding at a wheel and sweating as he ground, and grinding eternally. And when I perceived that he was the author of all our speed and that the music was of his making, that everything depended on his grinding wheel, I thought I would like to get off. But we were going too fast.

One of the most revealing of Huxley's earliest poems was 'Mole', written when he was little more than twenty and published in the first issue of the short-lived little magazine *The Palatine Review*, which he helped to found at Oxford in 1916.

> *Tunnelled in solid blackness creeps*
> *The old mole-soul, and wakes or sleeps,*
> *He knows not which, but tunnels on*
> *Through ages of oblivion;*
> *Until at last the long constraint*
> *Of each hand-hold is lost, and faint*
> *Comes daylight creeping from afar,*
> *And mole-work grows crepuscular.*
> *Tunnel meets air and bursts; mole sees*
> *Men as strange as walking trees. . . .*

The literary origins of the poem seem obvious; Kenneth Grahame's *Wind in the Willows* (1908), with its anthropomorphized animal character Mole, would certainly have been one of the books of Huxley's childhood, while the fabulist attempt to give a fresh aspect to meta-physical problems by seeing them through animal eyes had already been well exploited by English poets; one of the most recent examples had been Rupert Brooke's 'Fish', which attempted to criticize Christian cosmology by placing fish rather than man at the centre of the universe.

But there were also strains of more intimately personal significance in this poem. The emergence of 'the old mole-soul' into the daylight of understanding is linked with Huxley's own emergence from personal darkness into light; and light, by the end of the poem, is revealed in a curiously equivocal metaphor:

> The earth slopes upward, fold by fold
> Of quiet hills that meet the gold
> Serenity of western skies.
> Over the world's edge with clear eyes
> Our mole transcendant sees his way
> Tunnelled in light: he must obey
> Necessity again and thrid
> Close catacombs as erst he did,
> Fate's tunnellings, himself must bore
> Through the sunset's inmost core,
> The guiding walls to each-hand shine
> Luminous and crystalline;
> And mole shall tunnel on and on,
> Till night let fall oblivion.

The pessimism is heavy and opaque. Man, whether he believes he has achieved illumination or not, is still the creature of necessity. For all his visions of light, it is still the return to night that awaits him.

In such lines there is more than the echo of the French symbolists and their English disciples. There is also the influence of those Jacobean writers who profoundly affected Huxley's early work in every genre. One was Ben Jonson; in one of his *Athenaeum* middles, written when *Crome Yellow* was beginning to take shape, Huxley described Jonson's 'reduction of human beings to unpleasant humours' as 'sound and medicinal'. But Jonson's was mainly a formal influence; much more profound in shaping Huxley's thought in the years before his con-version were the poems of Francis Quarles (whose name, of course, was conferred on the anti-hero of *Point Counter Point*) and those of Fulke Greville, the self-proclaimed 'Friend to Sir Philip Sidney'. The reasons why Huxley was so interested in Greville are fairly obvious;

Greville resembled him in combining a melancholy but essentially compassionate view of the human condition, with the consciousness that once we recognize the worst of man's fate, we can proceed to consider the possibilities of alleviation, even of redemption. The passage from Greville that fascinated Huxley from 1915 when he studied it at Oxford under Walter Raleigh down to 1963 when he quoted it in his final book, *Literature and Science*, was the verse he used as the epigraph to *Point Counter Point*:

> *Oh, wearisome condition of humanity,*
> *Born under one law, to another bound,*
> *Vainly begot and yet forbidden vanity,*
> *Created sick, commanded to be sound.*
> *What meaneth nature by these diverse laws,*
> *Passion and reason, self-division's cause?*

It would be hard to think of any text more suited to the mood of Huxley's early works, more expressive of the dark irony with which he looked out on a world where men's actions were so different from their pretensions, and where even the most consistently virtuous human behaviour did not save a man from the caprices of a fate that seemed totally irrational. That man should have developed the kind of intellect that created the music of Bach and Mozart, and should spend his capacities on a murderous war such as that which gripped the world as Huxley came of mental age; that men should live and achieve only to die, and that goodness and intelligence like Julia Huxley's should not save them from bestial agonies: Huxley acknowledged these facts, and then turned aside and, even before he began to celebrate such cosmic injustices in the novels from *Antic Hay* to *Eyeless in Gaza*, wrote out his protest in didactic poems of rejection like 'Topiary', which appeared in 1918 in the volume significantly entitled *The Defeat of Youth*:

> *Failing sometimes to understand*
> *Why there are folk whose flesh should seem*
> *Like carrion puffed with noisome steam,*
> *Fly-blown to the eye that looks on it,*
> *Fly-blown to the touch of a hand. . . .*
> *Failing to see why God the Topiarist*
> *Should train and carve and twist*
> *Men's bodies into such fantastic shapes:*

> *Yes, failing to see the point of it all, I sometimes wish*
> *That I were a fabulous thing in a fool's mind,*
> *Or, at the ocean bottom, in a world that is deaf and blind,*
> *Very remote and happy, a great goggling fish.*

At such a time blindness seemed almost a blessing, a withdrawn world whose loss was to be regretted, for in another poem of the same volume Huxley represented himself longing to be

> *In tideless seas, uncharted and unconned*
> *Save by blind eyes: beyond the laughter and weeping*
> *That brood like a cloud over the lands of men. . . .*

His novels–like those of the French writers Malraux and Camus– were in fact to constitute a rejection of the desire to retreat into blindness, into darkness, that we encounter in the early poems. In those novels he chose to face the problem stated by Greville, that poet so like himself in the intellectuality that prevented most of his writings from being more than interesting verse. And Greville, after all, was not unrelievedly pessimistic, a fact that cannot have been lost on Huxley even at this time. For as Huxley eventually did, Greville believed that right knowledge could in some degree negate the condition of man expelled from Paradise.

> *The chief use, then, in man of that he knows*
> *Is his painstaking for the good of all;*
> *Not fleshly weeping for our own-made woes,*
> *Not laughing from a melancholy gall,*
> *Not hating from a soul that overflows*
> *With bitterness breathed out from inward thrall;*
> *But sweetly rather to ease, loose, or bind,*
> *As need requires, this frail, fall'n humankind.*

Similarly, if there are poems in Huxley's early books that turn away from life or–like those already quoted–look forward to the representation of the world as a meaningless wheel of existence as in *Antic Hay* and *Point Counter Point*, there are others which offer mysterious prospects, snatched away as quickly as a visionary's insights, like that poem of train travelling, 'Out of the Window' (one of the best of Huxley's early poems), in which he watches the sweeping drilled lines of the fields and market gardens until there is an instantaneous epiphany:

Each line deliberately swings
Towards me, till I see a straight
Green avenue to the heart of things,
The glimpse of a sudden opened gate
Piercing the adverse walls of fate . . .
A moment only, and then, fast, fast,
The gate swings to, the avenue closes;
Fate laughs, and once more interposes
Its barriers.

In 'Leda', the title poem, there is the reversal of the symbolism characteristic of Huxley's poems at this period. Darkness is no longer protection. It is the colour of the eagle that Aphrodite becomes, like Racine's 'Vénus toute entière à sa proie attachée'; she paradoxically prepares the way for Zeus, the white swan, to unite with Leda. This is an equivocal poem, in which the God is regarded with the kind of broad humour the Greeks themselves often adopted in telling tales of the Olympian deities, and we have no reason to believe that Huxley at this point (for the poem was published in 1920 and started in 1918) is presenting an allegory of the mystical life. Yet there is haunting ambivalence beneath the slightly decadent surface created by the Augustan diction and the neo-Gallic periphrases. It is true that the seduction of Leda makes an elegant and–as Huxley himself called it– 'luscious' narrative; though he described it at the time as 'a strange mixture of pure beauty and irony', it is likely that most of his contemporaries read it as an old tale amusingly retold for people with civilized and hedonistic tastes, and that few imagined the irony with which one now reads the final lines of this longest of Huxley's poems. For the imagery of the climactic passage is not unlike that of some of the more extravagant narratives of the mystics, and the terminal quatrain has a pure, haunting tone quite unlike the rest of the poem:

Hushed lay the earth and the wide, careless sky.
Then one sharp sound, that might have been a cry
Of utmost pleasure or of utmost pain,
Broke sobbing forth, and all was still again.

It might be taken for what it overtly is–the description of a sexual climax; but the experience is with a god, and that cry could pass just as easily for a metaphorical description of the mystic's unitive ecstasy. Perhaps this interpretation was wholly outside Huxley's mind, at this stage, but before assuming so we should remember that by the time *Leda* was completed Huxley had already published the volume of stories which included 'The Death of Lully', his first attempt to represent a conversion in fiction.

3

By 1916, when his first stories began to appear in *The Palatine Review*, Huxley had decided that his prose was essentially satirical. In that year at Oxford he won the Stanhope Prize with an essay on 'The Development of Political Satire in England from the Restoration to the Revolution'; his own satire was to be mainly social in character, but he never neglected politicians and their followers as inhabitants of the social landscape. The genre was suited to the temper of his approach to life, which was ironical. He saw not merely those incongruities between human pretensions and human actions which are the traditional province of the satirist; he placed them within a larger ironical frame which charted the inbred contradictions of the human condition.

All Huxley's fiction is dedicated in one way or another to the exploration of this landscape of contradictions; the difference between the early works and the later is not that what Huxley called the 'Essential Horror' of existence is removed. It is that while in the earlier works man appears to be caught without hope on the wheel of suffering and negation, in the later novels an escape through self-transcendence is offered. By the end, in *Island*, Huxley has reached the point of suggesting that self-transcendence may be not merely an individual matter; that it is possible to conceive a society arranged on the principles of Mahayanist Buddhism in which all men will have the chance to live in such a way that the physical and the intellectual, the moral and the spiritual facets of their natures will be fulfilled in total balance. The thematic progression of his novels closely follows Huxley's own pilgrimage in search first of intellectual and then of spiritual light. The equipment with which he begins, apart from his talents as a writer and his inherited hunger for knowledge, is the experience of his early years.

Huxley's writings are largely autobiographical; this applies in a double way. It is not merely that—like so many other writers who lack the powers of invention and visualization—he draws deeply on his own experiences for the material to build his novels and stories. His characters—where they are not caught inescapably in the circling patterns of habit and obsession—are bound on the same journey as he is.

The controversial nature of almost all of Huxley's novels, with their persistent concern with contemporary social and philosophical issues, has tended to create an impression of uniformity and to divert attention from their formal sophistication and variety. Even the novels can be divided into three main groups. There are the heavily populated neo-Peacockian novels of satire and social criticism: *Crome Yellow*, *Antic Hay*, *Those Barren Leaves* and *Point Counter Point*. There are the novels of conversion and regeneration—*Eyeless in Gaza*, *After Many a Summer* and *Time Must Have a Stop*. There are the Utopias, negative and positive, *Brave New World* and *Island*. All these works have in common the proliferation of characters and relationships, by means of which highly complex themes can be studied from a multiplicity of viewpoints. They are—with the possible exception of *Eyeless in Gaza*—novels which lack heroes in the ordinary sense of a central personage whose fate totally commands our interest. There are characters, like Denis in *Crome Yellow* and Gumbril in *Antic Hay*, who preserve a central thread, but their centrality is structural rather than psychological, while Philip Quarles in *Point Counter Point* is an essential chorus rather than a hero. This abandonment of the hero—or even the anti-hero—so far as most of the novels are concerned enables Huxley to abandon to a great extent the old linear plot. It is true that only in one novel, *Eyeless in Gaza*, is the traditional chronological time pattern radically disturbed; this, paradoxically, is the one case of a pronounced pattern of personal development within time, exemplified in Anthony Beavis's conversion. At the same time, though novels like *Crome Yellow*, *Antic Hay* and *Point Counter Point* take place within conventional chronological sequences, these are not the dominant patterns; both *Crome Yellow* and *Antic Hay* move in circular patterns of frustration, time having by the end solved or changed nothing in the landscapes of the human condition which they offer, while *Point Counter Point*, though it is crammed with action and ends with almost as many corpses as an Elizabethan tragedy of blood, still, because of its arrangement in imitation of the laws of classical music, leaves one with the sense that the pattern has been completed not through the action of time but through the appropriate balancing of fates and relationships.

There are some elements in Huxley's novels that are evident immediately. We realize after the first two chapters of *Crome Yellow* that he is dealing in moral and intellectual concepts and has the power of making them alive by his dramatic way of presenting them. His novels belong, from beginning to end, to the fiction of ideas; they are always resolutely didactic. We are also conscious that the excitement of the ideas makes up to a great extent for the shallowness of many of the characters, who are often little more than Jonsonian humours. It also disguises what David Daiches called the 'essentially inorganic quality of his technical apparatus': the mechanical patterning; the excessive use of coincidence and all too convenient accident in novels like *Antic Hay* and *Point Counter Point*; and the way in which, rather like de Maupassant's stories, the novels move always towards an ironic final twist, such as the scene at the end of *Point Counter Point* when, after we have been moved to pity and even unwilling admiration by Spandrell's deliberately chosen death, we are brought down to the muddy earth as Burlap and Beatrice romp together in their nuptial bath.

But apart from the merely stylistic similarities of individual novels, Huxley's fiction is embraced within a broader philosophic structure, which enabled him even at the end of his life, when he had moved far beyond the attitudes expressed in early novels like *Crome Yellow* and *Antic Hay*, to view their republication with equanimity; they were part of an *oeuvre* more unified for all its variation than that of most other writers.

Their unity was thematic, represented in that verse of Fulke Greville which to the very end, interpreted and reinterpreted, remained the leitmotiv of Huxley's imaginary world. To reconcile man's self-division, to recognize the predicament caused by the presence within the same being of passion and reason, of a body tied to time and a mind aspiring elsewhere, and then to move forward in this dialectic to a way of liberation: this is the developing thematic structure that conditions Huxley's novels and lifts them beyond mere passing satire into the realm of moral fables.

This combination of the satirical and the fabulous which appears in varying ratios in Huxley's books (with *Antic Hay* and *After Many a Summer* more satirical and *Eyeless in Gaza* and *Island* more fabulous) determines also Huxley's attitude toward literary style and towards experiment. Neither fabulists nor satirists are inclined towards naturalism, and in an early letter to H. L. Mencken, while he was still writing *Crome Yellow*, Huxley declared his distaste for 'Realismus'. The fabulist needs well-defined types, the satirist needs unbalanced, exaggerated natures, and Huxley's novels abound in both. At the same time, fable and satire always exist on the edge of plausibility, always possess, while rejecting complete realism, at least verisimilitude. Having created Lilliput, Swift rightly took pains to make it internally consistent in all its details. It is for such reasons that writers like Huxley–and one might quote Orwell as a similar case–are not interested in literary experiment *per se*, which is the field of the aesthetician, James Joyce or Valéry Larbaud. Huxley could appreciate Joyce, noting the 'slight flavour of excrement'; he could acknowledge Eliot's greatness; but he never felt the inclination to imitate them, and he regarded the more extreme and destructive forms of experiment with positive distrust. Apart from his often expressed disapproval of non-representational art, he declared himself–even as a young man–opposed to the theories and the practices of the Dadaists of which he remarked, as early as 1920, 'I see no point in destroying literature.' This is important to remember; at no stage was Huxley's satire intended to be merely destructive. It was meant as a corrective, or perhaps even more as a way of seeking and showing truth. 'A good satire is more deeply truthful and, of course, much more profitable than a good tragedy,' said Mr. Propter, the Mentor of *After Many a Summer*, and we can doubtless take this remark as expressing the author's own opinion. Certainly Huxley carried it out in practice, and, though he did at times experiment in fictional form, as in the time-pattern of *Eyeless in Gaza* and the structure of *Point Counter Point*, and even adapted the experiments of some of his contemporaries (notably Marcel Proust and André Gide), the experiment was always subordinated to thematic requirements, to the better teaching of the particular lesson of life with which Huxley was concerned at the time.

The satirical-fabulist attitude, which dominated the themes and structures of the novels and restrained experiment, had also a dominant effect on Huxley's choice of characters. Their essential similarities tended to be concealed in the earlier novels by his habit of giving his characters the mannerisms of living people well known in the contemporary intellectual world, so that in every novel up to (and including) *Eyeless in Gaza* the deeper intent was somewhat masked by the immediate interest of the *roman à clef*. But when one looks at the novels as a whole, it becomes clear that certain types of characters and even certain relationships recur from *Crome Yellow* in 1921 to *Island* more than forty years afterwards.

The key characters, despite their apparent modernity of thought and action, fit into archetypal patterns whose analogies can be found in classical mythology. The most strongly recurrent pattern is that of the experienced old man and the learning youth, Odysseus-Telemachus, the combination whose most celebrated example in recent literature is the relationship of Leopold Bloom and Stephen Dedalus in Joyce's *Ulysses*. In Huxley the pattern changes in a very interesting way. In the early books, the experienced elder—Mr. Scogan instructing Denis in *Crome Yellow*, Mr. Cardan criticizing Calamy in *Those Barren Leaves*—is Voltairian intellectuality personified in all its barrenness. In *Eyeless in Gaza* the change begins, the Odysseus figure is inverted and becomes the source of wisdom—Miller in *Eyeless*, Propter in *After Many a Summer* (with Pete Boone as his Telemachus), Bruno Rontini instructing Sebastian in *Time Must Have a Stop*.

Parallel to this central pair, there are other recurring characters. One represents an aspect of Huxley's own character of which he was always guiltily conscious—the intellectual whose cold concern with knowledge as an abstraction from existence detaches him from the reality of life. Appearing first in *Crome Yellow* as Henry Wimbush with his useless passion for the details of local history, he develops through the ob-sessed scientist Shearwater in *Antic Hay* to Quarles, the bloodless novelist, in *Point Counter Point*, and eventually expires as the bookworm Jeremy Pordage in *After Many a Summer*. The female complement of the cold intellectual is the Circe figure (her veins filled with passionate ice) who reduces her victims to animality or stupidity; Myra Viveash in *Antic Hay*, Lucy Tantamount in *Point Counter Point*, Veronica Thwale in *Time Must Have a Stop* and, at the end, Farnaby's remembered mistress Babs in *Island*. There are also the immoralists, carrying in their Satanism an implication of transcendental faith, from the peripatetic philanderer Ivor in *Crome Yellow*, through God-defying Coleman in *Antic Hay* and God-seeking Spandrell in *Point Counter Point*, and petering out in the self-indulgent hedonist, Eustace Barnack, whose descent into hell is the strange centre-piece of *Time Must Have a Stop*. And there are, finally, the detested sham hierarchs whom Huxley's enduring anticlericalism placed in almost every novel he wrote, beginning with the bigoted Mr. Bodiham in *Crome Yellow*, and taking such divergent forms as Burlap (the priest as writer) in *Point Counter Point*, the Arch-Community-Singer of Canterbury and his sexual acrobatics in *Brave New World*, the eunuch Arch-Vicar in *Ape and Essence*, and that most repulsive hierarch of science, Dr. Obispo in *After Many a Summer*, whose name—in Spanish—signifies 'bishop'. It is, in fact, the pattern of a morality, the seeker and his guru, with the tempting figures of the witch, the Satanist and the false priest in action around them, all travelling through time, that landscape of nightmares, with their destination the City of God. But for none of them are we sure that the trumpets sound on the other side, any more than we are sure that Huxley himself received the entry into light that became the goal of his personal journey.

While, considered individually, Huxley's novels may often seem, as Daiches has suggested, 'inorganic' and mechanical, considered as a whole they present a notably organic development, not premeditated or deliberately planned, yet acquiring a natural and valid form from the interplay of an incompletely realized artistic sensibility, a never satisfied intellectual curiosity and deep psychic needs that were given metaphorical shape by the varieties of suffering.

Within the greater structure which Huxley's novels sustain, the shorter works of fiction have their own functions. There are short stories in the usual sense, and also the novelle. Both adhere more closely than the longer novels to traditional patterns of fiction, though the novelle, with their small casts of characters, their restraint in description, their searchingly psychological approach, are much nearer to the French *récit* as developed by writers like Gide and Camus.

These novelle include two brief late works, *The Genius and the Goddess* and *Ape and Essence*, and several early works–some longer than those independently published books–which appeared only in collections of short fiction. Almost two-thirds of *Limbo* is taken up by the two novelle, 'Farcical History of Richard Greenow' and 'Happily Ever After'. 'Two or Three Graces' occupies more than two-thirds of the volume that carries the same title, 'After the Fireworks' occupies half of *Brief Candles*, and 'Uncle Spencer' over a third of *Little Mexican*. Apart from the major novels, there are thus at least six works of fiction by Aldous Huxley which are both too substantial and too complex to be counted as short stories. One, *Ape and Essence*, is a miniature anti-Utopia, and can best be regarded as a pendant to *Brave New World* or a fictional complement of *Brave New World Revisited*. The remaining five novelle have a special place in Huxley's work which has been rarely recognized because attention has been drawn away from them by the dramatically controversial nature of the longer works. They are close psychological studies of a kind which the elaborate intellectual patterning of the novels does not–except in the special case of *Eyeless in Gaza*–allow. Satire is never absent, but it is softer, the ironies are less mechanical, the settings less exotic, and the characters more fully and roundly developed, largely because the novelle have small casts and tend to concentrate around one or two central figures, following always a conventional time pattern, and usually involving what rarely happens in the longer works, a perceptible degree of character development, of evolution or sometimes – as in the case of 'Farcical History of Richard Greenow' – of devolution.

The novelle usually centre on some inner conflict, some duality of nature, within the leading character. Huxley wrote 'Farcical History of Richard Greenow' deliberately as a 'dual personality' story; it was, after all, an illustration of his theme of 'self-division'. He doubtless recognized in himself, in the combination of fascination and repulsion with which he regarded his world, in the demands of flesh and spirit that warred within him, the divisions that he portrayed with higher lights in his characters. A certain duality is implicit even in his definition of man within the context of the perennial philosophy, for he tells us that 'man possesses a double nature, a phenomenal ego and an eternal Self', and almost a decade before his conversion, in the mid Twenties just before he fell under the influence of D. H. Lawrence, he even played with the idea that duality of personality was not merely inevitable, but even something to be welcomed and cultivated.

> The only satisfactory way of existing in the modern, highly specialized world is to live with two personalities. A Dr. Jekyll that does the metaphysical and scientific thinking, that transacts business in the city, adds up figures, designs machines, and so forth. And a natural spontaneous Mr. Hyde to do the physical, instinctive living in the intervals of work. The two personalities should lead their unconnected lives apart, without poaching on one another's activities. Only by living discretely and inconsistently can we preserve both the man and the citizen, both the intellectual and the spontaneous animal being, alive within us. The solution may not be very satisfactory; but it is, I believe now (though I once thought differently), the best that, in modern circumstances, can be devised.

Later, when he comes to accept the perennial philosophy and to seek mystic enlightenment, Huxley regards duality as equivalent to imperfection and therefore evil. The knowledge of unity with the Divine Ground, of God as One and immanent, now seems to him the desirable goal, yet he realizes that it is the most difficult goal of all, for man inevitably lives in the imperfect time world, and that even the visionary's experience comprehends hell as well as heaven. Some of this consciousness of duality as a tragic condition appears even in his earliest work, and in his novelle it exists as evidence of the absurdity of human destiny.

In Huxley's shorter stories, there is naturally less development of character than in the novelle, and the structure tends to be episodic rather than narrative while the stress is less on duality of personality than on those other dualities between action and intent, between expectation and reality, which are the more usual province of the ironist. There are some stories in which two characters complement each other in interesting dialectic patterns, producing a similar effect to the portrayal of duality of personality within one character. In general, it is the sad and gentle ironist rather than the stringent satirist who is foremost in the Huxley of these shortest works of fiction, in some of which he reaches his highest points of achievement as a literary artist.

4

Limbo, Huxley's first volume of fiction, is a collection of the whimsical and bizarre, of stories that hover between real experience and the fantasy of the symbolists. Just as later in Huxley's career his *Point Counter Point* showed close resemblances to Gide's *Les Faux-Monnayeurs*, so at this early stage there are echoes, in manner rather than matter, of the earlier fiction of that writer, whom Huxley had met in 1918 in the dressing-room of Lydia Lopokova at the Russian Ballet. (Gide, Huxley recorded at the time, 'looks like a baboon with the voice, manners and education of Bloomsbury in French'.) Like Gide's first writings, *Paludes* and *The Notebooks of André Walter*, these juvenilia of Aldous Huxley seem to show a mind likely to escape into aestheticism. Yet, as in the young Gide, one can already in hindsight perceive the moralist concealed behind the self-conscious apprentice *littérateur*. There is not a story that does not contain its sombre irony.

'For this is not', says Huxley in the early pages of 'Farcical History of Richard Greenow', 'one of the conventional studies of those clever young men who discover Atheism and Art at School, Socialism at the University, and, passing through the inevitable stage of Sex and Syphilis after receiving their B.A., turn into maturely brilliant novelists at the age of twenty-five.' The *bildungsroman*, which had reached an early peak in Flaubert's *Sentimental Education*, had flowered again, degenerately, during Huxley's undergraduate days, in the *succès de scandale* of Compton Mackenzie's *Sinister Street*. This kind of sentimentalization of the bohemian life, misting over its follies with the hue of romance, Huxley disliked from the beginning for its untruth to the view of existence which experience had already shown him. His novels will not be without their romantics. But they will be men and women scarred and sometimes driven towards death, like Casimir Lypiatt in *Antic Hay*, by a hallucinatory view of life. At times, when their romance darkens into the Satanic, when the sardonic mood replaces the sentimental, Huxley can indeed sympathize with the romantics, can even dwell upon them with something near to love, as he does with Spandrell (that latter-day Stavrogin) in *Point Counter Point*, but he is pitiless, even then, in showing that romance, white or black, is destructive, of others and oneself, because it seeks to escape from the realities of both the phenomenal and the spiritual world.

'Farcical History' reproduces the pattern of the sentimental *bildungsroman*, but in mockery, as a jester might walk beside his victim and grotesquely mimic his gestures and his voice. Richard Greenow goes through the customary life sequence of the English upper-middle-class youth, leaving home at a tender age for a preparatory school (where 'shepherds grow to resemble their sheep and pedagogues their childish charges'); there (undoubtedly like his creator) Richard 'swallowed down *Robert Elsmere* in the three-volume edition at the age of eight' and 'used to sit and think about Things in General and Nothing in Particular'. He wins a scholarship to 'Aesop College, which is one of our Greatest Public Schools', where he begins to read omnivorously, and then, at the age of sixteen, is overwhelmed by the splendour of Lord Francis Quarles.

> He appeared like a revelation, bright, beautiful, and sudden, before Dick's eyes. A violent emotion seized him; his heart leapt, his bowels were moved within him; he felt a little sick and faint–he had fallen in love.

Again, Huxley's satirical finger is pointing at the sensational literature of the day; we have moved from *Sinister Street* to *The Loom of Youth*, Alec Waugh's novel about public school life which appeared in 1917, the year before Huxley began work on 'Farcical History', and created a sensation by its homosexual implications. But Huxley is ready with the ironist's twist. Richard Greenow is not a homosexual–even of the temporary kind that flourishes in public schools. It is his alter ego who falls in love with Lord Francis Quarles, and that alter ego, who shortly provokes Dick–or at least Dick's hand–to write a novel entitled *Heartsease Fitzroy: the Story of a Young Girl*, is a lady writer who calls herself Pearl Bellairs. In the musty room of an inn at Bablock Hithe, Dick realizes 'the strange truth about himself'. He is a spiritual hermaphrodite, 'a new William Sharp and Fiona MacLeod–a more intelligent William, a vulgarer Fiona'. From this point the novella proceeds into a dark Gogolian farce of dual personality, with madness at the end. Dick's male self–supported financially by the efforts of the Pearl Bellairs who is his sleepworking feminine double–is torn between 'knowing or doing, philosophy or politics', a dilemma with which his creator was at this time familiar, and here again he subdivides himself, writing pulp novels at midnight and in the day working on his Synthetic Philosophy and at the same time contributing money and articles to the *Weekly Internationalist* run by an indomitable paper revolutionary named Hyman, Huxley's first political fanatic.

The war comes, and Dick follows the course Huxley had come to consider by 1916 the only moral one: he becomes a conscientious objector, intending to stand out in absolutist defiance, but a softness within–undoubtedly the feminine influence of Pearl Bellairs–induces him to accept a conditional exemption and go off to do landwork, a decision which draws down upon him the moral furies of Hyman and the repulsive collection of lower-middle-class eccentrics–enthusiasts for craftsmanship and vegetarian feeding–with whom he has become alarmingly associated.[1] His political activities have bred in him, along with his idealism, an almost Swiftian horror of human physicality. ('How clear and splendid were the ideas of right and justice! If only one could filter away the contaminating human element . . .' he reflects like a latter-day Stendhal.) He sets off to carry out his landwork on the farm of a country estate. It is the first appearance of Garsington Manor in Huxley's fiction, and already it bears the name of Crome.

Dick soon discovers–as many city men seeking peace on the land before and since have found–that Tolstoyan self-abnegation is for him only a slow moral death. He finds the work unendurable. His fellow labourers hate him. The village children pursue and mock him, egged on by the jingoistic schoolmaster. The guests at the manor condescend to him. His ardently and efficiently patriotic sister Millicent and his

---

[1] There is an ironically prophetic touch about this and other aspects of 'Farcical History', for Huxley will describe more than a decade later, and in approving rather than mocking terms, the essentially similar pacifist activities of Anthony Beavis in *Eyeless in Gaza*. These early stories are filled with touches that read ironically in view of the mature Huxley's beliefs and attitudes, e.g. 'The consolations of religion do not console the less efficaciously for being illusory.'

former friend Hyman visit him and both condemn him for not standing by his principles and going to prison. He feels immersed in earth and dung, yet at the same time Pearl Bellairs, that ardently belligerent lady writer, has been busily engaged in writing recruiting propaganda and articles on the delights of being a land-girl: 'dewy dawns, rosy children's faces, quaint cottages, mossy thatch, milkmaids, healthy exercise'.

As Dick's sanity breaks down, so does the division between his two personalities, until he suddenly begins to introduce his ostensibly male self to strangers as the well-known lady novelist. He is taken to a lunatic asylum, where his protests during moments of clarity are of no avail and where, when he starts a hunger strike, he is forcibly fed with the brutality meted out to British conscientious objectors during World War I. He dies in delirium, shouting at phantoms, gesticulating wildly with his left hand while his right automatically pours on to the page the patriotic vapourings of Pearl Bellairs. The last words he writes as Dick Greenow are these:

> World will always be hell. Cap., or Lab., Engl. or Germ.–all beasts. One in a mill. is GOOD. I wasn't. Selfish intellect. . . .

It might serve as a baldly simplified expression of Huxley's own view of existence in those months after the Armistice when it became evident that even the horror of a world conflict had not driven sense into the heads of statesmen of any party.

'Farcical History of Richard Greenow' is a dark, disturbing story; its 'farce' is not in the least amusing, and the final impression it leaves is one of black pessimism. It reveals a number of characteristic Huxleian preoccupations–the horror of war, the sterility of merely intellectual activities, and the bitter contradiction between the ideals of philo- sophers and the creations of artists on the one hand, and on the other those realities of suffering and mere human weakness, which at that time Huxley felt to by irreconcilable.

In these respects 'Farcical History' sets the tone for the whole group of early writings. Even more bizarre is the short closet play, 'Happy Families', in which the division of personality is further developed. Huxley borrowed the essential trick of the play from Leonid Andreyev, whose symbolist plays were popular with the intellectuals of 1918 and who had developed the idea of actually embodying in characters on the stage the various facets of a hero's nature. The scene, of Firbankish grotesqueness, is a conservatory filled with revolting and fleshly 'fabu- lous flowers', in which all the action goes on in 'a greenish aquarium twilight'–the sort of twilight through which during these early years of writing Huxley must have observed his fellow beings. Aston Tyrrell and Topsy Garrick, two typical young products of the intellectually fashionable currents of the time, come on stage, fresh from a dance, trailing with them grotesque ventriloquist's dummies of themselves. They begin to converse through the dummies, while Aston's two brothers, Sir Jasper and Cain (a Mendelian throwback revealing the family's 'touch of the tarbrush') and Topsy's sisters, Belle and Henrika, peep out from among the tropical plants. It becomes obvious that they are in fact other selves of the two protagonists, Sir Jasper projecting the cynicism and Cain the carnality that exist under Aston's polite and cultured surface, and Belle and Henrika projecting the sensuality and naïveté that lurk behind Topsy's public persona, the accomplished young bluestocking. As the conversation goes on the puppets of polite formality are set aside, and the siblings advance from the background to make their remarks in which they identify with the protagonists. The action is inconsequential. Talk goes on at cross purposes, Belle and Henrika comment from their various viewpoints as if what happens to Topsy were happening to them, Sir Jasper offers cynical advice to Aston who takes Topsy on a tour of the fantastic plants, Cain hovers in fascination, stroking Topsy's arm and provoking reactions of curiosity and fear from her sisters. Finally the play moves to its bizarre climax as Topsy inadvertently sniffs the chloroform flower. Aston opens the conservatory door, the flowers scream, drip blood and flash lights as the cold wind sweeps in, and Cain–Aston's carnal self–begins to kiss the unconscious Topsy, who awakens to see 'the black, greasy face, the chryselephantine smile, the pink, thick lips, the goggling eyeballs of white enamel'. There are confusions and reproaches before Topsy and Aston resume their social surface, talking through their dummies. The characters leave the stage. Sir Jasper is the last. 'Charming evening, charming evening,' he remarks. 'Now it's over, I wonder whether it ever existed.' And as he goes out the flowers flash and wink and chuckle 'while the Alochusia, after whistling a few derisive notes, finally utters a loud, gross Oriental hiccough'.

It is rather surprising that, in our age of the revolutionary theatre, this curious little play has not aroused more interest, for it presents a kind of blackly meaningful meaninglessness very similar to that one encounters in the contemporary plays of Ionesco and Beckett. It is a piece of the theatre of the absurd which antedates the rise of absurdism as a self-conscious literary movement.

None of the items included in *Limbo* is in fact without its interest in the context of Huxley's whole career. 'The Bookshop' is a fragile little story about a bookseller who simulates a great enthusiasm for the music of Berlioz, and sits down at a piano to play for his customer a score of *Robert the Devil*, singing the arias in a ghostly old man's voice. The ambiguities of the scene are obvious and multiple. The old man puts on the performance to sell the score for a mere five shillings, yet his love of the music is at the same time genuine. The customer is moved by the performance in 'this peaceful, abstracted place', and the music seems – as it often does in later Huxley books – to establish momentarily the feeling of an existence apart from the phenomenal world, 'safe from things, living at a remove from equality'. And as he goes out, having realized the ironies in the situation, the customer decides that: 'The wisest thing, perhaps, is to take for granted the "wearisome condition of humanity, born under one law, to another bound," and to leave the matter at that, without an attempt to reconcile the incompatibles.' The familiar Fulke Greville quotation, making its first appearance, established the attitude Huxley would sustain until the unendurability of those unreconciled incompatibles led him to his conversion and to the search for the unifying principle, which is curiously anticipated, in the poignant Huxleian imagery of sight, in another story.

This is 'Eupompus Gave Splendour to Art by Numbers', published in 1916 in *The Palatine Review* and strongly symbolist in flavour. It describes the career of a lost Hellenistic painter who believed that in numbers lay the clue to link all art with reality by giving it a mathematical foundation. The story is clearly intended to satirize the various schools of painting which, from the Impressionists to the Futurists, had sought to find a scientific basis for painting. Eupompus specialized in vast pictures representing crowds of people carefully grouped in numerical patterns; the most famous was an amphitheatre scene:

> Tier upon tier of seats are seen, all occupied by strange Cyclopean figures. Each tier accommodates more people than the tier below, and the number rises in a complicated but regular progression. All the figures seated in the amphitheatre possess but a single eye, enormous and luminous, planted in the middle of the forehead: and all these thousands of single eyes are fixed, in a terrible and menacing scrutiny, upon a dwarf-like creature cowering pitiably in the arena. . . . He alone of the multitude possesses two eyes.

In terms of satire on modern art, the intent of this passage is evident: the single-eyed are the cubists who, in reducing the painting to two dimensions, abandon the stereoscopic two-eyed vision which gives objects their appearance of three-dimensional solidity. In more personal terms, the less conscious implications of the image are even more interesting. First, there is the relevance to Huxley's own predicament. And then, anticipating Huxley's later arguments, there is the idea of light and unity associated in mystical understanding, with duality as a characteristic of the unregenerate.

But perhaps the most astonishing anticipation in *Limbo* of the later, mystically inclined Huxley is the one historically based story, 'The Death of Lully'. A Genoese boat lies offshore from an African city, with a Spanish libertine nobleman and his mistress as passengers. A clamour goes up in the city; the Moslems are attacking Raymond Lully, the Illuminated Doctor, who has been preaching among them. The captain of the ship tells the story of Lully: how as a young man he had been a profligate – like the Spaniard who is listening – and, after seeing the body of his most desired mistress eaten with cancer, was overwhelmed with horror and abandoned his rakish pleasures to set out on his missionary career that would lead to martyrdom.

The captain goes ashore to find the body of a martyr so that he can take it back to Christendom and gain credit and perhaps profit by it. But the old man is not dead, though he is dying. He is put to lie on his bier, and asks the young Spaniard to stay with him. 'We are countrymen and of noble blood, both of us. I would rather have you near me than anyone else.'

And as the libertine and his woman watch and listen, the old man talks in his thin weak voice, first to them, and then as if to himself, telling how God 'opened my eyes' (the stress once again on sight), and how, an alchemist, he had 'essayed that more difficult alchemy, the transformation of man', the recovery of that perfection in which God had made all things. Everything but gold will corrode under the bitterness of life. To quell passion and hatred, to overcome pain and illusion, needs 'the golden perfection of pure knowledge'.

The old man falls asleep. The captain wonders whether he will make more profit if he sells the saint's body in Genoa or in Minorca. The young Spaniard shrugs. 'I have no advice to offer.'

The story, based in general outline on the known history and teachings of the Dominican alchemist Raymond Lully, was derived from Huxley's readings in the mystics while an undergraduate at Oxford. What makes it so interesting in the general pattern of Huxley's works is that it reads like a sketch for the story of Anthony Beavis in *Eyeless in Gaza*, with the same shift from a profligate to a religious life, precipitated in each instance by a shock of horror–in Anthony's case the falling from the sky of a dog which bursts like a bomb of blood and defiles him and his mistress as they are making love on the roof of his house. But there is more to it than that, for the story contains further curious dualities. Read now, with Huxley's life in the past, it gives the impression of the author's two selves meeting. When he wrote the story, Huxley shared the young Spaniard's feeling that the horror of life was gratuitous and inescapable, and he was fascinated by those who regarded a bright hedonism as the only way of dealing with the Essential Horror. At the age of forty, when the Spaniard had decided he would kill himself, Huxley was to go through the metaphorical death and rebirth of conversion, and to emerge with an attitude to life much like that of Raymond Lully–a proselytizing mysticism which eventually refused to accept that enlightenment should be the privilege of the few. But beyond this biographical irony, there is the story's own particular irony. For Huxley has given us no hint of the young Spaniard's reactions. He leaves the story an enigma. We do not know which death the libertine will choose as his youth draws towards an end.

I have left till the last the second of the longer pieces in *Limbo*, the novella called 'Happily Ever After', because more than any other of the early pieces it serves as the crude prototype in miniature of Huxley's novels. It differs from them, and undoubtedly suffers, from having been written, during 1918, in the actual shadow of the war which was the first great mental watershed of Huxley's journey, and which was to a very great extent the subject of the story. Huxley had started it as a play, found it 'wholly undramatic' and decided to turn it into a 'long-drawn Henry Jamesian' story. In fact, all that survives of that intent is an American scholar, visiting his former tutor, who is at best a caricature of the Jamesian introvert. The story into which he has found his way is the earliest of Huxley's Peacockian experiments.

The title 'Happily Ever After' gives the clue to the satiric target of the novella. Huxley maintained a lifelong hostility to the literature of romantic love, and the very idea of idyllic love relationships seemed especially absurd in the conditions of the war. 'Happily Ever After' is not merely ironical in the way it emphasizes this point; it is positively bitter in its portrayal of the conflict of the generations that had developed by the end of the war.

All Huxley's early novels involve arrivals, and most of them departures. Denis Stone visits Crome, Gumbril returns to London, Calamy arrives at the Cybo Malaspina; Denis departs as *Crome Yellow* ends, Gumbril is about to leave London as *Antic Hay* ends and Calamy effectively terminates *Those Barren Leaves* by retiring to his hermitage. 'Happily Ever After' is not quite so neatly contrived. It begins with the arrival of the Norwegian-American scholar Jacobsen in June 1917 at the house of his old tutor Alfred Petherton in Oxford. But the departure that ends the novel is not, as we shall see, Jacobsen's.

Jacobsen provides one of the points of view through which we see the action of the novella. The other is that of Marjorie, old Petherton's daughter, the unwilling prisoner of Edwardian inhibitions. Between Petherton and Jacobsen exists the guru-pupil relation repeated in the novels, but Jacobsen, unlike later Telemachus figures, is not the *jeune premier* of the story.

That role is given to Guy Lambourne, Petherton's ward, whom Marjorie has known 'almost as long as she can remember'. Guy, an apprentice poet, an omnivorous reader, tireless in his attempts to educate Marjorie, is an ancestor of the young men whom Huxley later inserts into his novels as self-caricatures of the artist as a young man. Guy has been trapped into the army–the fate Huxley was by now glad to have escaped–but when he slips out of uniform on leave it is evident that military life has had no perceptible effect; he resembles Huxley as others must have seen him in 1917:

> . . . he still looked like a tall, untidy undergraduate; he stooped and drooped as much as ever; his hair was still bushy and, to judge by the dim expression of his face, he had not yet learnt to think imperially. . . .

He is a troubled young man, as Huxley himself was during the months of teaching at Eton when he wrote the novella and became involved in the left-wing politics that had spread through the College owing to the radical enthusiasm of young Lord de la Warr, abetted by George Lansbury, whom Huxley met when he came down to Eton to address the Political Club.

> . . . I had meant [Guy tells Jacobsen] to spend my life writing and thinking, trying to create something beautiful or discover something true. But oughtn't one, after all, if one survives, to give up everything else and try to make this hideous den of a world a little more habitable?

All Guy has the chance to do is to quarrel with his uncle Roger, a hearty clergyman schoolmaster full of fervour for a war he is far too old to fight, but which he expects Guy and his athletic young friend George White to accept without question. There is a tense scene at dinner on the eve of Guy's return to the front. Mr. Petherton has complained of being positively incapacitated by poor digestion.

> Roger turned and seized once more on the unhappy George. 'White,' he said, 'let this be a lesson to you. Take care of your inside; it's the secret of happy old age.'
> Guy looked up quickly. 'Don't worry about his old age,' he said in a strange harsh voice, very different from the gentle, elaborately modulated tone in which he generally spoke. 'He won't have an old age. His chances against surviving are about fourteen to three if the war goes on another year.'
> 'Come,' said Roger, 'don't let's be pessimistic.'
> 'But I'm not. I assure you, I'm giving you a most rosy view of George's chance of achieving old age.'
> It was felt that Guy's remarks had been in poor taste. There was a silence; eyes floated vaguely and uneasily, trying not to encounter one another. Roger cracked a nut loudly. When he had sufficiently relished the situation, Jacobsen changed the subject. . . .

Fathers and sons: the theme appears now in the form of Turgenev's generations; in Huxley's novels, it is not the biological fathers who will be positively significant, but the surrogate spiritual fathers.

But more than art, more than the future of humanity, more even than death, it is sex that disturbs Guy and now makes its first ambivalent appearance as a prime factor in Huxley's fiction. Guy has already written agonized letters to Marjorie, talking of his desire for her, and Marjorie, half hating herself for the vulgarity of it, has replied: 'Sometimes I long for you in the same way.' That night, after the tenseness of dinner, they go out into the moonlit garden where everything is black and white in the 'bright pale light that could not wake the sleeping colours of the world'. The light and the night play on their emotions. Saying 'We must make this the happiest hour of our lives,' Guy sees suddenly, as Huxley undoubtedly did at one time in his recovery of sight, that the moon is not a flat disk on a nearby wall but 'a sphere islanded in an endless night', and he feels suddenly insignificant, filled with 'an infinite dreariness'. Then they go into a tunnel of darkness between tall hedges, and Marjorie experiences an effect of blindness with which her creator was familiar. Guy, to her, 'had become nothing but a voice, and now that had ceased; he had disappeared.' It is in this protecting darkness, looking towards the light, that she implicitly offers herself, and then, out in the moonlight, Guy begins to kiss her, and suddenly, with contemptuous words, thrusts her away, remembering his one sexual experience with a prostitute. Marjorie flees in tears. They are both the victims of their repressions and their culture, which have offered Guy only 'dismal and cloistered chastity–broken only once, and how sordidly!'

Guy and his friend George go back to the war. George returns with one leg, and Jacobsen reflects with bitter irony that this once perfect young man is thought lucky to get away with so little damage. 'One thanks God because he has thought fit to deprive one of His creatures of a limb.' That is in the autumn. At Christmas, Guy is dead. The older people react with conventional mourning. Jacobsen sees it from his own viewpoint of self-protective and rational calm, now threatened by the disasters that afflict others around him. Marjorie's reaction is rendered with the cruellest of Huxleian irony; as she weeps there is a self observ-ing her sorrow, noting for future use the thoughts that provoke tears, and when George limps in to offer consolations they drift from sharing misery into sharing kisses–all in memory of darling Guy! The first of the Huxleian women who mingle despair with cynicism, their wounds with their pleasure, has appeared–the elder sister of Myra Viveash and Lucy Tantamount. In miniature, the characteristic Huxley novel first emerged with the publication of that long and bitter story 'Happily Ever After'.

5

It was not, however, for three more years that *Crome Yellow*, the first avowed novel, was published. They were years of diversified experience during which Huxley learnt a great deal about literary techniques, and came under a great many intellectual influences, all of which he gladly absorbed, for he was never one of those writers who disdain to borrow and turn to their own purposes whatever may be congenial to their talents. In 1920 he began an arrangement with the Condé Nast publi-cations which was to last longer than any of his early associations with periodicals. It brought him at first a great deal of drudgery, when he worked for *House and Garden* and *Vogue*, but through the articles he wrote from 1922 to 1930 for *Vanity Fair*, it provided him with the means to live economically in Italy and France, and concentrate on his novels away from the London literary world, which he found fascinating in his early twenties but later tediously distracting.

Huxley's early periodical articles, with their widening interests in human manners and eccentricities, in the arts, in politics, in philosophy and eventually, by a process of fascination that at last became irresistible, in changing facets of religion and mysticism, are a part of his work that cannot be ignored, and later I shall consider them in relation to the works of fiction which develop the ideas already partially worked out in the essays. It is superficial to dismiss Huxley as a mere essayist, as some critics have done, but it is impossible to ignore the expository development of ideas he later used in novels which, however didactic they may be, fulfil the only foolproof definition of authentic fiction: that they present worlds of the imagination convincing and self-consistent.

One of these worlds is the microcosm of *Crome Yellow*, which Huxley created when he escaped from London in 1921 for the first of a series of long writing periods abroad. He spent it mainly at Florence and in Forte dei Marmi near Carrara; economy attracted him there, as well as the abundant light that filled the Italian landscape; he estimated he could live as well in Forte dei Marmi for £300 as he could in England for £750 or £800 a year; it was the age when the shores of the Mediterranean offered an abundant existence to those who could command even a modest sterling income.

Announcing the advent of *Crome Yellow* to his friends, Huxley referred to it as 'my Peacockian novel'. Indeed, in a number of ways it adhered to the Peacockian model. Its setting was a country house, its occasion the gathering of a group of people of varied temperaments and of strong, not always compatible, points of view. Like every Peacock novel it had its elements of farce–lovers clambering over roofs, elderly gentlemen posing as fortune tellers–and its interpolated romances. Finally, most important, it used ideas dramatically and moved forward on the wings of discussion as much as of episode.

Yet there are a mellowness and fulness about *Crome Yellow*–slight though it may be in action and sometimes shallow in psychology–that distinguish it from all Peacock's novels, except *Gryll Grange*. Unlike most of Peacock's characters, Huxley's are not mere crotcheteers, one-opinion men arguing their points at everlasting cross purposes like those indomitable bores of *Headlong Hall*, Mr. Foster the perfectibilarian and Mr. Escot the deteriorationist. Huxley's characters have their limitations, their areas of blindness, but these are the accidents of temperament and experience that make one man a romantic and the other a cynic. Later, Huxley's interest in psycho-physiological typologies was to lead him into the acceptance of Jung's doctrines of psychological types and, more important, of W. H. Sheldon's theories linking temperament with physique, and even in this first novel the physical descriptions of the characters strike one as appropriate to the idiosyncrasies they display – the cynical rationality and the dry wit of the lizard-like Mr. Scogan, the bland and cultured futility of Henry Wimbush, whose handsome unageing face is 'like the pale grey bowler hat which he always wore, winter and summer – unageing, calm, serenely without expression'.

Crome Yellow is distinguished from Huxley's later adaptations of the Peacockian model by the gentler mood, the tone of mild pessimism that underlies the play of irony and humour. And in this distinguishing quality it resembles the book which acted as a filter for the Peacockian influence, Norman Douglas's *South Wind*, published in 1917, and undoubtedly the novel of the time that most strongly influenced Huxley's development. Cyril Connolly, in *Enemies of Promise*, has correctly pointed out how Douglas – in opposition to the vulgar success strain in the *bildungsromanen* that derived from Mackenzie's *Sinister Street* – developed the novel that 'stated for the first time the predicament (when anxious to be successful in love or at making a living) of the Petrouchka of the Twenties, the Clever Young Man'. In his first four novels Huxley was Douglas's best disciple; the two novelists became friends in Italy and remained so until Huxley's departure for the United States in 1937.

In *Crome Yellow* the echoes of *South Wind* are clear and ringing. It is not merely a question of form – the symposium-with-action that both novelists share with Peacock and W. H. Mallock – and not at all a question of setting; not until *Those Barren Leaves* four years later did Huxley follow Douglas in exploiting the exotic appeal to the Georgian English of an Italian scene. Nor does Huxley produce anything quite so magnificently bizarre as *South Wind*'s antics of Russian sectarians and drunken English spinsters in a violently coloured landscape whose sun is always in danger of being obscured by rains of volcanic ash. Yet, in the serene English country setting – Garsington Manor modified – which Huxley has chosen, the characters remind one constantly of their predecessors in Douglas's Island of Nepenthe. The hero has the same name as Denis of *South Wind;* he is a product of the same academically genteel background; and the misfortune of Huxley's Denis is identical with that of his namesake–to fail in love because of his lack of brute initiative. Scogan, that knowledgeable sceptic who is Denis's father surrogate so far as the novel is concerned, resembles closely the equally garrulous and cynical Keith of *South Wind*, though here a shift has occurred, for Scogan is poor and dependent where Keith is rich and independent; in compensation, where Mr. Eames, the indefatigable local historian of Nepenthe, is proudly poor, Henry Wimbush, who plays the corresponding role in *Crome Yellow*, is comfortably rich.

There are other influences at work in *Crome Yellow*: Swift among them, in such allusions as Henry Wimbush's remark that he enjoys 'seeing fourteen pigs grow where only one grew before' and in the interpolated story of Sir Hercules Lapith, the midget lord of Crome, whose attempt to create a self-contained Lilliputian world is destroyed by the invasion of Brobdingnagians of his own breeding. And throughout the novel are scattered exotic displays of knowledge which display the breadth and depth of Huxley's reading: for example, the treatise on water closets, *Certain Privy Counsels*, written by the Elizabethan owner of Crome, Sir Ferdinand Lapith, is modelled on Sir John Harington's treatise written on the same subject at the same period, *The Metamorphosis of Ajax*, but Huxley gives the concept a wide-ranging satirical application, and where Harington merely tells us that, by the use of his invention, 'your worst privy may be as sweet as your best chamber', Sir Ferdinand constructs the great towers that distinguish Crome in order to install his privies at their summit. For he argues:

> ... the necessities of nature are so base and brutish that in obeying them we are apt to forget that we are the noblest creatures of the universe. To counteract these degrading effects he advised that the privy should be in every house the room nearest to heaven, that it should be well provided with windows commanding an extensive and noble prospect, and that the walls of the chamber should be lined with bookshelves containing all the ripest products of human wisdom. ...

Here, of course, in grotesque form, was another Huxleian comment on the incongruities of the human condition, the division in man between animal functions and sublime speculations.

Given the kind of talent which Huxley possessed, supremely eclectic and assimilative, these literary influences are a more profitable matter of discussion than the idiosyncrasies borrowed from his acquaintances with which he graced his characters. Already it is a great deal less interesting than it was to people in the Twenties to know that Mr. Scogan resembles Bertrand Russell as Huxley had encountered him at Garsington, and Gombauld is a heavily touched-up likeness of the painter Mark Gertler, or that in deaf Jenny Mullion and earnest Mary Bracegirdle there survive memories of two other regular Garsington guests, Dorothy Brett and Dora Carrington, or that the preoccupation of the absurd inspirational writer Mr. Barbecue-Smith with his daily production of words may well be a fragment culled from Huxley's observation of Arnold Bennett, with whom he had become friendly in 1919. Huxley, despite the ingenuity with which he rearranged patterns taken from life, had an uninventive and unvisualizing mind; it was inevitable that he should take the materials that experience offered him, borrowing characteristics from his acquaintances, adapting scenes with which he was familiar, and endlessly mining his own life and his own mind for usable material.

The essential point to remember is that *Crome Yellow*, despite its autobiographical elements and its tantalizing resemblance to the *roman à clef*, is not as a whole an autobiographical novel and is avowedly unrealistic. Plot and character are used less for their customary purpose of telling a convincing tale about convincing people than to present, along with the ideas that emerge in discussion, other thoughts–less amenable to direct expression–on the nature of human motives and human relationships. It is not a novel of personal development, since none of the characters has by the end perceptibly changed, but it is at least a novel in which people learn lessons about life. But in *Crome Yellow* the mellowness of atmosphere and the lightness of treatment make the lessons sufficiently unobtrusive, so that it is possible here, as it is not in Huxley's later novels, to admire the grace of writing and the play of fancy for their own sakes. In this novel alone–to quote another of Cyril Connolly's insights–can Huxley be regarded as the literary dandy in the sense accepted in the Nineties, though I disagree with Connolly that 'the irony and lyricism are unadulterated.' They are both abundantly there and no later work displays them in such wistful eloquence, yet among them germinate the seeds of Huxley's later moralism.

In plan the novel is neatly united. The action takes place in the great house and its immediate environs; it lasts a little over a week, and is bounded by Denis's arrival at the nearest railway station and–at the end –by his abrupt departure, quoting Landor, from the porch of Crome.

The cast of characters is as carefully limited, in numbers and in class. There is the family at Crome–Henry Wimbush, his wife Priscilla with her spiritualist dabblings, and his coolly emancipated daughter Anne. There are the guests, Mr. Scogan and the painter Gombauld, the flirtatious Ivor and the unctuous Mr. Barbecue-Smith, Jenny and Mary, and, of course, Denis. Mr. Bodiham, the Low Church vicar with a sense of impending apocalypse, plays a peripheral role, as does his wife, with her watchful puritanism. And from the past the ghosts of ancestral Lapiths and Wimbushes are brought in through historical interpolations to set the present against a lost age seen through the golden veils of nostalgia. In the theatrical ambiance created by Huxley's rather formal description of the great house and its grounds, the poor enter as mainly voiceless extras: a guard at the railway station, some servants, the villagers who attend the great annual Fair in the grounds of Crome. And never does Huxley take us into their minds; to *Crome Yellow* as to all of Huxley's novels applies the comment which the novelist Quarles noted in *Point Counter Point*.

> The chief defect of the novel of ideas is that you must write about people who have ideas to express–which excludes all but about ·01 per cent of the human race. Hence the real, the congenital novelists don't write such books.

In this respect Huxley never changed. His characters were always drawn from a minority of the population distinguished by either prosperity or intellectuality, and this was not merely because these were the people among whom–because of class and occupation–his life had been led; it was because, whether he was discussing the life of art or the life of the spirit, the kind of people who could plausibly voice his thoughts were even rarer than the people who could read them with understanding. The characters who carry on the running symposium of *Crome Yellow* all have access to sweeping landscapes of ideas available to a leisure society with an implicit faith in aristocratic values.

But the novel is not all talk, despite the efforts of Mr. Scogan and Henry Wimbush and Barbecue-Smith to make it so. Indeed, the role of the talkers is strictly limited to exposition. They are excluded from the function of viewing. One never sees what is going on through the eyes of Mr. Scogan, and through Henry Wimbush's eyes one only sees the past that he has reconstructed in those episodes from the History of Crome which he reads aloud to entertain his guests. Mr. Bodiham is a hostile outside observer, bringing the deteriorationist eye of a moralistic bigot straight out of Peacock, to bear on the obviously useless and presumably immoral activities of the occupants of Crome. And from the inside we see that microcosmic world through several pairs of eyes, and all of them eyes of the young who have not yet acquired the narrowing of vision that comes to the Scogans whose minds are already hardened by habits of thought. We look through Denis's eye, through Anne's eye, through Mary's eye; we look with disconcerting indirect-ness through the critical eye of Jenny Mullion, when Denis opens her book of drawings and sees himself cruelly caricatured therein.

Jenny Mullion exemplifies more clearly than any other character the central ironic theme of *Crome Yellow*–a theme well explored by Peacock–that no matter how much we may talk, we never really understand each other. Jenny, in 'the ivory tower of her deafness', which is the equivalent of the dark tower of blindness Huxley once inhabited, in fact sees people more clearly than those who try to under-stand them by their words, a process which leads Denis to the melan-choly reflection: 'Parallel straight lines . . . meet only in infinity. . . . Did one ever establish contact with anyone?' Denis, inveterately romantic, sees everything through the spectacles of his infatuation for Anne, and yet sees wrongly, for he has no inkling until the end, when it is too late, that her flirtation with Gombauld has masked a growing tenderness for him. Anne in her turn is caught within her own hedonist pattern, that of an intelligent but mentally lazy girl who enjoys her power over men and cherishes the independence it gives her, yet is capable of genuine affections; her failing of perception is that she does not realize–again until it is too late–how Denis is likely to interpret her actions. As for Mary Bracegirdle–descended directly from that other Huxleian bluestocking with a theatrical name, Topsy Garrick in 'Happy Families'–she is caught entirely in the trap of false intellectuality, feeling bound to accept everything that seems to her authentically modern, from free love to cubism; this makes her an easy prey to Ivor's carefree amoralism, and inspires her to advise Denis to leave because Anne is indifferent to him, disastrous advice as Denis realizes when he stands in the library, having announced his intention to depart.

'I'm wretched you should be going,' said Anne.

Denis turned towards her; she really did look wretched. He abandoned himself hopelessly, fatalistically to his destiny. This was what came of action, of doing something decisive. If only he'd just let things drift! If only. . . .

The mood of the end is set, the mood of resigned irony, as Denis climbs into the car that seems to him like a hearse, and the turn of the wheel of existence that has been his stay at Crome is ended. It is, like the mood of the rest of the book, an irony without anger; the imperfections of life and of human nature have been observed and noted, not condemned. Only here and there in *Crome Yellow* does one get a hint of the dark satire that haunts the later novels of the Twenties–in the swingeing anti-clerical portrait of Mr. Bodiham, for example, and, more ironically, the Sludge-like portrait of the fake mystic, Mr. Barbecue-Smith, disreputable elder brother of the benign spiritual teachers, Miller and Propter and Rontini, in Huxley's post-conversion novels.

The monologues, discussions and readings which occupy so much of *Crome Yellow* are set out more deftly and more plausibly than the bare dialogues, voice shouting against voice, opinion clashing with opinion, that fill so many pages of Peacock. The ideas they express are drawn from the breadth of Huxley's varied interests. There are entertaining discussions of the purpose of literature in which Scogan sketches out a theory of non-realistic fiction that might be taken as a model for the novel in which he speaks, a fiction in which: 'All the ideas of the present and of the past, on every possible subject, bob up . . . smile gravely or grimace a caricature of themselves, then disappear to make place for something new.' Gombauld, tiring of abstract painting, constructs a masterpiece of mannerist fantasy that (as Sir Kenneth Clark has pointed out) is a remarkably accurate parallel to Caravaggio's painting of the Conversion of St. Paul which Huxley's poor eyes had remarkably well perceived in the church of Santa Maria del Popolo. There are discourses on the way in which a political environment will produce a leader appropriate to it. The hard scepticism of Scogan conflicts with–at the opposite end of the scale–the false spirituality of Priscilla Wimbush, who longs for and never achieves the extra-sensory experiences in which she believes.

If, in this essentially agnostic book, Huxley mocks the mysticism towards which he was later attracted, it is clear that he is not giving his approval to Scogan, who, with his love of the intellectual and the mathematical, his withdrawal from Nature, his lack of any feeling for art, is a precursor of those scientific and intellectual half-men who haunt the later novels. Nowhere is the link between the portrait of Scogan and Huxley's later attacks on the scientific attitude shown more clearly than in the speculations in which, a decade before that book was written, Scogan sketches out the basic concepts of *Brave New World*, and particularly the manipulative nature of its society.

Scogan's sketch begins early in *Crome Yellow* with a speculation on what might be done by the application of eugenics. 'In vast state incubators, rows upon rows of gravid bottles will supply the world with the population it desires.' Since mothers are no longer necessary, the family will cease to exist; since breeding is divorced from copulation, 'Eros ... will flit like a gay butterfly from flower to flower through a sunlit world.' But the Brave New World must be governed, and half way through *Crome Yellow* Scogan adapts the Platonic vision by arguing that: 'If you're to do anything reasonable in this world, you must have a class of people who are secure, safe from public opinion, safe from poverty, leisured, not compelled to waste their time in the imbecile routines that go by the name of Honest Work.' And later again he elaborates this pseudo-Platonic thought into the vision of a 'Rational State', whose population is divided into 'distinct species', their membership determined by psychological examination and appropriate education. The species will be 'the Directing Intelligences, the Men of Faith, and the Herd', and the Herd will be carefully conditioned by the scientific exploitation of its suggestibility. 'Systematically, from earliest infancy, its members will be assured that there is no happiness to be found except in work and obedience; they will be made to believe that they are happy, that they are tremendously important beings, and that everything they do is noble and significant.'

The necessary outline of the central vision of *Brave New World* is here presented, and one can admire the foresight with which, as early as 1921, Huxley was moving towards his conviction of the 1930s, that the greatest danger to man's freedom lies in the power to exploit his infinite suggestibility.

There are other Utopian thoughts in *Crome Yellow*. Henry Wimbush, that mild dilettante, with so much of Huxley in his nature, who believes that 'the proper study of mankind is books', dreams like a truly Peacockian character of the perfectibility of machinery, and likes to imagine himself living 'in a dignified seclusion, surrounded by the delicate attentions of silent and graceful machines, and entirely secure from any human intrusion'. And there is the fragile private world of Sir Hercules Lapith, who tries to create a microcosm for people of his kind into which the gigantic, which he equates with evil, cannot enter. But in a world where brutality exists those who try to give substance to fragile dreams are doomed, and, pathetically, brutally, the fate of Sir

Hercules, whose Utopia for midgets is destroyed when his normally human son returns with his companions from the grand tour, anticipates the fate of the Utopians of Pala at the hands of their militaristic neighbours in Huxley's last novel, *Island*.

CHAPTER FOUR

Circe's Realm

I

Wars end on waves of relief, and the relief spreads into ripples of optimism, which die away when it is realized that nothing has apparently been learnt in the school of destruction, that the world has not become a better place, that peace is no more inviolable than it was before, politicians no more incorruptible, mankind no less gullible. This process usually takes a few years, and during that time the survivors try to forget the horror they have witnessed and endured. It is still there of course, seeping irresistibly into consciousness, but most people, including writers, try to ignore it. They write–as Huxley did–books like *Crome Yellow*. Not until the later Twenties did the important novels of World War I begin to appear; Aldous Huxley, who lacked the direct experience of physical combat, wrote only in 1923 what we must consider his war book. *Antic Hay*, set in an England already four years away from the last battle of 1918, concerned itself with what the war had wrought. To his father, Leonard Huxley, who found the book distasteful and said so, Aldous replied: 'it is a book written by a member of what I call the war-generation for others of his kind; and . . . it is intended to reflect–fantastically of course, but none the less faithfully– the life and opinions of an age which has seen the violent disruption of almost all the standards, conventions and values current in the previous epoch.'

It was the air of challenge that made *Antic Hay* so much an emblem for the generation of the 1920s. Yet Huxley is not seeking to convert so much as to reveal. He is the social and moral critic; he is–in a way that still makes *Antic Hay* and *Point Counter Point* required reading for those who wish to understand the intellectual temper of the Twenties–the historian of attitudes; in this sense he is undoubtedly the teacher, but in the sense of offering the vision of an alternative world, as he was to do so frankly in most of the later novels from *Eyeless in Gaza* to *Island*, he is not. In using his satirical talent to arrange and present in a striking way what he observes rather than constructing a model of what he would like to see, he preserves that contact with the actual and concrete out of which spring the flowers of art.

Crome Yellow and *Antic Hay* resemble each other like fair and dark siblings. They share the same circular pattern, the same relative unity of place and time, the same mixture of humours, types and true characters, the same abundant and casually displayed erudition, the same use of discussion and idea as dynamic elements, the same ironic observation of the divisions and dualities of human life. Yet the two years that divide them changed Huxley's attitudes profoundly, so that already in *Antic Hay*, under the acerbic wit and the gathering pessimism, one can see the Huxleian dialectic beginning to work, the first glimmerings of a philosophy of eternity appearing in the gloom of a world dominated by time. For conversions, as Huxley was to remark in 'Uncle Spencer', are 'secretly and unconsciously prepared for, long before the event'.

2

An insight into the transition that Huxley underwent in the two years between the completion of *Crome Yellow* and *Antic Hay*, almost entirely written in two months – again mainly at Forte dei Marmi – during the summer of 1923, is offered by his second book of stories, *Mortal Coils*, which appeared in the spring of 1922.

Mortal Coils covers the spectrum of styles from his early neo-symbolist period to the baroque lyricism which is one of the prominent elements in his third novel, *Those Barren Leaves*. Neo-symbolism is represented in the one-act farce, 'Permutations among the Nightingales', completed early in 1920 and published in *Coterie*, a short-lived literary periodical with which Huxley was closely associated. Huxley told Arnold Bennett that he doubted if it were actable, and in that opinion he was undoubtedly correct. Today it seems a stilted and artificial comedy of rococo accidents of love that might have made a good scenario for the Russian Ballet (which perhaps inspired it) but is incapable of stirring an imaginative response in the reader.

The other four pieces in *Mortal Coils* are short stories – 'The Gioconda Smile', 'The Tillotson Banquet', 'Green Tunnels' and 'Nuns at Luncheon' – and they are among the best pieces of fiction Huxley ever wrote, showing a level of craftsmanship which he never equalled consistently in his larger works, and, at their best, a lyrical intensity that the novels only rarely—and in their least typical passages—approach.

'The Gioconda Smile' has a particularly significant place in the Huxley canon, for Huxley felt it important enough a quarter of a century later to turn it into a play and a film scenario, altering it radically to accord with his changed philosophy. Since Huxley did this with no other of his early works, it provides a touchstone of the differences between his literary aims in 1921 when the story was written and published by Ford Madox Ford in the *English Review* and those he held in 1946 when he carried out his adaptation.

In its first version 'The Gioconda Smile' is a stark little study of human evil. It is a story of crime and its reasons within the human heart, of the irony of motives misunderstood, of the ways in which our own actions doom us. The central character, Henry Hutton, is an aesthetically minded hedonist married to a permanent invalid; with Janet Spence, a spinster of thirty-five, he carries on a flirtatious friendship which she interprets as a tentative love affair; his real love affair is with Doris, a girl of vulgar prettiness, of trivial mind, and half his age.

One afternoon, when Janet is at his house and the nurse is going out for the evening, Hutton takes up to his invalid wife a cup of coffee Janet has poured. Afterwards, he goes out to spend the evening with Doris. Returning at night, through 'a bright and narrow universe of forms and colours scooped out of the night by the electric head lamps', he gets home to find Dr. Libbard there and his wife dead. It is assumed she has died from eating stewed red currants the nurse had given her, which set off an attack of indigestion and triggered a heart attack. Dr. Libbard is portrayed as a tired cynic who 'spoke of death as he would speak of a local cricket match. All things are equally vain and equally deplorable.'

Up to now, Hutton has been a totally selfish man. 'Instead of pitying, he loathed the unfortunate.' But the evening after his wife's funeral, having read a life of Milton picked at random out of his bookshelves, he goes out through the French windows into the quiet, clear night. There he has a momentary experience of bitter self-knowledge.

> He began to think with a kind of confused violence. There were the stars, there was Milton. A man can be somehow the peer of stars and night. Greatness, nobility. But is there seriously a difference between the noble and the ignoble? Milton, the stars, death, and himself—himself. The soul, the body; the higher and the lower nature. Perhaps there was something in it, after all. Milton had a god

on his side and righteousness. What had he? Nothing, nothing whatever. There were only Doris's little breasts. What was the point of it
all? Milton, the stars, death, and Emily in her grave, Doris and
himself—always himself. . . .

Oh, he was a futile and disgusting being. . . .

He resolves never to see Doris again. He fails to keep his resolution,
discovering 'in irresponsibility the secret of gaiety', and less than two
weeks after his wife's death he is secretly married again. He returns
home to receive a confession of love from Janet Spence. Now, she says,
they are both free. He leaves her sobbing and steals guiltily away. And
so, by the discrepancy between his resolutions and his actions, he has
played into the hands of fate; having made his marriage public and gone
abroad with Doris, he is pursued to Italy by the news that Janet is putting
about the story that he has poisoned his wife. Even at this moment of
peril he cannot resist the temptations offered by an Italian servant girl
with the profile of 'a Sicilian coin of a bad period'.

> 'Ha chiamato?' she asked at last.
> Stupidity or reason? Oh, there was no choice now. It was imbecility
> every time.
> 'Scendo,' he called back to her. Twelve steps led from the garden
> to the terrace. Mr. Hutton counted them. Down, down, down,
> down. . . . He saw a vision of himself descending from one circle of
> the inferno to the next–from a darkness full of wind and hail to an
> abyss of stinking mud.

Such a passage, with its view of the hell of self-knowledge preceding
the earthly paradise of self-enjoyment, makes it evident why Huxley
should have picked for re-use the story filled with premonitions of his
later speculations, and remarkably anticipating–in Hutton's life and
fall–the fate of the hedonist Eustace Barnack in *Time Must Have a Stop*.
For Hutton receives his punishment, even in this life, though not for the
sins he has committed. He returns to England for the inquest; it is
demonstrated that his wife actually died of arsenic poisoning. Henry is
the obvious suspect, and in due course the machine of the law works out
his doom. 'Confusedly he felt that some extraordinary kind of justice
was being done. In the past he had been wanton and imbecile and
irresponsible. Now Fate was playing as wantonly, as irresponsibly, with
him. It was tit for tat, and God existed after all.' In the end, after Hutton
has been hanged, it is Dr. Libbard who indifferently wrings out of
Janet Spence the confession that she poisoned Mrs. Hutton.

It is an extraordinary kind of story for Huxley to have written as early as 1921, full of the overtones of a kind of religion that had played no part in his youth. Reading it without knowing its author, one might easily assign it to a Catholic writer of the following decade: Graham Greene was to write many similar stories. It was the very elements which suggest the idea of an implacable divine justice–a God of the kind later to be postulated by Spandrell in *Point Counter Point*–that Huxley eliminated when a quarter of a century later he turned the story into a play with a happy ending.

In the play, also called *The Gioconda Smile*, the basic situation remains–the invalid wife, the cynical husband, the platonic woman friend, the fluffy little mistress. But the action is complicated by the nurse instead of Janet accusing Hutton of murder, though Janet gives her evidence so as to make sure of a condemnation. Most significantly Dr. Libbard is changed from the inactive cynic of the story into a version of the mystical guru of later novels. Deploring Hutton's way of life, he believes him innocent. He appears in prison to fill Hutton with the wisdom of 'letting go', and he pursues outside prison a strategy of enlightened action, winning over the nurse, establishing contact with the Home Secretary and, by a combination of trickery and hypnosis, gaining a confession from Janet Spence just in time to save Hutton from the drop. The changed role of Libbard and the contrived happy ending rob the piece of its original sombre impressiveness. It is clear, when one reads the two pieces together, that the early Huxley aimed at combining the presentation of moral *facts* with the achievement of aesthetic proportion, and usually succeeded. The later Huxley was willing to sacrifice aesthetic proportions to moral *lessons*, and by doing so he often failed even as a teacher.

The last letter that has survived from Aldous Huxley, written on the 17th November 1963, five days before his death, concerns the other story from *Mortal Coils* that was first published in 1921; this, 'The Tillotson Banquet', he was considering for adaptation into a television drama. The effort to reach an ever wider audience for the socio-moral lessons of his later years by dramatizing his books and stories became almost an obsession in Huxley's final decades, but 'The Tillotson Banquet' missed this fate, and it remains as one of Huxley's most humanly moving stories and one of his many psychological studies of painters.

'The Tillotson Banquet' is centrally concerned with the ironical relationship between the artist and his work. The artist moves on towards decay and death, caught in the time cycle of human existence.

The work, if it is true art, remains lodged in a different temporal world, its physical substance still subject to decay, its form an emanation of eternity. So, when the art critic Spode sees in Lord Badgery's collection an impeccable painting by Tillotson, a pupil of Benjamin Robert Haydon, and realizes that Tillotson, who painted the picture in 1846, must still be obscurely alive, Badgery imagines a whole room covered with great Tillotson frescoes, and the search for the artist begins. Spode eventually runs him to earth among the black-beetles of a Holloway slum. There is no prospect of the great murals, for Tillotson, who vanished for decades in the Middle East and returned to a London that had forgotten him, is not only down to his last ten pounds; he is also ninety-three, senile and purblind. In one of the private jests in which he often refers obliquely to his own condition, Huxley makes Tillotson say: 'The eyes of memory don't grow dim. But my sight is improving, I assure you; it's improving daily.' Since he will get no paintings, Badgery settles instead on the idea of a great Tillotson Banquet where he can amuse himself by mixing all the great enemies of the London art world.

Spode's attitude towards the whole affair is ambiguous. He hopes the banquet will be a means to his own advancement. Yet, when he is with Tillotson, other thoughts move him. 'Spode felt strangely moved, he hardly knew why, in the presence of this man, so frail, so ancient, in body three parts dead, in the spirit so full of life and hopeful patience. He felt ashamed.' But he still goes on with the preparations for the banquet, and in due course this great gathering takes place in a room filled with patrons and patronesses, with critics and dealers, and even a few painters. It was Huxley's first foray into that metropolitan half-world where the Bright People of Mayfair meet the Bohemians of Chelsea and Bloomsbury; he was shortly to anatomize it in *Antic Hay* and *Point Counter Point*. In 'The Tillotson Banquet' the satire on the predators of culture is sharp but brief; the banal and excruciatingly pathetic climax comes when Tillotson is presented with the silk purse containing fifty-eight pounds, the proceeds of the subscription on his behalf, and speaks in prolix response on the hard life of the artist, repeating himself endlessly, and telling over and over again the sad history of his great master Benjamin Robert Haydon. Ironically, of course, as Spode had realized, Tillotson was the better painter; Haydon played a great part in Huxley's thoughts at this period as the prime example of the artist whose views on art and life were impeccable, whose conceptions of individual paintings were magnificent, but who failed completely to realize his ideas or his plans. Packed into Badgery's second Rolls-Royce, Tillotson returns to his basement, his black-beetles, the morning-after reproaches of his landlady. So far as the art world is concerned, oblivion has closed over him again after this brief, embarrassing interlude. He has become irrelevant to his works, which live on unchanged while change submerges the artist.

The last two stories in *Mortal Coils*, 'Green Tunnels' and 'Nuns at Luncheon', are remarkable for their felicitous combination of the satiric and the lyrical. In 'Green Tunnels', deeply disguised, lies the experience of Huxley's youth, for it is really a study of the equivocal character of all our romantic imaginings. It is also Huxley's first exploration in fiction of the terrain of *Those Barren Leaves*, the Tyrrhenian coastline of Italy which he sees, not through the eyes of its native inhabitants, but through those of the English expatriates who form a colony projected by the world of *Crome Yellow* and *Antic Hay*. Mr. Buzzacott, and his guests, Mr. and Mrs. Topes, are monied people, involved in endless conversations on the arts, but basically concerned with the preservation of their status and their financial security. Mr. Topes is one of Huxley's relentless talkers, expounding his lore of paintings and sculptures until Barbara, Buzzacott's adolescent daughter, asks him: 'Why do you always talk about art? You bring these dead people into everything. What do I know about Canova or whoever it is?' And Mr. Topes, a long time after, when they have looked together over the sea with its 'mysterious air of remoteness', answers her in words that might have been spoken by Mr. Scogan if only he had been still concerned with art, or by almost any other Huxley elder until the appearance of Miller in *Eyeless in Gaza*:

> Most of one's life is one prolonged effort to prevent oneself thinking. Your father and I, we collect pictures and read about the dead. Other people achieve the same result by drinking, or breeding rabbits, or doing amateur carpentry. Anything rather than think calmly about the important things.

The basic irony of the story is that Barbara and Mr. Topes, who is sixty, 'with all a life immensely long and yet timelessly short, behind him', are akin without knowing it. Barbara resembles one of Huxley's own past personae, the poet of his student years. When her father talks in the affected bilingual language of the Italianate Englishman about the green tunnels which thirteenth-century Italian gardeners loved to create, her mind echoes the preoccupation with underwater worlds which was a characteristic of early Huxley poems. In 'The Reef', there are 'the green/Idiot fishes of my aquarium,/Who loiter down their dim tunnels. . . .' Barbara in her turn 'pictured caverns in a great aquarium, long vistas between rocks and scarcely swaying waves and pale, dis-coloured corals; endless dim green corridors with huge lazy fishes loitering aimlessly along them. Green-faced monsters with goggling eyes and mouths that slowly opened and shut. Green tunnels. . . .' For Barbara too is avoiding reality, not by studying paintings, but by living in a fantasy world where her dreams centre in the romantic-looking young Marchese Prampolini, one of their neighbours. One day, swimming back to the beach where the marquis has been sun-bathing only a moment before, she sees scrawled in the sand before her bathing cabin the mysterious evocative words, 'O Clara d'Ellébeuse'. Immediately she thinks of the marquis, and her head fills with yearning dreams. But one day when she is strolling with Mr. Topes, she meets him in the company of a scandalous Russian woman from the hotel, and suddenly they seem like the artificial figures of 'Permutations among the Nightingales'. Mr. Topes, meanwhile, has been stirred by Barbara's loveliness (which he can only liken to a Mantegna madonna) 'with the sea and the westering sun, the mountains and the storm, all eternity as a background'. He thinks of death and beauty, and of tenderness, and does not know what to say until, stumbling through grand and clumsy generalizations, he comes back to the literary allusions that are his most congenial way of expressing himself:

'. . . Certain poems express it. You know Francis Jammes? I have thought so much of his work lately. Art instead of life, as usual; but then I'm made that way. I can't help thinking of Jammes. Those delicate, exquisite things he wrote about Clara d'Ellébeuse.'
   'Clara d'Ellébeuse?' She stopped and stared at him.
   'You know the lines?' Mr. Topes smiled delightedly. 'This place makes me think, you make me think of them. "J'aime dans les temps Clara d'Ellébeuse. . . ." But, my dear Barbara, what is the matter?'
   She had started crying, for no reason whatever.

No reason—except that the romantic sensibility which had induced a man to write about Clara d'Ellébeuse outside her bathing cabin is hidden, not within a young and dashing Italian noblemen, but within a dry scholar who resembles an elderly cat. This conjunction of the awakening girl and the old man who cannot think of beauty without thinking of death is a masterpiece in its mingling of multiple ironies with a lyrical tenderness rare in Huxley's work.

'Nuns at Luncheon' is another of the stories of European wandering, full of recollections of those adolescent days which Huxley spent in Germany before the war while he was recovering from his blindness. Though it was written about the end of 1921, before *Antic Hay*, it is, like 'Green Tunnels', more closely linked to *Those Barren Leaves*, both by its locale, and by the presence of a lady writer, Miss Penny, precursor of Mary Thriplow in the novel, who over lunch tells the narrator of the double possession of the unfortunate Melpomene Fugger. Having been sexually assaulted by her father's old friend, Professor Engelmann of the 'red Assyrian beard', Melpomene takes to religion and self-mortification and ends up as a nun. Persuaded that the self-mortification stemmed from spiritual pride, she becomes an efficient and cheerful nurse, her smile enhanced by a 'grand new set of imperishable teeth, all gold and ivory', which she gains after losing all her own teeth through neglect during her period of hysterical devotion.

But Sister Agatha—as she has now become—is not proof against temptation. She has already converted several of her patients, and when an Italian thief comes from prison to be treated in the hospital she sets out to repeat the process, only to fall unwittingly in love with him. Kuno, at first indifferent, soon sees a chance of escape, plays up to Sister Agatha, and on the day before he is about to be taken back to the prison, escapes with her, disguised in nun's robes. On the tram riding out to the country Kuno steals an old lady's purse, but it does not contain enough to enable him to escape. He and Sister Agatha reach a shepherd's caravan; he breaks the lock, they enter, and he forcibly deprives her of her golden teeth. With that grim comic irony ends the first of Huxley's studies of the phenomenon of possession which he was later to elaborate so dramatically in *The Devils of Loudun*. It is a story executed with splendid craftsmanship, in which the to and fro of the dialogue and the freaks of Miss Penny's memory are used for Huxley's first experiment in breaking the strictly chronological pattern. The story begins with Miss Penny in a German hospital, and the sudden disappearance of one of the nuns, who returns a couple of days later, infinitely miserable and attired as a hospital charwoman; it continues with the presentation of various scattered facts as they are reluctantly surrendered to Miss Penny's avaricious curiosity, until in the end the fragments of memory are assembled and stitched together by the imagination of the story teller and the conjectures of the colleague with whom she is lunching.

3

If one were fitting Huxley's novels into a mythological pattern, the best way to describe *Antic Hay* would be as a Circead, for it is a pilgrimage in the company of the presiding spirit of an infernal circle where men are universally seen as less than they might be, half bestial. 'My men, like satyrs grazing on the lawns,' runs the epigraph from Marlowe's *Edward II*, 'Shall with their goat feet dance an antic hay.'

The Circe of the novel is Myra Viveash; the anti-Odysseus who chooses a witch for a companion is Theodore Gumbril, like Huxley himself a master at a public school, who decides to abandon his tedious profession and to seek liberty not through writing but by means of a fantastic invention which sets the serio-comic tone of the novel— Gumbril's Patent Small Clothes, a new type of trousers equipped with an inflatable seat. The Small Clothes, besides making Gumbril a fair amount of money through his dealings with the rascally speculator, Mr. Boldero, are also the basis of the disguise–completed by a great golden false beard–through which Gumbril seeks to create a new persona, Toto the Rabelaisian man, who will accomplish the adventures which Gumbril, a brainy ineffectual in real life, has never been able to realize. Indeed, adventures do follow, with ironic conclusions; for the girl with the serpentine figure whom Toto picks up in Bayswater turns out to be the wife of Gumbril's friend, the physiologist Shearwater, and Emily, the wounded innocent whom he encounters in the National Gallery, only begins to love him when he removes his beard and becomes his own weak self.

Such episodes suggest the mood of the book, which is a great deal more complicated in tone, theme and action than *Crome Yellow*. Huxley described it, when he made its excuses to his disapproving father, as 'a very serious book'. 'Artistically, too,' he went on, 'it has a certain novelty, being a work in which all the ordinarily separated categories– tragic, comic, fantastic, realistic–are combined so to say chemically into a single entity, whose unfamiliar character makes it appear at first sight rather repulsive.'

This combination of the various 'categories' gives effective expression to two of the important themes of the book–delusion (things are never what they seem) and imperfection (things are never what they should be). Gumbril's disguise is one of the more obvious but also one of the more innocent examples of delusion in *Antic Hay:* he is, after all, the Holy Fool of the book, who deludes himself as much as he does others.

The more sinister forms of delusion are almost always accompanied by the reminders of bitter reality. In the opening scene of the book there is a magnificently anticlerical representation of Mr. Pelvey ('Mr. Pelvey knew; he had studied theology') thundering away at his mechanical liturgy in the school chapel while, as a harsh comment on this pompous religiosity, the recollection of his mother's apparently pointless agonies as she died of cancer come surging up out of memory into Gumbril's consciousness. Rosie Shearwater's fantasies of being a fastidious lady, the muse-mistress of young poets, seem to be fulfilled when she meets Toto the Complete Man, but as she passes on through the voluptuary hands of Mercaptan and finally reaches Coleman, with his Dostoevskian passion for arousing self-disgust in the partners of his amorous games, she has learnt the difference between daydream and reality; it is a lesson that had been learnt long ago by Myra Viveash.

One deludes, as Gumbril deludes Rosie and Rosie deludes Shearwater, but always one ends in self-delusion, and it is the patterns of self-delusion that are the more deeply bitten. Casimir Lypiatt, like Benjamin Robert Haydon, has laudable views, and mounts a criticism of the intellectual world around him that Huxley undoubtedly in part endorses.

> You disgust me [he shouts at the slimy, complacent and lascivious Mercaptan], you disgust me—you and your odious little sham eighteenth-century civilization; your piddling little poetry; your art for art's sake instead of for God's sake; your nauseating little copulations without love or passion; your hoggish materialism; your bestial indifference to all that's unhappy and your yelping hatred of all that's great.

Lypiatt's denunciation is sincere and accurate. He knows, clearly enough, all that is wrong with the world. And his bluster conceals real passions and a power to love devotedly, as he loves Myra Viveash. Yet, when Lypiatt put his brush to a canvas the result, as Myra tactlessly tells Mercaptan, is like that of a Cinzano advertisement; all his burning sincerity, expressed in painting, seems flashy and insincere, yet to self-deluding Lypiatt it is the greatest art of its time.

Shearwater is another victim of self-delusion, the prototype of the mentally crippled scientist, seeing only the statistics of his research and the abstractions he derives from them, but ignoring his young wife and unaware that she is industriously cuckolding him. An encounter with Myra Viveash suddenly shatters his closed world.

'You don't seem to take much interest in us, Mr. Shearwater,'
Myra called expiringly. Shearwater looked up; Mrs. Viveash
regarded him intently through pale, unwavering eyes, smiling as she
looked that queer downward-turning smile which gave to her face,
through its mask of laughter, a peculiar expression of agony. 'You
don't seem to take much interest in us,' she repeated. . . .

Shearwater, who had hesitated before replying, was about to
speak. But Coleman answered for him. 'Be respectful,' he said to
Mrs. Viveash. 'This is a great man. He reads no papers, not even
those in which our Mercaptan so beautifully writes. He does not
know what a beaver is. And he lives for nothing but the kidneys.'

Mrs. Viveash smiled her smile of agony. 'Kidneys? But what a
memento mori! There are other portions of the anatomy.' She threw
back her cloak, revealing an arm, a bare shoulder, a slant of pectoral
muscle. She was wearing a white dress that, leaving her back and
shoulders bare, came up, under either arm, to a point in front and
was held there by a golden thread about the back. 'For example,'
she said, and twisted her hand several times over and over, making
the slender arm turn at the elbow, as though to demonstrate the
movement of the articulations and the muscular play.

Such an exhibition turns even Shearwater's head, and he becomes one
of Myra's vain suitors, to be shrugged off after he has sufficiently shown
his captivity to her Circean charms. And in the very last scene of the
book, when Myra looks through the window of the chamber in which
he is pedalling to prove some scientific point, he sees her as a hallucin-
ation haunting him on 'the nightmare road'.

In a sense his vision is true, for Myra is the centre of the whole pattern
of delusion. When Gumbril abandons the school and decides to return
to London, he meets in a restaurant the friends who personify the
various pretences of the intellectual world: Mercaptan, writer of
'delicious middles' who represents shallow literary aestheticism and
obliquely mocks Huxley's own past at the *Athenaeum;* Lypiatt, who
represents the hollowness of the grand visions that seem the alternative
to Mercaptanism; Shearwater the scientist whose knowledge, unlinked
to a wider view of life, is as much a pointless ride to nowhere as his
efforts on the captive bicycle; Coleman, the blasphemer and corrupter
derived from the tragic Philip Heseltine (better known under his
composer's nom-de-plume of Peter Warlock) and anticipating the full-
fledged Satanist Spandrell in *Point Counter Point.* The dinner is an
introductory symposium in which the five characters expound, in fury
or jest, their points of view and so delineate their various temperaments.

It is the most Peacockian part of the book; a real dialogue of ideas, carried on between men who have one thing in common, that they have been or will be captivated by Myra Viveash. And their meeting ends when they stroll out to Hyde Park Corner, and encounter Myra standing at a coffee stall with Bruin Opps, her incumbent lover, eating a snack after a disastrous expedition to dine at Hampton Court. Opps completes the circle of the world where Mayfair and Bohemia meet, the world of all of Huxley's earlier novels. Wearing his 'tall tubed hat and silk-faced overcoat', he makes no attempt to conceal his dislike of the working people who surround him at the stall; his snobbery and prejudice are frank.

> 'I loathe them,' said Bruin. 'I hate everyone poor, or ill, or old. Can't abide them; they make me positively sick.'

All these men delude themselves into imagining they can stir Myra's love. But it is she who induces in them that phenomenon of crystallization which Stendhal defined so ably, and which Gumbril, who has already gone through the process, redefines as he observes Shearwater imagining that somewhere under the apparent Myra, with her poses and frivolities, there must be a 'real Mrs. Viveash'.

> Most lovers, Gumbril reflected, picture to themselves, in their mistresses, a secret reality, beyond and different from what they see every day. They are in love with somebody else – their own invention. And sometimes there is a secret reality; and sometimes reality and appearance are the same. The discovery, in either case, is likely to cause a shock. 'I don't know,' he said. 'How should I know? You must find out for yourself.'

Yet everything about Myra – her faint, expiring voice, her pale, fixed eyes, the expression of agony on her face, her very name with its bilingual suggestion of 'living ash' – suggests the burnt-out heart, a nature that can occasionally be capable of a decent thought but nothing more. Myra brings the meaning of the book, as stated by Huxley, into focus since she is the character who most of all embodies the inner death of disillusionment that is the result of war. Her lover, Tony Lamb, was killed in France; his name, of course, echoes that of the other war victim, Guy Lambourne, in 'Happily Ever After', and Myra resembles Marjorie in that she too was once able to reawaken her grief by mentally repeating the words 'never again'. But she is Marjorie a stage farther on; something has died inside her, and nothing has grown to replace it.

. . . Never again, never again. She repeated them slowly now. But she felt no tears behind her eyes. Grief doesn't kill, love doesn't kill; but time kills everything, kills desire, kills sorrow, kills in the end the mind that feels them; wrinkles and softens the body while it still lives, rots it like a medlar, kills it too at last. Never again. Instead of crying, she laughed, laughed aloud.

Incapable any more of love, Myra half unwillingly attracts men to her, and makes them—while they are under her Circean spell—less than themselves, giving her favours, taking her lovers away, and with negligent hand whipping them into their circus acts to amuse her. Thus even Gumbril, who imagines himself free from her, submits when she capriciously demands that he stay to lunch with her in London rather than joining in the country the girl—Emily—for whom he has developed a real tenderness during his Toto adventures, and so the idyll is destroyed, for when Gumbril does go the next day Emily has vanished. And to Lypiatt, lightly—and without real malice—she brings that disillusionment which is his searing moment of truth. For, when Lypiatt goes in fury to reproach Mercaptan for the latter's sneering remarks about the art show from which he has expected so much, Mercaptan reveals that it is Myra—whose faith in his greatness he had always assumed—who has jestingly insisted that his paintings were like vermouth advertisements. He decides to shoot himself, and begins to compose—for Myra—a great apologia for his life. He writes on, at times contemplating the muzzle of his service revolver, until at night there is a knock on the door of his dingy mews flat. He hears the voices of Myra and Gumbril, but does not answer. They talk of him with a compassion that is almost more horrifying than the derision of the Mercaptan. He stands silently listening until they go.

Lypiatt walked slowly back to his bed. He wished suddenly that he had gone down to answer the last knock. These voices—at the well's edge he had turned to listen to them; at the well's extreme edge. He lay quite still in the darkness; and it seemed to him at last that he had floated away from the earth, that he was alone, no longer in a narrow dark room, but in an illimitable darkness outside and beyond. His mind grew calmer; he began to think of himself, of all that he had known, remotely, as though from a great way off.

We are not told that Lypiatt actually kills himself; nevertheless, he has died to his past, and goes on into that dark night of the spirit which, in certain later Huxley characters, is the prelude to enlightenment. Again, inner crisis is associated with the imagery of light and darkness.

But if Myra and her 'men like satyrs' are individually the victims of
delusion and self-delusion, so is the Bohemian-Mayfair society to which
they belong; for it is trying in its cynical pastimes to forget the realities
of misery and poverty, of the great other nation on which it floats like
a raft upon a quaking swamp. On the most brutal level, its attitude is
represented by Bruin Opps and his hatred of the poor and the unfortunate which–as Gumbril shrewdly realizes–is intensified by guilt.
On the highest level it is represented by Gumbril Senior, who resents
that his imagination as an architect should be utilized in designing
houses for the workers, and dreams of constructing the palaces and
cathedrals for which he can only make models.

But there are times when the nation of the poor demands attention;
indeed, *Antic Hay* has in it more of the elements of social awareness than
any other of Huxley's early novels. During the scene at the coffee stall
Gumbril becomes conscious of the conversation among the cab drivers
and workmen who are the regular patrons of the stall, and what he
hears is counterpointed with the frivolities of Mrs. Viveash, the
blasphemies of Coleman and the obtusenesses of Shearwater (named
after a large-headed seabird incapable of lofty flight):

'I used to do cartin' jobs,' the man with the teacup was saying.
' 'Ad a van and an old pony of me own. And didn't do so badly
neither. The only trouble was me lifting furniture and 'eavy weights
about the place. Because I 'ad malaria out in India, in the war. . . .'

'Nor even–you compel me to violate the laws of modesty,–nor
even,' Mrs. Viveash went on smiling painfully, speaking huskily,
expiringly, 'of legs?'

A spring of blasphemy was touched in Coleman's brain. 'Neither
delighteth He in any man's legs,' he shouted, and with an extravagant
show of affection he embraced Zoe, who caught hold of his hand
and bit it.

'It comes back on you when you get tired like, malaria does.' The
man's face was sallow and there was an air of peculiar listlessness and
hopelessness about his misery. 'It comes back on you, and then you
go down with fever and you're as weak as a child.'

Shearwater shook his head.

'Nor even of the heart?' Mrs. Viveash lifted her eyebrows. 'Ah,
now the inevitable word has been pronounced, the real subject of
every conversation has appeared on the scene. Love, Mr. Shearwater!'

'But as I says,' recapitulated the man with the teacup, 'we didn't do
so badly after all. We 'ad nothing to complain about. 'Ad we,
Florrie?'

The black bundle made an affirmative movement with its upper extremity.

This is a good example of Huxley's method of setting off against each other the frivolities of the artificial world and the grimnesses of the real one, with the further irony that for Myra Viveash and Lypiatt and Shearwater and all the others life holds its special grimnesses. Huxley's comedy–for there is a laugh to be wrung out of even this situation–is not essentially that of verbal wit (which explains the dullness of his plays) but rather that of the incongruities of situation.

Gumbril appeals to his friends on behalf of the carter, who has lost his old horse and tramped to Portsmouth and back with his pregnant wife. They salve their consciences by contributing five pounds between them (a fraction of what they have together spent on dinner) and Gumbril, walking away with Shearwater, whose head is full of physiological experiments and Mrs. Viveash, broods over the fact that 'the majority of one's fellow-beings pass their whole lives being shoved about like maltreated animals!' He thinks of legless soldiers grinding organs, of wretched street hawkers, of hanged men and despairing suicides and ruined shopkeepers. And then, luxuriating in this melancholy, he remembers an earlier melancholy with which he had walked the same streets; the images of human degradation pass from his mind and he begins to talk of the time when he was in love with Myra Viveash and for a brief two or three days possessed her.

Few of the other characters, except Lypiatt on occasion, think of the poor or of social justice, but the grim spectre of revolution is aroused on the unlikely lips of Mr. Bojanus, the Savile Row tailor who confides to Gumbril his theory that the basis of revolution is not economic envy but cultural resentment.

'When the revolution comes, Mr. Gumbril–the great and necessary revolution, as Alderman Beckford called it–it won't be the owning of a little money that'll get a man into trouble. It'll be his class-habits, Mr. Gumbril, his class-speech, his class-education. It'll be Shibboleth all over again, Mr. Gumbril; mark my words. The Red Guards will stop people in the street and ask them to say some such word as "towel". If they call it "towel", like you and your friends, Mr. Gumbril, why then . . .' Mr. Bojanus went through the gestures of pointing a rifle and pulling the trigger; he clicked his tongue against his teeth to symbolize the report . . . 'That'll be the end of them. But if they say "tèaul", like the rest of us, Mr. Gumbril, it'll be "Pass Friend and Long Live the Proletariat." Long live Tèaul.'

Mr. Bojanus, one of the wiser characters of *Antic Hay*, does not believe that revolutions bring liberty. He maintains that true freedom is something only a few independently-minded people achieve, and that the concept of political and social liberty is a swindle because necessity still demands of men 'the fundamental slavery – the necessity of working'. As for sexual freedom, 'It's an 'orrible, 'ideous slavery.' The fate of Myra's 'satyrs' bears him out.

Parallel with this complex of delusions which traps Huxley's characters, and which misleads whole societies with illusions of security and freedom, the pattern of the ideal world versus the actual world is developed much more complexly than in *Crome Yellow*.

This pattern is reflected in the very structure of the novel. It plays its due part in the central linear narrative of Gumbril's symbolic adventures, but it also affects the overall circular construction, which manifests itself in concrete terms as the portrait of a city conceived in the spirit of Shelley's line, 'Hell is a city much like London.' The novel begins with Gumbril leaving his school in the Home Counties and coming into London. It finishes, after he has discarded Rosie and in turn been discarded by Emily, with his going abroad. During the weeks of action, many parts of London, from Lypiatt's Piranesian mews to Myra Viveash's Mayfair home, are visited, and the novel ends in a last melancholy tour of the city, time and again traversing Piccadilly Circus, as Myra and Gumbril vainly seek even one of his friends to share in his farewell.

Within this great infernal circle the relationships of the characters are arranged in peculiar Huxleian patterns. Once, in an interview published in the *Saturday Review of Literature* during the 1930s, Huxley described explicitly the multiple viewpoints he sought to establish in his novels:

> I have a literary theory that I must have a two-angled vision of all my characters. You know how closely farce and tragedy are related. That's because the comic and the tragic are the same thing seen from different angles. I try to get a stereoscopic vision, to show my characters from two angles simultaneously. Either I try to show them both as they feel themselves to be, and as others feel them to be; or else I try to give them rather similar characters who throw light on each other, two characters who share the same element, but in one it is made grotesque.

In both categories one might take Lypiatt as the most striking example of this technique. He is both tragic and comic; tragic in the sense that he is destroyed by his own flaw of failing to match achievements with pretensions; comic because of that very incongruity. We see Lypiatt in terms of the grandeur he feels within himself; we see him mocked and decried by Coleman and Gumbril and Mercaptan in the dinner scene; we see Myra Viveash's ambivalent attitude towards him – pity mingled with involuntary mockery; we see the critics misunderstanding his intentions but all too clearly assessing his painterly shortcomings; we see Gumbril performing the most cruel criticism of all by sending the egregious Mr. Boldero to persuade Lypiatt to design a poster for Gumbril's Patent Small Clothes; finally, when Lypiatt recites his inflated poems, we, the readers, are able to make our own judgement on the gulf between the sincerity of his ideals and the ineptness with which he renders them. Finally, there is the inevitable comparison between Lypiatt and Gumbril Senior: both see quite accurately the degeneracy of the intellectual and artistic world in their time. But, where Lypiatt seeks to thrust his values upon that world, Gumbril Senior remains aloof; where Lypiatt seeks to project himself through vast and tormented expressionist images Gumbril Senior is content to immerse himself in the impersonal greatness of classical architecture; while Lypiatt achieves merely grandiloquence, Gumbril Senior achieves genuine grandeur even if he does so in the miniature form of the models which represent the buildings he has never been able to erect on their full scale. In that sense, Gumbril Senior is as much a failure as Lypiatt; but Lypiatt is a grotesque failure, because his ability was never equal to his ambitions; Gumbril Senior is a dignified and admirable failure because his ability was always greater than his opportunities. One might draw up similar charts for the other main characters, with certain special differences. Coleman, that supreme extrovert, is shown only through his own actions and the perceptions of others; there is never any inkling of an inner life. Myra is shown through the eyes of her three main admirers who all live out their sufferings in character-istic ways, Gumbril by the tear-soaked pillows of the 'weak, silent man', Lypiatt by the vast apologia he writes before what may or may not be his suicide, and Shearwater by retreating into the most obsessional of scientific routines. She is also seen from within, barely able to extract from her chronic indifference any reaction other than a vague pity towards these men she fatally fascinates to their undoing. And she is contrasted with the naïvely corrupt Rosie and the spoilt innocent Emily; by the sheer strength of her negation she remains the one really memorable feminine character in the whole book.

There is a symbolic centre to Huxley's city; it is the plane-bowered square where Gumbril Senior lives and where he sits at his window to listen to the starlings who fly homing each night to nest there like birds in a desert oasis. Gumbril Senior is perhaps the one happy man in the novel; he has renounced success and turned himself into an urban hermit, giving private form to public visions. Dwarfed by the circumstances of his age, the old man is the direct heir of Alberti, Brunelleschi, Wren and the other great neo-classical architects whom Huxley himself admired for their sense of mass, for their splendid manipulation of light and shadow. This architecture Gumbril Senior sees as the product of a vision that transcends both actuality and history.

> . . . And he thought of Alberti—Alberti, the noblest Roman of them all [Huxley uses the same phrase in his splendid essay on 'Rimini and Alberti' in *Along the Road*], the true and only Roman. For the Romans themselves had lived their own actual lives, sordidly and extravagantly in the middle of a vulgar empire. Alberti and his followers in the Renaissance lived the ideal Roman life. They put Plutarch into their architecture. They took the detestable real Cato, the Brutus of history, and made of them Roman heroes to walk as guides and models before them. Before Alberti there were no true Romans, and with Piranesi's death the race began to wither towards extinction.

It is appropriate that Gumbril Senior should be the creator of the Utopia embedded within *Antic Hay*, the ideal city which stands in contrast to the apocalyptic vision of the real city that Coleman presents earlier in the novel, a vision of seven million people, each one living his separate life indifferent to the existence of the rest, each thinking himself as important as any one of his fellows:

> Millions of them are now sleeping in an empested atmosphere. Hundreds of thousands of couples are at this moment engaged in mutually caressing one another in a manner too hideous to be thought of, but in no way different from the manner in which each of us performs, delightfully, passionately and beautifully, his similar work of love. Thousands of women are now in the throes of parturition, and of both sexes thousands are dying of the most diverse and appalling diseases, or simply because they have lived too long. Thousands are drunk, thousands have over-eaten, thousands have not had enough to eat. And they are all alive, all unique and separate and sensitive, like you and me. It's a horrible thought. Ah, if I could lead them all into that great hole of centipedes.

This is, as it were, the real Rome compared with Gumbril Senior's

ideal Rome. Theodore Gumbril visits his father three times–once
immediately after he abandons his teaching career and goes to London,
a second time with Shearwater, and a third with Myra Viveash on the
last journey around London. On the second occasion old Gumbril
comes upon the two young men talking about proportion. He interprets the word architecturally, and leads them into a room where the
floor is covered by the enormous model of a river-traversed city
dominated by a great dome. Theodore Gumbril imagines it is the
capital of Utopia, and in a sense it is the crystallization of a Utopian
vision, for it represents London as it might have been if Wren's plans
of reconstruction had been carried out after the unique opportunity
offered by the Great Fire.

> '... Wren offered them open spaces and broad streets [Gumbril
> Senior explains]; he offered them sunlight and air and cleanliness; he
> offered them beauty, order and grandeur. He offered to build for the
> imagination and the ambitious spirit of man, so that even the most
> bestial, vaguely and remotely, as they walked those streets, might
> feel that they were of the same race–or very nearly–as Michelangelo;
> that they too might feel themselves, in spirit at least, magnificent,
> strong and free. He offered them all these things; he drew a plan for
> them, walking in peril among the still smouldering ruins. But they
> preferred to re-erect the old intricate squalor. . . .'

And he goes on to show how literally ideal Wren's vision was by
remarking that modern men would be no more likely than Restoration
men to accept a city or a life based on reason and order. On Theodore's
last visit to his father, the model is no longer there; it has been sold–
the novel's unique act of noble self-sacrifice–to help an old friend in
difficulties. But the image lives on, in Shearwater's mind, and dominates
the last page of the book as Myra and Gumbril turn away from the
window where they have been watching him on his wild stationary
race. He continues to sweat and pedal. 'He was building up his strong
light dome of life. Proportion, cried the old man, proportion! And it
hung there, proportioned and beautiful in the dark, confused horror of
his desires, solid and strong and durable among his broken thoughts.
Time flowed darkly past.'

Shearwater's epiphany, like Lypiatt's, is set in darkness. Gumbril's,
which presents the other great contrasting pattern of the novel, is set in
light, but cannot escape that fatal conjunction of Heaven and Hell
which in his later works Huxley was to regard as the result of the
merely visionary as distinct from the true mystic experience of union

with the Divine Ground. If the early chapters of *Antic Hay* centre on Lypiatt's failure to project the genuine passions that lie within him through the artistic persona which he has created, the middle of the novel is dominated by Gumbril's attempt at self-transformation, by the creation of the Complete Man. This leads him through the adventure with Rosie Shearwater to the meeting in the National Gallery with Emily. In this relationship the novel mounts nearest to real spirituality, contrasted with the bogus spirituality which Mr. Boldero regards as an indispensable element of good advertising. ('Combine spirituality and practicality and you've fairly got them. Got them, I may say, on toast.') A tenderness enters into the relationship, as Gumbril strips off his beard and returns to his own, gentler self, and a tremulous kind of confidence is established. Emily and Gumbril go to a concert, where the music (Mozart played impeccably by a quartet of ungainly men)weaves the pattern of intellectual order which is its function in Huxley's earlier novels. They go on to Gumbril's rooms, and lie together in bed, in a kind of eternity, as Emily's fears vanish, lapsing into a desireless enchantment. As Gumbril sees the scene in guilty recollection: 'Emily's breasts were firm and pointed and she had slept at last without a tremor. In the starlight, good, true and beautiful became one.' It is an experience never to be repeated; all along Gumbril has known in his heart that his illusion of eternity would never last.

Gumbril's fragile interlude with Emily (which some critics have unjustifiably exaggerated into a 'conversion') is the sole incident in *Antic Hay*–apart from Gumbril Senior's act of sacrificial generosity–in which the negative pattern of the book is broken. And it is itself negated by the ugly passage in which, on the night when Gumbril should have been in the country with Emily, he accompanies Myra Viveash to a nightclub and deliberately mars his vision by describing his relationship with Emily jestingly for Myra and the Satanic Coleman. 'Well, let everything go,' he thinks. 'Leave it there, and let the dogs lift their hind legs over it as they pass.' In that act of besmirching what is tender and lyrical in life the pervading darkness of *Antic Hay* is re-established. The images of the ideal, the ordered, the spiritual, belong to a world only briefly to be perceived. And outside those perceptions life in *Antic Hay* is meaningless and brutish, as befits the existence of Circe's creatures. All of them imagine they are free. But, as Mr. Bojanus points out, their freedom is illusory and all of them are trapped within the limitations of their natures, which from the outside often make them seem, like Mercaptan and Coleman, mere types set in narrow moulds of speech and behaviour. Yet there are, at least in the two Gumbrils, in Lypiatt, even in Myra Viveash, depths and distances that make multidimensional beings, and Huxley has gone far toward the exploration of human motives and reactions that reaches its climax in *Eyeless in Gaza*.

CHAPTER FIVE

Death in a Sunlit Landscape

I

For Aldous Huxley the 1920s were a decade of almost constant travel. He never spent more than a few months at a time in England, and always moved towards the Mediterranean with that almost instinctual northern urge which impelled those whom the Restoration called Italianate Englishmen and continued to send its devotees southward through the ages of Beckford and Byron and Ruskin. Between the great wars, when phenomenal sunshine combined with phenomenal cheapness, Italy and the Midi de France became the uneasy resting-places of British *rentiers* impoverished by wartime inflation and of writers seeking to escape the Grub Street drudgery in which Huxley had passed his literary apprenticeship. In the earlier part of the decade it was in Florence and Fonte dei Marmi that Huxley mainly spent his time, taking trips into Austria, Tunisia and his wife's native land of Belgium, and visiting London for increasingly short periods. Success as a journalistic essayist made life abroad more easy. In a variety of magazines that stretched all the way from *Vanity Fair* and the *Saturday Review* to his father's *Cornhill* he published the increasingly sophisticated essays, combining travel, art and philosophy in novel permutations, which, in volumes like *Along the Road*, *Proper Studies* and *Do What You Will*, provide the background of thought for his novels.

Huxley's works immediately after the publication of *Antic Hay* are greatly influenced by his Italian surroundings. Having produced his infernal picture of London, he turns to the light-filled south in order to write the gentler books that follow *Antic Hay*. *Those Barren Leaves* was described by Huxley when he wrote it as 'a gigantic Peacock in an Italian scene'. In fact it is Huxley's last and nearest approach to Norman Douglas's *South Wind;* it was written when Huxley was seeing a great deal of Douglas, then resident in Florence. It also shows a strong influence of Proust in the treatment of both love and time. (The volumes of *A la recherche du temps perdu* were appearing at this period, with *La Prisonnière* published the year before Huxley started work on *Those Barren Leaves* and *Albertine disparue* in the year he finished it.)

The influence of continental settings and literatures is also evident in the essays, poems and shorter fiction of the same period. *Along the Road* celebrates those great journeyings, usually in the Citroën which Maria drove with much verve through the hills of Italy and over the great solitary plains of France, when he explored most of Latin Europe, gathering impressions for his travel pieces and painfully observing the paintings and buildings and sculptures on which he based the first of his remarkable essays on the fine arts. The book of short fiction, *Little Mexican*, which appeared in 1924, contains a novella – 'Uncle Spencer' – set in Belgium and of its five short stories the two most interesting are set in Italy and a third in France. Many of the poems later published in *Arabia Infelix* (1929) and in some cases republished in *The Cicadas* (1931) were written at this time, with Mediterranean settings; some of them were published first in *Those Barren Leaves*, a fact which Huxley's bibliographers have failed to notice.

The dominance of the Mediterranean setting in the works of this period distinguishes them from Huxley's later work and gives them – like their precursors 'Green Tunnels' and 'Nuns at Luncheon' – a lyrical quality more intense than one encounters in any other period of his writing. There is a glow in an essay like 'The Palio at Siena', in a story like 'Young Archimedes', in some of the passages of scenic description in *Those Barren Leaves*, which one rarely encounters in the later works when the light seems to be colder and harsher. The dominant impression of the time and its works is that of a pause in a landscape of sunlit splendour between the dying city of *Antic Hay* and the spiritual black country of *Point Counter Point*. For it was after completing *Those Barren Leaves* that Huxley set out on the Asian journey which made inevitable that quest in darkness towards a mystical religion that before had been merely one of many possibilities.

2

One is always surprised that Huxley did not publish separately his best novelle, and often seemed anxious to conceal their merits. 'Uncle Spencer' appears in a volume, *Little Mexican*, whose title comes from one of the shorter stories, and one of the best of them.

'Uncle Spencer' is one of those unexpected and untypical pieces of writing which surprise one with the versatility of Huxley's talent and the extraordinary competence of his craftsmanship. It is a long, linear tale, far more simply constructed than any of the novels. The early part is told by a young man remembering his boyhood, when he would spend every school holiday with his Uncle Spencer, an Englishman who by some freak of fortune had inherited a sugar-beet mill which he ran, none too competently, in the little Belgian town of Longres.

Years pass, the boy grows up, but the background of his holidays at Longres is little changed; there are still his uncle's yearly panics as the beet season comes round, still the salty insights into Flemish life provided by Antonieke the housekeeper and her sister Louiseke, a holy spinster privileged to clean gold and silver ornaments and vessels of the church; the great event of the year is the kermesse, when life takes on a Rabelaisian vividness and vigour, and it is through the kermesse that one year a momentous novelty enters the life of the small town. A troupe of 'Tibetan Devil Dancers' appear, consisting of two swarthy Frenchmen from Marseilles and a couple of Tamil cobblers, who have devised a ritual phallic and obscene enough to captivate even Flemish peasants. The most captivated of all is the pious and shrivelled Louiseke, who falls in love with one of the Tamils, 'a stout coffee-coloured man, whom the schoolboys of Longres, like those three rude boys in *Struwwelpeter*, pursued at a distance, contorting themselves with mirth'.

The Tamil's name is unpronounceable in Flemish, but when he settles down to ply his cobbler's trade and occasionally read the hands of pretty girls, he is accepted as Monsieur Alphonse. As such he plays a notable part in the second phase of the story, which takes place during the First World War. The narrator, having vainly tried to overcome Uncle Spencer's view that the war will end in a few days, makes his way back to England; they do not meet again until it is all over. The narrative shifts to the third person as Uncle Spencer and Monsieur Alphonse, British subjects both, are taken to the internment prison which the Germans have created in the top floor of a Brussels ministry building.

It is interesting, and perhaps indicative of Huxley's inclinations as well as his inexperience, that his only war story should have contained no fighting and only a couple of natural deaths. Like E. E. Cummings in *The Enormous Room*, he deals rather with the wartime dislocations of normal life that can throw a large number of incompatible people together in conditions of daily proximity over long periods and create relationships that in peacetime would be impossible. Huxley's prisoners are not entirely the kind of social outcasts and criminal riffraff with whom Cummings populated his enormous room. They are, rather, a cross-section of the people of all classes that a policy of internment sweeps together: an opera singer on tour, a Brussels journalist, a couple of Belgian counts and a lusty Russian countess, an anarchist, a pimply London bank clerk and 'a little gold-haired male impersonator', slightly vulgar and indubitably cockney, called Emmy Wendle. In his normal life, Uncle Spencer would never have encountered such a strange collection of people, and certainly he would never have felt a tenderness for an Emmy Wendle that steadily developed into infatuation and thence into obsessive love.

Despairing of being released, Monsieur Alphonse declines like a wild animal pining for freedom; just before he dies he utters a series of prophecies regarding the length of the war and the fates of the people around him. All are fulfilled except one. Uncle Spencer is released and then imprisoned again and sent to Germany. Others are set free or die according to the Tamil's prophecy. The war lasts, to Uncle Spencer's surprise, exactly as long as Monsieur Alphonse has foretold. But there is one oracle that remains tantalizingly unfulfilled: Monsieur Alphonse has promised that in the end Uncle Spencer will marry Emmy Wendle and live happily ever after; the story ends with Uncle Spencer, and his nephew, now grown to years of knowledge in such matters, combing the theatrical agencies and lodging houses of London, enquiring at endless stage doors, but failing to find more than the most elusive clues of Emmy's whereabouts. 'And yet the Indian,' murmurs Uncle Spencer, 'he was always right. . . .'

It is a story whose ultimate effect is pathetic, for Uncle Spencer is one of Huxley's few characters for whom one feels the warmth of compassion rather than the chill of pity. He belongs outside the world of intellectuals, Bohemians and snobs who populate most of Huxley's other works of fiction. He is a man of confused but vast general knowledge, and in this aspect of him there is a little ironic self-mockery of Huxley's own ardent eclecticism, sustained as it was by the perpetual reading of encyclopaedias. But at the same time Uncle Spencer is an English eccentric in a comic tradition one associates with Dickens, or perhaps even more with the lower-middle-class novelists of the early part of this century; there is a touch of Wells—even of Bennett—about him. Even in Huxley's longer novels the kind of comic character-ization which belongs properly in the Wells-Bennett-Priestley world is liable to appear, but only in minor figures; Bojardus and Boldero in *Antic Hay*, and even, in a more sombre way, Illidge in *Point Counter Point*, are inhabitants of that world rather than of typical Huxleyland, and their presence suggests that, even if Huxley knew that the world of the real workers was as impenetrable as Orwell later found it, he did try to understand that great petit-bourgeois stratum which was represented for him in the flesh by writers he knew and liked (in the case of Bennett) or disliked (in the case of Wells).

Like many of Huxley's novelle, 'Uncle Spencer' can be regarded as a study in the mutability of personality, for there is nothing in the early life of the central character to suggest that a change in circumstances would turn him into the doting lover pursuing as his lost Eurydice a brainless little music-hall star whose profession itself emphasizes the theme of the instability of human patterns. 'Uncle Spencer' is also an exercise in the Proustian idea, derived in its turn from the Stendhalian theory of crystallization, that the lover creates the person he loves. Uncle Spencer endues Emmy with virtues she does not possess and even transmutes the faults he discovers in her to create the image of the desired woman he had not known he needed, in his unawakened past before the war and the enormous room.

The whole novella is in fact impregnated with Proustian atmosphere. It is true that the act of recollection, detailed though it may be, is not contained within a great epiphanous experience of time regained. But the reminiscent narrative that brings back the scenes and episodes of childhood reminds one in tone of *Du côté de chez Swann*, and Antonieke, the Flemish peasant housekeeper of Uncle Spencer, is the spiritual sister of Françoise, the housekeeper of Marcel's family in Proust's novel.

It is also true that Longres, the village where Uncle Spencer lives, was immediately modelled on St. Trond, the village in Belgium where Maria Huxley's parents, who were manufacturers, lived—like Uncle Spencer—in a house in the Grand' Place. And, when one reads of the weekly pig market and the great annual kermesse with its sideshows and excitement one is reminded that at this period Huxley was an admirer of Pieter Breughel, whose painting (then unfashionable) he defended in one of the best essays of *Along the Road*, pointing out that Breughel

> was perfectly qualified to be the natural historian of the Flemish folk. He exhibits them mostly in those moments of orgiastic gaiety with which they temper the laborious monotony of their daily lives: eating enormously, drinking, uncouthly dancing, indulging in that peculiarly Flemish scatological waggery.

All that Huxley perceived in Breughel he projects into his description of the kermesse, with its vulgar pleasures and its crudely enjoying peasants, even down to the scatology represented in the chocolate chamber-pots which the narrator in his childhood crunches with such relish.

Yet, as the taste of that chocolate melts into one's imagination, it is Proust who comes back, the Proust whose rich perceptions enabled him to evoke not merely sight, but all the five senses, in his splendid nostalgic descriptions of the landscape of Marcel's childhood, and its centre, the village of Combray. And of what place but Combray, that quintessential heart of memory, is one reminded as the narrator and his uncle drive–so many times and at so many seasons–from the station into the Grand' Place at Longres?

> . . . Even in the winter, when there was nothing to be seen of it but an occasional green gas-lamp, with a little universe of pavement, brick wall and shuttered window dependent upon it and created by it out of the surrounding darkness, the Rue de la Gare was signally depressing if only because it was so straight and long. But in summer, when the dismal brick houses by which it was flanked revealed themselves in the evening light, when the dust and the waste-paper came puffing along it in gusts of warm, stale-smelling wind, then the street seemed doubly long and disagreeable. But, on the other hand, the contrast between its sordidness and the cool, spacious Grand' Place into which, after what seemed a carefully studied preparatory twisting and turning among the narrow streets of the old town, it finally debouched, was all the more striking and refreshing. Like a ship floating out from between the jaws of a canyon into a wide and sunlit lake, our carriage emerged upon the Grand' Place. And the moment was solemn, breathlessly anticipated and theatrical, as though we were gliding in along the suspended calling of the oboes and bassoons, and the violins trembling with amorous anxiety all around us, rolling silently and with not a hitch in the stage carpentry on to some vast and limelit stage where, as soon as we had taken up our position well forward and in the centre, something tremendous, one imagined, would suddenly begin to happen–a huge orchestral tutti from contrabass trombone to piccolo, from bell instrument to triangle, and then the tenor and soprano in such a duet as had never in all the history of opera been heard before.

The musical conceit continues, elaboration after elaboration, for another five pages of the story; this kind of vast metaphorical construction is unusual in Huxley's writings, and if one considers it in connection with the parenthetical complexity of the sentences and the slightly Gothic exaggeration of the other images (the ship floating from the jaws of a canyon, for example) it can be recognized as parody, even if it is high parody; the master is clearly Proust.

The five stories that complete *Little Mexican* are of varied quality. 'The Portrait', a tale of a fraudulent art dealer, is no more than a competent piece of dialogue with an over-emphatic twist to its tail. 'Fard' is a brutal little piece which develops Huxley's realization that those who fear misfortune are cruel to the unfortunate; a vain French-woman cannot endure the sight of her sick maid and makes her rouge her cheeks so that she herself will not feel uncomfortable while the other woman slaves for her.

'Little Mexican' and 'Young Archimedes' are the best of the stories, and both are set in Italy. 'Little Mexican', whose inconsequential title comes from a black sombrero that sets off the events which make the story, is a curious and amusing study of the unpredictable effects of time, the uncertainty of durability. A fictional 'Oosselay' (or Huxley), old enough and healthy enough to have been an art-watching tourist in 1912 (which the real Huxley was not) is accosted in Padua by a young Italian count who imagines (on the strength of the black hat) that he is an artist. Count Tirabassi claims to be the owner of frescoes of im-measurable value, all painted on the walls of his country house, and the astonished 'Oosselay' indeed discovers that the Count's great rooms are covered with splendid murals by Veronese and Tiepolo. The Count and his father are anxious to sell them to American collectors who will be able to strip them off the walls by a recently invented process and smuggle them out of the country. Talking with the old Count, the narrator discovers a parasitical relationship, for the father has managed to saddle the son with a marriage that keeps him near Padua tending the family estate, while he himself continues, into his sixties, into his seventies, to sow youth's wild oats at the expense of his toiling progeny.

'Oosselay' never finds a buyer for the paintings, but he does keep up the connection with the two Counts, and returns occasionally to visit them. His last return is in 1921. The young count is still there, worn down by work and a great family. The frescoes which had seemed such symbols of the permanence of art are also there, half ruined by the vicissitudes of wartime billeting and post-war peasant revolution. But in Salzburg, not long after, 'Oosselay' encounters the old Count, more sprightly than ever, with his current *bella grassa*. In a figure of double paradox, age thrives while youth declines, life is long while art is short.

From this sardonic comedy one passes to the brutal tragedy of 'Young Archimedes', one of Huxley's best and most rarely moving stories. The narrative centres upon music, the most abstract of the arts, and geometry, the most abstract visualization of man's world.

The narrator and his wife settle in the hills above Florence, in a rented villa whose situation makes worth enduring the discomforts of the house and the impositions of Signora Bondi, the landlady. The relations between Signora Bondi and the couple in the house are guarded, but the latter live on cordial terms with the neighbouring peasant family, whose boy, Guido, plays with their own smaller child.

Guido is a strange, meditative child, subject to sudden fits of pensiveness when his eyes become like 'clear, pale lakes of thought'. When a gramophone with records of classical music arrives, Guido's quality begins to manifest itself positively. He sits rapt while Bach and Mozart are played; he reasons out his preferences, and when the narrator imports a piano he shows an immediate aptitude for playing. By chance Signora Bondi hears of this, and, since he is her tenant's child, conceives the idea of educating him in music so that she can become the patroness of a prodigy. In the meantime the boy has suddenly revealed something quite different – a natural sense of geometry, a power to scratch with a stick in the sand and by original thinking to work out Euclidean problems. For him, it is clear, the harmonies of music have only been a way to reach the even greater beauties of geometry, of mathematical relations. But Signora Bondi insists on taking him to Florence to teach him music, and, away from home, deprived of his Euclid, he pines and in the end throws himself out of a window. With him dies something unique, a fineness of spirit smashed by the crudity of human ambition.

What is extraordinary about 'Young Archimedes' is the way the opposing elements constantly play against each other, the landscape and the events illuminated by a clear, sublime light, yet evil always impending, like the long dark shadows that come over the earth at evening and deepen under the hills. For even in this civilized Tuscan landscape the 'fiendish influences' which the narrator identifies with the wilderness find a place to lodge in the hearts of men. Yet the story ends with a sense of triumph that the unique child should have lived. The narrator looks out over the valley after he has seen Guido's grave.

It was a day of floating clouds – great shapes, white, golden, and grey; and between them patches of a thin, transparent blue. Its lantern level, almost, with our eyes, the dome of the cathedral revealed itself in all its grandiose lightness, its vastness and aerial strength. On the innumerable brown and rosy roofs of the city the afternoon sunlight lay softly, sumptuously, and the towers were as though varnished and enamelled with an old gold. I thought of all the Men who had lived here and left the visible traces of their spirit and conceived extraordinary things. I thought of the dead child.

Guido is exceptional among Huxley's earlier characters; life has not had time to twist him. Huxley will return to this theme of the meaningless destruction of children, by sickness if not by human beings, but the others will remain merely children, whereas Guido stands as well for that in Huxley which was always seeking, beyond phenomena, the essential outlines of reality.

3

Huxley's earlier essays, the weekly 'Marginalia' which he wrote for the *Athenaeum*, and which he mocked as Mercaptan's 'delicious middles' in *Antic Hay*, were passable literary journalism for their day, but now, preserved in his earliest collection, *On the Margin*, they seem singularly dated, with their Georgian air of playful erudition. Here and there one detects an interest that will develop into something more substantial and mature; an essay on 'Advertisement' which will blossom into the outrageous commercial fancies of Mr. Boldero in *Antic Hay;* a note on 'Accidie' which charts the beginning of Huxley's interest in Baudelaire; an appreciation of Sir Christopher Wren that reflects his enduring admiration for the neo-classical in architecture. And here and there emerges one of those youthful points of view which Huxley will invert long before the end of his career. I think particularly of the essay on Tibet in which–reviewing the book on that country, written by the Japanese monk Kawaguchi–he mocks what to him in his mid-twenties seems 'an ancient and elaborate civilization of which almost no detail is not entirely idiotic . . .'.

If such fragments are interesting merely as early works of a man who later did better, there is evident progress in *Along the Road*, which Huxley sub-titles 'Notes and Essays of a Tourist'. Not all the essays are concerned with travel: there are pieces on 'The Mystery of the Theatre', drawing on Huxley's days as a dramatic critic; a discussion of 'Popular Music' and its origins; a disquisition on plebeian culture and the cult of the amusing entitled 'The Pierian Spring'; and a consideration of 'Work and Leisure' looking forward to Huxley's later preoccupation with the problems of a technologically exploding culture. But even in these pieces one is aware of the broadening of interest and the growing flexibility of thought that Huxley had acquired partly by an assiduous practice of the craft, partly by the experience of travel, and most of all by the rapid development of his creative and critical insights.

Some even of the essays in *Along the Road* are jocular trivialities written for middlebrow magazines on the lighter aspects of travel. The best are either substantial travel pieces like that admirable description of a custom surviving from the Italian middle ages, 'The Palio at Siena', or studies of works of art in their settings, such as 'The Best Picture', Huxley's eulogy of Piero della Francesca's great Descent from the Cross at Borgo San Sepolcro.

In all the essays on the visual arts one is aware first of the peculiar interest in pictures filled with solid and almost geometrical forms like Piero's, or with strong tonal patterns of light and shade like Breughel's, but it is never the form alone that is important to Huxley. He argues this question ably in 'Breughel', and defends the 'great dramatic and reflective painters' against the mere formalists. In fact, his approach is eclectic in the better sense.

> The contemporary insistence on form to the exclusion of everything else is an absurdity. So was the older insistence on exact imitation and sentiment to the exclusion of form. There need be no exclusions. In spite of the single name, there are many different kinds of painters and all of them, with the exception of those who cannot paint, and those whose minds are trivial, vulgar and tedious, have a right to exist.

This approach not only makes Huxley responsive, given the limitations of his vision, to the formal excellences of painters as different as Piero and Breughel and Patinir, but also enables him to understand what a painter may be saying outside the formal pattern, and to relate that statement to the age for which it was made. Such a receptivity to the extra-formal elements in painting came naturally to a writer himself so didactically inclined.

Huxley's enthusiasm for neo-classical architecture, as opposed to the Ruskinian Gothic he was taught to respect in his Arnoldian youth, is shown in 'Rimini and Alberti', perhaps the best essay in *Along the Road*, which discusses the background in which the great Renaissance builders worked, aspiring to equal a Rome that existed only in their own minds, as a 'retrospective Utopia'. In its idealizing intellectuality, in its manipulation of splendid masses, its dramatic use of sunlight and shadow, such architecture made a special appeal to Huxley. But there was another way in which architecture fascinated him. It was a public activity that helped to humanize the earth, planting its geometric shapes as symbols of man's control over the apparent indiscipline of Nature. Indeed, this liking for all that tames Nature without destroying it extends beyond architecture to a fascination with landscapes patterned by man. In 'Young Archimedes' he had already praised the civilizing effect of ancient cultivation, and in his essay, 'Views of Holland', he shows how the 'criss-cross of perfect parallels' of meadow and ditch and dyke respond to the abstracting element in his mind, and motion gives a further intensity to the experience.

> And all the time, as one advances, the huge geometrical landscape spreads out on either side of the car like an opening fan. Along the level skyline a score of windmills wave their arms like dancers in a geometrical ballet. Ineluctably, the laws of perspective lead away the long roads and shining waters to a misty vanishing point.

And in a Wildeian appreciation of the curious interworking of our perceptions of Nature and of art he notes, in 'Patinir's River', how one can find in Nature a scene even to reflect the luminous paintings of Joachim Patinir, which Huxley had thought represented 'a river of the mind, out of the world' until, driving from Namur to Dinant and Givet, on a wet day in the autumn, he found himself beside Patinir's river and gloried in that strange interplay between Nature and fanciful art.

Though Huxley kept up with whatever was new in writing and the arts, and was able to make the appropriate allusion to Picasso's colour schemes when describing the costumes of the banner-bearers at the Sienese palio, he was not concerned with the new or the fashionable as such. The craze for new fashions in art he mocked later with biting sarcasm in 'Two or Three Graces'. Another tendency that was emerging in the Twenties led him to give a judicious warning which places him among the more responsible of modern art critics.

> Knowledge has enabled us to sympathize with unfamiliar points of view, to appreciate artistic conventions devised by people utterly unlike ourselves. All this, no doubt, is a very good thing. But our sympathy is so vast and we are so much afraid of showing ourselves intolerant towards the things we ought to like, that we have begun to love in our all-embracing way not merely the highest, in whatever convention, when we see it, but the lowest as well. ('The Pierian Spring.')

The lowest sometimes interested Huxley, as a product of the endless variousness of human nature, but he never, at any period, fell into the error of considering it anything else than low. What he admired was always of the best. Indeed, if–considering all that Huxley wrote on the visual arts–there is a fault one can find with him, it is that he was too unadventurous in terms of the present and too consistently inclined to make his discoveries in the past. He wrote at length and in depth on no painter–with the sole exception of Toulouse-Lautrec–later than Goya. He was certainly aware of the great painters of the modern age, he even appreciated them, but Cézanne and Seurat and Renoir and all the others appear merely as passing names in his books. What he needed to sustain his interest in a painter long enough to produce an essay upon him was a strong dramatic or intellectual interest. Mere formal accomplishment, however splendid, was not enough to release the springs of his eloquence.

4

The basic idea of *Those Barren Leaves* occurred to Huxley in August 1921, after he had finished writing *Crome Yellow* during the first of his Italian summers. Inspired by a visit to the mountain fortress which the Sitwells occupied at Montegufoni, he thought of it as taking place in 'an incredibly large castle ... divided up, as Monte Gufone [sic] was divided till recently, into scores of separate habitations, which will be occupied, for the purposes of my story, by the most improbable people of every species and nationality.' When he actually did write his novel set in a historic Italian castle, the Cybo Malaspina, the cast was in fact greatly curtailed, consisting of Mrs. Aldwinkle, the current châtelaine, her niece Irene, her six house guests, and that strange couple, the appropriately named Elvers, who emerge from the marshes of the Maremma to deepen the theme of death which hangs obsessively over the book.

Like Crome, the Cybo Malaspina is totally removed from the city of dreadful night which is the London of *Antic Hay* and *Point Counter Point*. The setting is dramatic–almost melodramatic–with the great fantastic castle, its walls covered with splendid medieval frescoes, set in a landscape of theatrical splendour; that landscape becomes an important element as the scene shifts from the hills down into the marshes and the seacoast, and then over the mountains into Umbria, and emphasizes the comparison between the green and living leaves of the natural world and the barren leaves of the life of arts and letters which forms one of the book's important themes.

The social problems that rumble subterraneously in *Antic Hay*–even if no positive consideration of them is offered, are distant in *Those Barren Leaves*. An elderly and puritanical trade union leader, the former engine driver Mr. Falx, is one of Mrs. Aldwinkle's guests, but he is a minor character, rarely allowed to utter his booming homilies, and easily defeated by little Irene, Mrs. Aldwinkle's niece, in the contest for domination over young Lord Hovenden, his disciple. Otherwise, we are made only distantly aware that a world of injustice and massive distress exists somewhere beyond the crenellated walls of the Cybo Malaspina, a world from which the barren existence presided over by Mrs. Aldwinkle draws its sustenance.

And at this very moment, Mr. Falx was meditating, at this very moment, on tram-cars in the Argentine, among Peruvian guano-beds, in humming power-stations at the foot of African waterfalls, in Australian refrigerators packed with slaughtered mutton, in the heat and darkness of Yorkshire coalmines, in tea-plantations on the slopes of the Himalayas, in Japanese banks, at the mouth of Mexican oil-wells, in steamers walloping along across the China Sea–at this very moment, men and women of every race and colour were doing their bit to supply Mrs. Aldwinkle with her income. On the two hundred and seventy thousand pounds of Mrs. Aldwinkle's capital the sun never set. People worked; Mrs. Aldwinkle led the higher life. She for art only, they–albeit unconscious of the privilege–for art in her.

The wretched of the earth–at least in their masses–are mentioned and forgotten, and not without reason, for *Those Barren Leaves* makes evident that the exploiters are as wretched as the exploited. In this novel we come close to the Buddhistic legend of the achievement of enlightenment through the knowledge of the suffering inseparable from existence: suffering in all its forms even to death.

Love, age and death are the forces that preside over *Those Barren Leaves*. The theme of love divides the characters into four pairs, with Mr. Falx the unimportant odd man out, and the central part of the book is in fact entitled 'The Loves of the Parallels'. These 'loves' result from the conjunctions of characters engineered in the earlier chapters. The first chapter, 'An Evening at Mrs. Aldwinkle's', centres on the arrival at the Cybo of Calamy, a handsome but weary amorist, welcomed in Mrs. Aldwinkle's absence by Mary Thriplow, a young lady novelist who is one of the house guests. At this time the party consists of Mrs. Aldwinkle, Irene and Mary, of Mr. Falx and Lord Hovenden, and of Mr. Cardan, who in this novel takes the place of Scogan in *Crome Yellow* as the cynical elderly dilettante ('one of the obscure Great' in Mrs. Aldwinkle's view). Having lived through almost all the money he ever had, Cardan is reduced to accepting the board and bed offered by his hostess, in younger days his mistress. Despite his endless and over-powering talk, which might seem to establish him as a Peacockian type, Cardan is a major character, developed in considerable depth and essential to the unfolding of the major themes.

Francis Chelifer is the second figure to appear from outside. The 'Fragments' from his 'Autobiography' which form Part II of the novel, introduce the device of the interpolated memoir or journal which henceforward Huxley will often use to vary the tone, texture and viewpoint of his novels. It is balanced by the author's journal which Mary Thriplow keeps and the rambling, sentimental letters she writes in secret to her dead cousin Jim, descendant of the slaughtered Tony Lamb and Guy Lambourne in earlier works. Yet the 'Autobiography' differs from Mary's journal in being no day-to-day narrative of events, but a sweeping look back from a certain point in time over a whole life; this not only deepens the temporal recession of the novel by strengthening the scattered memories of the other characters, but also establishes Chelifer as the most elaborately presented character in the book and possibly the most important.

A rather drily intellectual young man, Chelifer echoes much of Huxley's own past, and in some ways anticipates his future. In a book[1] filled with those quaint notions that spawn so freely in American graduate schools, Professor Jerome Meckier of the University of Massachusetts has put forward the curious and unsupported theory that Chelifer was modelled on Middleton Murry and *The Rabbit Fancier's Gazette* he edits on *The Adelphi*. In fact, Chelifer bears no resemblance to the real Murry, whom I knew, and just as little to the fictional Murry whom Huxley introduced as Burlap in *Point Counter Point*. But there are significant resemblances between him and Huxley. Chelifer's task as editor is of the same sub-literary character as Huxley's when he was editing *House and Garden*. His father closely resembles Leonard Huxley, and the family goes on the same kind of vigorous Alpine excursions as Aldous Huxley remembered from his own child-hood. Chelifer, like Huxley, works during the war in the offices of the

[1] *Aldous Huxley: Satire and Structure.*

Air Board. He even writes a number of poems which Huxley later published as his own, including early versions of 'Caligula: or The Triumph of Beauty' and the two 'Nero and Sporus' poems which eventually appeared in the verse collection *Arabia Infelix* (1929).

At the same time, Chelifer is not Huxley whole, and his adventures take him into sub-worlds that have their evident origin in literature. The owners and staff of *The Rabbit Fancier's Gazette* seem to emerge from the world of *Tony-Bungay*, and the boarding house operated by Miss Carruthers in Chelsea is an English version of the boarding house where Rastignac lived the months of his initiation into Paris in *Père Goriot;* the resemblance is not accidental, for at this time Huxley had just abandoned work on a study of Balzac which he had promised Constable in 1919 and had worked on sporadically and unsuccessfully for five years.

In his infatuation for the beautiful and amoral Barbara Waters– latest in the chain of Huxley women who are incapable of real love– Chelifer endures the amorous bondage that marks the Huxley anti-hero, but his disillusionment is more scarifying than that experienced by Denis Stone or Gumbril, since unlike them he realizes the Proustian truth that he has created his own misery by loving Barbara as a symbol, thus feeding artificially his desire for her as a woman.

Chelifer has come to look cynically not merely on love, but also on art.

> Art for art's sake, halma for halma's sake. It is time to smash the last and silliest of the idols.

The habit of writing continues, like a tic, but Chelifer withdraws himself from the Bohemian world to a microcosm marked out by the magazine office in Gog's Court and the lodging house in Chelsea, where he can live among people who are without literary or artistic pretensions.

There is an extraordinary anticipation of the tone of French absurdist novels written a decade and more later in the passages in which Chelifer criticizes all doctrines of progress, all offerings of hope.

> It was then that I learned to live only in the moment–to ignore causes, motives, antecedents, to refuse responsibility for what should follow. It was then that I learned, since the future was always bound to be a painful repetition of what had happened before, never to look forward for comfort or justification, but to live now and here in the heart of reality, in the very centre of the hot dark hive.

This apprehension of reality Chelifer presents in terms familiar to existentialists and to Buddhists alike as a kind of nausea.

Q. What did Buddha consider the most deadly of the deadly sins?
A. Unawareness, stupidity.
Q. And what will happen if I make myself aware, if I actually begin to think?
A. Your swivel chair will turn into a trolley on the mountain railway, the office floor will gracefully slide away from beneath you and you will find yourself launched into the abyss.

Down, down, down! The sensation, though sickening, is really delightful. Most people I know, find it a little too much for them and consequently cease to think, in which case the trolley reconverts itself into the swivel chair, the floor closes up and the hours at the desk seem once more to be hours passed in a perfectly reasonable manner; or else, more rarely, flee in panic horror from the office to bury their heads like ostriches in religion or what not. . . . The proper course, I flatter myself, is that which I have adopted. Having sought out the heart of reality–Gog's Court, to be explicit–I have taken up my position there; and though fully aware of the nature of the reality by which I am surrounded, though deliberately keeping myself reminded of the complete imbecility of what I am doing, I yet remain heroically at my post. My whole time is passed on the switchback; all my life is one unceasing slide through nothing.

Here Huxley's mood of disillusionment is carried to its ultimate point. All his early sense of the meaningless of the universe, of the hopelessness of all our forays into illusion, is contained in this passage. It is the dark night through which the mystic must pass, and perhaps the most curious aspect of *Those Barren Leaves* is that it is not Chelifer, but Calamy, who proceeds towards enlightenment. Perhaps it is because Chelifer has become fixed in the pride of his nihilism, of his stance as a man knowing that he is facing the absurd.

But Chelifer and Calamy remain linked, not only because they have advanced in their various ways out of illusion, but also because they realize that their actions do not entirely accord with their convictions. 'On principle', notes Chelifer, 'I disapprove of writing; on principle I desire to live brutishly like any other human being. The flesh is willing, but the spirit is weak.' And Calamy, who has learnt the futility of the sensualist's life and wishes no longer to pursue it, is forced to the reflection: 'Now I'm free; I have every opportunity for doing exactly what I like–and I consistently do what I don't like.' The consequence, in Calamy's case, is that out of habit he finds himself starting up a love affair with Mary Thriplow whom he does not even desire. As for Chelifer, the repute he has gained from following his bad habit of writing poetry has long made Mrs. Aldwinkle anxious to add him to her menagerie; he has successfully evaded her, until coincidence plays its part; while floating in the Tyrrhenian Sea he is almost drowned by a yacht that sails over him, and, having been rescued, is triumphantly captured by Mrs. Aldwinkle, who happens to be there at the right moment and carries him off to the Cybo Malaspina. She immediately falls in love with him. The desperation of her fifties, and of her nostalgia for a youth long slipped away, makes her perform the Proustian miracle of turning into a romantic hero this young man with a spider's surname.

The names of Huxley's characters, sometimes suggesting onomato-poeically the natures of their possessors, as in the cases of Aldwinkle and Thriplow, and sometimes picked carefully from the pages of diction-aries and encyclopaedias, are always interesting and usually significant. This is particularly so in the case of the three men who are thematically the most important characters in *Those Barren Leaves*. That all their names begin with the same letter–C–suggests a special link between them, and in fact their individual names are chosen to illuminate their varying attitudes towards the problem of the purpose and destination of life. The small spider whose name Chelifer bears is also called 'the book scorpion'; he bears minute claws like the real scorpion, but lacks his poisonous tail. Not only is Chelifer's dry bookishness suggested, but also his rebellion against the world from which he defends himself with the claws of a desperate philosophy, and, finally, the lack of active evil within him. Calamy bears the name of two celebrated seventeenth-century divines, and there is a relevance to the nature of his search in the fact that one of his namesakes, Benjamin Calamy, wrote a *Discourse about a Doubting (scrupulous) Conscience*. Cardan, of course, bears the anglicized version of the name of Girolamo Cardano, a noted figure of the Italian sixteenth century, a 'Renaissance man' who combined with great success the roles of mathematician, physician and astrologer, and left two important works, *De Subtilitate Rerum* and *De Varietate Rerum*, in which he speculated daringly if obscurely on the possibility that inorganic as well as organic matter may be animated. Huxley's Cardan, with his great and miscellaneous knowledge and his habit of lecturing like a medieval professor, could well pass as an inglorious (though not mute) Cardano, unable to spread his wings in a modern world that has no use for universal men. Certainly the connotations of the three names closely fit their functions in presenting three facets of the problem that in the end the novel leaves unsolved: Chelifer that of the existentialist, Cardan that of the rational hedonist, and Calamy that of the contemplative and mystic.

With Hovenden and Irene shyly aware of each other, with Calamy playing his half-willing part in Mary's fantasies, and Chelifer pursued by Mrs. Aldwinkle, three of the 'Loves of the Parallels' are established. The pattern is only complete when Mr. Cardan makes his curious expedition into the Maremma, descending from the wind-cleansed hills into the marshes which tradition and Dante have associated in history with malaria and in symbolism with death. Mr. Cardan is in search of an antique sculpture which he is told has been discovered by a grocer in a marshland village. He hopes with its sale to earn enough money to replenish his depleted means. The sculpture turns out to be worthless, but Cardan discovers a treasure that seems far more valuable. Beside one of the dank waterways, when he has lost his way the first evening, he meets an odd English couple–a certain Elver and his half-witted sister Grace. Elver has brought Grace to the marshes on the strength of what he had read long ago in the *Inferno*, in the hope that she will die of ague and he can enjoy the fortune a relative has inconsiderately left to her rather than to him. He is unaware that the progress of preventive medicine has made his scheme impracticable. Cardan cynically views the situation. He has recently been oppressed with visions of disease, decrepitude and death, of being left alone and poor in his old age, and Grace's twenty-five thousand pounds, even with Grace herself, seems extraordinarily enviable. He contrives to captivate and elope with the ecstatic half-wit, and adds her to Mrs. Aldwinkle's household while he sets about arranging the marriage. But it is her funeral not her marriage that he attends, for on the trip into Umbria Grace eats rotten fish and dies in agony. All Cardan's efforts–he realizes bitterly–have been lost. He has merely fulfilled Elver's ambition, and is left with a deeper consciousness of the nearness of death.

The other loves, all but one, prove equally ludicrous and sordid. Having pursued Chelifer relentlessly from day to day, Mrs. Aldwinkle in desperation at last bursts into his bedroom and Chelifer is saved from a virtual rape only by the coincidence of Grace Elver's death throes setting the house in an uproar. The relationship between Calamy and Mary is one of people united only by physical lust; Calamy does not enjoy what he does from habit, and Mary, even when she is most subdued to him by sexual ecstasy, is playing in her mind one of the endless series of fantasy roles that make her life. Only the idyllic relationship between Irene and Hovenden breaks the pattern. It is one of the very few occasions when Huxley allows a romantic love relationship to develop without mocking or destroying it; perhaps he does it to demonstrate the falseness of the other sexual relationships. Some day, he seems to suggest, even these innocents will be corrupted.

Like all of Huxley's books, *Those Barren Leaves* has several themes: the Proustian delusiveness of love, the animal ugliness of sex, the inevitability of age and death, all these are sharply delineated. And the problem of freedom is strongly stated; how can man free himself from the necessities of his flesh and his nature? For, as Cardan reflects, 'Sooner or later every soul is stifled by the sick body.'

But despite these dark thoughts upon dark things, despite the gratuitous brutishness of Grace's death, one is aware of the splendour of the landscapes in which the characters live and travel, and sharp and clear on the vision gleam the Etruscan tombs where long-dead men had left an image of their vitality that delighted and puzzled their successors more than two millennia afterwards. For all its exhibition of those horrors of ageing, sickness and death beloved of Tibetan Buddhists and medieval Christians, *Those Barren Leaves* is not only a gentler book than *Antic Hay;* it also offers more genuine hope than Gumbril's fleeting epiphany.

There is a parody of Stavrogin's marriage in *The Possessed* in Cardan's courting of Grace, and there seems an even fuller reflection of that Dostoevskian hero in the strange choice of Calamy as the potential convert to a mystical religion. For Calamy, in his proud handsomeness, seems hardly the kind of material out of which saints are made. Mary sees him looking down at her 'through half-closed eyes, with that air of sleepy insolence, of indolent power, characteristic of him, especially in his relations with women', and later she sees in him 'a formidable and Satanic beauty'. Calamy would seem more convincing as the precursor of Spandrell than of Anthony Beavis, yet the Satanic is after all merely the Godly inverted, and the man who has once come into that circle of existence where powers of good and evil compete has the possibility of choosing either direction.

Calamy arrives at the Cybo Malaspina already nurturing the conviction that his old life is at an end, and his affair with Mary is the final diversion from the true path that teaches him the detachment he must practise, if he is to solve the questions that pursue him.

Calamy lay on his back, quite still, looking up into the darkness. Up there, he was thinking, so near that it's only a question of reaching out a hand to draw back the curtaining darkness that conceals it, up there, just above me, floats the great secret, the beauty and the mystery. To look into the depths of that mystery, to fix the eyes of the spirit on that bright and enigmatic beauty, to pore over the secret until its symbols cease to be opaque and the light filters through from beyond – there is nothing else in life, for me at any rate, that matters; there is no rest or possibility of satisfaction in doing anything else.

The novel reaches its climax and its thematic conclusion in Calamy's departure from the Cybo Malaspina, which represents all the pretensions he now rejects, to a retreat in the mountains where he can make his attempt to attain the truth 'by relentless and concentrated thought'. His going spells the end of the long party at Mrs. Aldwinkle's. Irene and Hovenden will marry, Chelifer is going back to his particular reality at Gog's Court, Grace is dead, Falx is immersed in an International Labour Congress, and Cardan will be setting off in Mrs. Aldwinkle's entourage to Monte Carlo. As the novel closes, Cardan and Chelifer go up to visit Calamy, and the three central male characters are together for the last time, without those pursuing women who – with rare exceptions – are the enemies in Huxley's world. In the splendid setting of the Apennines they talk of religion and of the necessities of decay and death with which the novel has been filled, and Calamy puts the mystic's answer that all this, and even the thought of life after death, are irrelevant because eternity can be experienced here and now. He does not convince his friends, nor does he convince the reader. And it is in a bathos on the verge of sentimentality that the novel ends, without the ironic twist to which its predecessors had accustomed one. Chelifer and Cardan have gone; Calamy stands awhile, having watched them passing down the hill.

Looking up the slope he could see a clump of trees still glittering as though prepared for a festival above the rising flood of darkness. And at the head of the valley, like an immense precious stone, glowing with its own inward fire, the limestone crag reached up through the clouds into the pale sky. Perhaps he had been a fool, thought Calamy. But looking at that shining peak, he was somehow reassured.

Perhaps the most striking thing about that ending is the opposition of light and darkness, and the image of the crag as a kind of jewel of wisdom. Such will be the dominant imagery of Huxley's later work.

The conclusion of *Those Barren Leaves* is as tentative as Calamy's final thoughts. A great deal of Huxley goes down the hill with Chelifer and Cardan, and the next few years will see him tending to seek a solution to the problems of human existence elsewhere than in mystical philosophy. Perhaps it is for this reason—for its lack of final certainty—that *Those Barren Leaves*, though the weakest of Huxley's earlier novels, is still superior to the post-conversion works which replace its poignant question with the kind of dogmatic answer that mars *Time Must Have a Stop* and ruins *Island*.

Huxley himself took great pride in *Those Barren Leaves* immediately after he had completed it. He told his American publisher Eugene Saxton that it 'cuts more ice, I think, than the others and is more explicit and to the point'. But within four months he was writing to Naomi Mitchison that he felt it to be 'jejune and shallow and off the point'. All his works so far, he went on to say, had been 'off the point'. He wished he could stop writing for a while, could put an end to all 'this fuss in the intellectual void'. His mind was ripe for changes, and, shortly afterwards, they came.

CHAPTER SIX

Time's Baleful Face

I

'A sensitive man can't go round the world and come back with the same philosophy of life as the one he started with.' So said Kingham in 'Two or Three Graces'. It is a telling remark when one remembers that in May, 1926, when the novella was published, Huxley was still in the United States on the last stage of the world journey that would profoundly change his attitude to existence and lead him into the interlude, dominated by the vast edifice of his most ambitious novel, *Point Counter Point*, that separated the virtual nihilism of *Antic Hay* from the acceptance of mystical religion reflected and recorded in *Eyeless in Gaza*. The mood Kingham's remark implies is revived in the last pages of *Jesting Pilate*, the volume of travel notes which Huxley published in October 1926, four months after his return to Europe.

> I set out on my travels knowing, or thinking that I knew [says Huxley] how men should live, how be governed, how educated, what they should believe. I knew which was the best form of social organization and to what end societies had been created. I had my views on every variety of human life. Now, on my return, I find myself without any of these pleasing certainties.

He describes some of the illusions he has lost, and goes on:

> But in compensation for what I lost, I acquired two important new convictions: that it takes all sorts to make a world, and that the established spiritual values are fundamentally correct and should be maintained.

In Asia Huxley learnt the Asian philosophy of acceptance; if men—as his novels up to now had palpably demonstrated—are foolish, the reason may lie partly outside themselves, in the nature of the existence they must encompass, and if this is so they deserve more compassion, more understanding, than the purely Peacockian approach allows. Already, in exploring the philosophic fashions of the generation his earlier novels represented, he had recognized the existence of chronic human miseries for which there was no easy solution, and had learnt the virtues of responsible conservatism. He was prepared for the process that would replace the cult of the new by the perennial philosophy.

'Two or Three Graces' was prophetic in a double sense. Not only did Kingham anticipate Huxley's reactions to a global journey, but the fascination his personality wielded over the narrator, Dick Wilkes, bore such a strong resemblance to that which D. H. Lawrence wielded over Huxley for a few years in the late 1920s, that critics have freely assumed that Kingham was intended as a fictional portrait of Lawrence.

This was denied by Huxley. In 1930 he told a correspondent that when Kingham was 'concocted' he had only seen Lawrence on one occasion, at their meeting in 1915 when the project for the colony of Rananim was abortively discussed. The two men did not encounter each other for a second time until 1926 in Florence. Lawrence had written to Huxley in India from Spotorno, suggesting that they might meet again. By this time Kingham had been created and the story he obsessively dominated had appeared in print. This fact needs emphasis, for the case of Kingham is only one example of the way in which Lawrence's influence over Huxley's writings during the later 1920s and the early 1930s has been exaggerated.

Huxley was indeed impressed and puzzled by a personality so unlike his own. Lawrence was one of the few people towards whom he broke his reticence so far as to use the word 'love' to describe retrospectively his own side of the relationship. As early as 1927, when their acquaint-ance had been renewed for little more than a year, he noted in his diary: 'Lawrence is one of the few people I feel real respect and admiration for. Of most other eminent people I have met I feel that at any rate I belong to the same species as they do. But this man has something different and superior in kind, not degree.'

Huxley's feelings were not reciprocated with the same intensity. Revealing a mild hypocrisy, Lawrence was inclined to praise Huxley's books when writing to him–and condemn them when writing to their common friends. He was far too egocentric to have a real respect for a writer so far removed in attitude, and the affection he did feel for Huxley was directed towards the man rather than his works.

But as I say [he remarked once to Lady Ottoline Morrell] there's more than one self to everybody and the Aldous that writes those

· novels is only one little Aldous amongst others—probably much
nicer—that don't write novels. . . . No, I don't like his books: even if
I admire a sort of desperate courage of repulsion and repudiation in
them. But again, I feel only half a man writes the books—a sort of
precocious adolescent. There's surely much more of a man in the
actual Aldous.

A grudging acknowledgement of brilliance, combined with the
curiously intense affection that often appears when opposing characters
come together: this appears to have been the extent of Lawrence's
reactions to Huxley.

Huxley's attitude was more complicated because the encounter with
Lawrence fulfilled the intellectual needs he was experiencing at the
time. He was seeking a positive philosophy to replace his unwilling
nihilism, and Lawrence's vitalism seemed for a time to fill the moral
vacuum. He was also (and this is the true clue to Kingham and his
influence over Wilkes in 'Two or Three Graces') looking for a quasi-
religious teacher, a guru, in whom he could personify his new approach
to existence. Lawrence, in fact, led Huxley to no destination other than
that he had already found necessary. This is why he was able to shed
Lawrence so easily, and to write in 1931, a year after his friend's death,
that, in spite of his admiration and love, 'in reading him I often suffer
from a kind of claustrophobia; I have the impression of being swallowed
up like the unfortunate prophet.' In the same way, the journey to India
only confirmed a shift in his world view whose necessity he had already
realized when Gumbril, leaving London at the end of *Antic Hay*, does
not return to the past represented by his schoolroom, but goes abroad
to destinations unknown.

On Huxley's actual writings Lawrence's influence consists mainly in
the contribution of a few ideas to be processed in the great digestive
machine of Huxley's intellect and to be regurgitated in the essays of
Do What You Will and in Rampion's tedious monologues in *Point
Counter Point*. In terms of the larger artistic and psychological elements
which make up a work of fiction, in terms even of dominant themes,
Lawrence's influence was no greater than Dostoevsky's (which has been
much underestimated) and probably less than that of contemporary
French writers, like Proust, Malraux and especially Gide.

English and American critics have in fact been surprisingly un-
perceptive of the extent of Huxley's immersion in continental European
literature, and of the affinities he discovered there. With some French
writers, like Paul Valéry and the unfortunate Drieu de la Rochelle, he

maintained close personal contact; for many others, from Stendhal and Baudelaire in the past to Rimbaud and Cendrars more recently, he felt an intense admiration (Baudelaire was for him the greatest of modern poets). And it is in his work of the Middle Twenties–*Those Barren Leaves, Point Counter Point*, his later poems and some of the stories and essays of the time–that their influence is most penetrative.

2

The novella and the three attendant short stories which form *Two or Three Graces* demonstrate Huxley's growing philosophic restlessness, his discontent with the kind of social picture he had presented in his earlier novels. They also show the variations he was developing on the lessons he had learnt from Proust. For he deals not merely with the nature of love, but also with those psychological discontinuities of which the author of *A la recherche du temps perdu* was so highly conscious, and with the complexities of that vital factor of snobbery which holds together the world of the privileged that Huxley like Proust regarded with the ambiguity of contempt combined with addiction.

In all the stories of *Two or Three Graces* the mental agonies of the lower middle class, who accept upper-class values but have neither the money nor the breeding to live up to them, form a dominant element. Unlike Orwell, Huxley knew from the beginning that so far as he was concerned the barrier dividing Disraeli's Two Nations was too high even to make the effort of surmounting it. But experience did bring him into contact with people born into the working class or the lower strata of the lower middle class, who had contrived by merit, luck or cunning to achieve some kind of foothold in the world of wealth and intellect in which he himself moved with birthright ease. Lawrence, of course, was one of them; so in Huxley's earlier experience, had been Wells and George Lansbury, and by the 1920s he had become acquainted with many of those young men of talent who were rising socially and in the process taking revenge for the slights which they had suffered on the way up.

As a laboratory to study this phenomenon there was, of course, no country like England before 1939, with its infinite variations of class behaviour. And so, in *Two or Three Graces*, Huxley returns from the continental scene of *Those Barren Leaves* and *Little Mexican*, to the London of *Antic Hay*. To the emotional furies which tear the characters of that novel (in which the lower classes were kept resolutely on the outside) are added the mental torments bred of a sense of social in-feriority – the collective paranoia which is one of the attendant sicknesses of poverty.

The lyrical irony, the controlled pathos, that characterize the best work in *Little Mexican* have already vanished in *Two or Three Graces*. The three shorter stories are all rather bitter little studies in class humiliation. In 'Half Holiday' the beginning is lyrical enough; it is one of those splendid spring afternoons when London lies under the hazy sunlight like 'a city of the imagination', and the inhabitants of the city walk in Hyde Park, stirred by the impulses of the season. Even Peter Brett, the wretched Lancashire-born clerk with his respectable up-bringing and his miserable job, feels the spirit that moves in the air like pollen, and longs for the romantic accident that will break his solitude.

> But of course, as a matter of fact, no accident ever did happen and he never had the courage to tell anyone how lonely he was; and his stammer was something awful; and he was small, he wore spectacles, and nearly always had pimples on his face; and his dark grey suit was growing very shabby and rather short in the sleeves; and his boots, though carefully blacked, looked just as cheap as they really were.

Peter follows two impeccably dressed Mayfair girls who are taking their dog for a walk and making flapper chatter about parties and beaux. The miracle appears to happen, for their dog becomes involved in a fight with another of its kind, and Peter – at the cost of an unpleasant bite – pulls the two beasts apart. He believes he has proved himself; the girls smile well-bred smiles and congratulate him on his bravery. The more beautiful, the owner of the dog, puts out her hand; when Peter, in fearful ecstasy, takes it, a pound note is slipped into his palm. Wretched with humiliation, he tramps about London, picks up a tart, suddenly realizes that this is the bitter end of all his romantic dreams and flees as she shouts abuse, leaving the pound note in her hand. The effect is overdone; Peter is more pathetic than a writer from his own class would have made him, and the whore is unnecessary. Brutality dissolves into sentiment.

'The Monocle' views the class situation from a slightly different angle. Gregory – the anti-hero – is not poor; he is the son of a prosperous business man, but his wealth, and the monocle he wears as an outward and visible sign of the position to which he aspires, do not make him feel secure. He always arrives at parties feeling that the servants despise him. The story is of one such party at which he defers to people whose intelligence he despises, feels himself socially rejected even when he is not, becomes the butt of a drunken colonial, hankers after a Viveash-like girl with a 'cold and steady grey eye' who has a taste for 'ruffians', and finally, leaving the gathering, succumbs ludicrously in the street to the drink that has given him the courage to carry his monocle with a dash: with variations, one suspects, the evening's events will be often repeated.

'The Monocle' is a more sardonic and more successful story than 'Half Holiday', but the best of the shorter stories in *Two or Three Graces* is 'Fairy Godmother', which brings Huxley on to his own social ground. For Mrs. Escobar, the central figure, is a rich woman moved by caprice and condescension, and the portrait that Huxley paints of her relationship as a demanding benefactress with her two protégées is drawn with sure and delicate satirical lines.

Susan and Ruth are well-brought-up girls suddenly orphaned into poverty. Mrs. Escobar took Susan into her household, as a pet to be ruled by whim, but Ruth, the older girl, preferred to marry a young man with no income and a future to make. In revenge, Mrs. Escobar visits her on superior slumming expeditions, and the story tells of one of these occasions when the benefactress strains every drop of satisfaction out of exercising her patronage and proving her power. But not all beings acknowledge the superiority of even a Mrs. Escobar, and when she condescends to read 'The Owl and the Pussy Cat' to Ruth's small child, he interrupts her affected elocution with a clamour that turns the reading into a highly amusing conflict of two kinds of infantility. And all the time, beneath the comedy, one is aware of the tension between the characters, the resentment of the two girls against the selfish benevolence of Mrs. Escobar.

'Two or Three Graces', the major work of the collection, is a casually told *récit* whose appearance of narrative simplicity disguises the complexity of its themes. The action is simple enough. Through accidentally meeting in Paris an old schoolfellow–a dull amiable bore named Herbert Comfrey–the music critic Dick Wilkes makes the acquaintance of John Peddley and his wife Grace, who is Herbert's sister. Grace is a charmingly ugly girl with an indeterminate temperament which, as Dick soon discovers, tends to take on shape and colouring from the people with whom she associates. With Peddley she is the dedicated if incapable housewife, a perfect foil to his loud, overbearing personality. With Dick, she turns into a devotee of music, and when he introduces her to the meretriciously fashionable painter Rodney Clegg, she is transformed as quickly into a passionate follower of the arts and the

Bohemian life, becoming Clegg's mistress while maintaining at home—without any sense of hypocrisy—the guise of the faithful bourgeois wife. Rodney jilts her for a richer woman, and on the rebound she falls in with Dick's friend Kingham, a neurotic writer who combines intelligence and a charm that captivates even his enemies with a passion for hysterical scenes; to live in peace is virtually impossible for him, and the most innocent love relationship becomes in his mind a maze of calculation and betrayal, in which every act seems planned to dominate or to degrade. With Grace, Kingham proceeds through every variation of bliss and damnation, until he tires of it all and walks out on her. Grace threatens to commit suicide; but for Dick's providential arrival, she would probably have carried out her threat.

Into this fairly simple plot are woven a whole series of themes related to Huxley's current preoccupations. The portrayal of Herbert Comfrey and his fellow bore John Peddley is a mocking revelation of the pointlessness of ordinary upper-middle-class life, the life followed, as Huxley realized, by the majority of his schoolfellows and university companions, who sank what individualities they might have had when young into careers in the City and unmentionable suburban recreations. Yet how much worse is this life than the trivial Bohemian half-world of Rodney and his companions which Huxley dexterously opposes to it, mocking equally the routines in which many of his fellow artists are trapped? Dick and his wife Catharine, with their dedication to music and their periodical withdrawals to a light-ridden Italian oasis, represent the rational just as Kingham represents the irrational opposition to both routines.

'Two or Three Graces' presents a compact microcosm of the social world as Huxley saw it in 1925, and the social theme is extended, in the portrayal of Kingham, to show the explosive nature of the frustrations that afflict a man who has climbed out of poverty into the snobbish ambiance of the artistic and literary worlds; Orwell was later to explore the same theme with more relentless bitterness in *Keep the Aspidistra Flying*.

But Kingham is more than a frustrated petit bourgeois. He projects a philosophic viewpoint, and one of the reasons why critics once imagined him a portrait of D. H. Lawrence was that his attack on rationalist philosophies and his insistence on wringing the maximum emotional experience out of life superficially resembled attitudes Lawrence was defending at the time. But only superficially, for Kingham stands in opposition to Lawrence in more ways than he resembles him. His drinking would have aroused Lawrence's disapproval; his promiscuous sexual relationships, which humiliated both himself and his partner, had a sado-masochistic violence of a kind Lawrence would have found atrociously perverted. But Dostoevsky would not, and one of the clues to Kingham's origins is presented when Grace, at the height of her affair with him, brings *Letters from the Underworld* as a present to Catharine, with the remark: 'You must read it. . . . It's so damnably true.' True, certainly, of her relationship with Kingham. For all the Dostoevskian passion for sin and remorse, with its attendant paranoia, is present in Kingham, as is a bitter anti-Utopianism reminiscent in mood of *The Possessed*, the novel by Dostoevsky that impressed and appalled Huxley more than any other; it is certainly a parody of Dostoevsky rather than of Lawrence that appears in Kingham's writing:

> Only those who know the Holy Ghost are tempted to sin against him—indeed, can sin against him. One cannot waste a talent unless one first possesses it. One cannot do what is wrong, or stupid, or futile, unless one first knows what is right, what is reasonable, what is worth doing. Temptation begins with knowledge and grows as knowledge grows. A man knows that he has a soul to save and that it is a precious soul; it is for this very reason that he passes his time in such a way that it must infallibly be damned.

Reading such a passage, one realizes that Kingham's descendant in *Point Counter Point* is not Rampion, that spouter of Lawrencian phrases, but the God-seeking Satanist Spandrell.

Flamboyantly as Kingham may attract one's attention, the title of the novella accurately indicates the principal character. Not only is Grace Peddley a woman of many lives; she draws together reminiscences of many past Huxley characters. There is a shadow of the undeveloped child that was her namesake Grace Elver. There is the naïve vanity that led Rosie Shearwater into her increasingly disturbing adventures. There is—acted out in life rather than in the brain—the parade of fantasy selves that filled the mind of Mary Thriplow in *Those Barren Leaves*. And it is appropriate that Grace should resemble so varied a group of characters, since in her Huxley develops most strikingly his own version of a conception of character explored by earlier novelists.

Duality of personality—which Huxley himself exploited in 'Farcical History of Richard Greenow'—had found its place in the Gothic novelists, in Russian writers like Gogol and Dostoevsky, and in such later exotic works as *The Picture of Dorian Grey*, and that book read in childhood and so often mentioned by Huxley, R. L. Stevenson's *Dr. Jekyll and Mr. Hyde*. To this established literature of the instability of personality, Proust had added the doctrine of 'the intermittences of the heart'; our minds do not act, he suggested, in regular, structured ways, and so we do not always feel the impact of events when we may be expected to do so. Huxley extended these ideas into a doctrine of the discontinuity of 'the psychological materials out of which the individual must construct his personality'. Grace never does construct a consistent and stable personality, but under the diabolic impact of Kingham she comes near to constructing a self-destructive anti-personality. What she normally presents instead of a personality is a persona in the original sense of a mask, borrowed from the individual under whose influence for the moment she lives, and sometimes she uses two different personae at the same time–e.g. her Rodney persona and her Peddley persona. She is incapable of real continuity of thought, and this emerges even in her speech, which is inconsequential, proceeding without logical transition from one unrelated subject to the next. Huxley never again presented a character so unstructured as Grace; she represents the extreme point of his rebellion against the mechanical consistency of characters in the Peacockian tradition.

Huxley used his early novelle to try out experimentally ideas later developed in his true novels, and 'Two or Three Graces' reveals several of the preoccupations that later shaped *Point Counter Point*. Just as Quarles in *Point Counter Point* is a novelist within the novel, taking part in the action and writing about what he helps to create in real life, so Dick Wilkes not only records the adventures of Grace, but also acts as the impresario–the Pandarus of his own definition–as he leads Grace out of her life with Peddley and is instrumental in introducing her first to Rodney Clegg and then to Kingham. In a number of ways–again like Quarles–Wilkes resembles Huxley himself: in his lack of the power to visualize, in his passion for Italy and his use of light as a metaphor for life, and possibly in the detachment that prevents him from becoming Grace's lover. But perhaps the most interesting anticipation of *Point Counter Point* is the way 'Two or Three Graces' develops through the narrator's musical consciousness. Wilkes is a critic of music, author of a life of Mozart, something of an amateur musician; he begins Grace's series of transformations by taking her to concerts. Through these musical expeditions Grace meets Rodney; it is at the Queen's Hall that Dick meets Kingham and takes him home to the encounter with Grace which begins their disastrous affair. But it is not merely that Dick's musical occupations direct the action. The very structure of the novella imitates that of music, for the narrator explicitly delineates the four movements – domesticity with Peddley, music with Dick, the *scherzando* of Bohemian life with Rodney, the *molto agitato* of passion with Kingham. He sits, as the story ends, playing Beethoven's opus III. 'The miracle of the Arietta floated out from under my fingers. Ah, if only the music of our destinies could be like this!'

And here emerges an irony that recurs in Huxley's works at this period. For, to the early Huxley, music is the quasi-Platonic metaphor for that perfection with which the human condition is rarely in tune. By giving works like 'Two or Three Graces' and *Point Counter Point* the structure of music without its essence, he is emphasizing more strongly than ever the discord between the ideal and the actual.

3

When Huxley set out in September 1925 on the first of the great journeys which marked important transitions in his life, he sailed from Naples via Port Said and the Red Sea to Bombay. Thence he went to Kashmir, and afterwards through Peshawar and Taxila to Lahore. He visited Agra and the medieval principalities of Rajputana. He saw nothing of the Deccan, or of the Dravidian south of India, so different in character from the great plain of Hindustan, over which he proceeded, through Delhi and Cawnpore, through Lucknow and Benares, to Calcutta, where he boarded a ship which took him to Burma. He sailed up the Irrawaddy, went inland to the Chinese border; then to Malaya, Java and Borneo, to the Philippines, Shanghai and Japan. Crossing the Pacific, he landed at San Francisco, but inexplicably left that attractive city to immerse himself in the fascinating monstrosities of Los Angeles. Chicago and New York were his other destinations in North America. He returned to London in June, 1926, after more than nine months of travel.

The experience of those seasons of voyaging gave Huxley the material for his first travel book, *Jesting Pilate*, became embedded in the action of *Point Counter Point*, and influenced the essays in *Do What You Will*; more diffusely it emerged in his Gandhian pacifism during the mid Thirties and in the oriental elements that became increasingly preponderant in his religious attitudes after he settled in California in 1937; it surfaced at the end of his life, a whole generation after that first trip to the Orient, when he chose the Malayan archipelago as a setting for his last novel, *Island*, and gave its society a religio-philosophic basis combining Indian and European elements.

Jesting Pilate is described as 'The Diary of a Journey', and it reads like the edited jottings of a writer with a constantly available notebook. It is a mosaic of impressions; the continuity is implied instead of being expressed in a linear narrative. The author withdraws as an acting person, though not as a reflective observer. The book lacks anything that might be called adventure, and is niggardly in its presentation of episode. Its characteristic component is the particular observation which the author broadens into a generalization that illuminates the local culture he is experiencing and, if possible, reflects on the human condition in general.

Jesting Pilate begins in Port Said with some traveller's commonplaces on the touts who sell dirty postcards. It ends with the author back in London, making his final generalizations on the way the traveller, observing the characteristic excesses to which every culture is subject, himself moves nearer to a stable and comprehensive view.

> In certain parts of the world he will find spirituality run wild; in others a stupid materialism that would deny the very existence of values. The traveller will observe these various distortions and will create for himself a standard that shall be, as far as possible, free from them–a standard of values that shall be as timeless, as uncontingent on circumstances, as nearly absolute as he can make them. Understanding diversity and allowing for it, he will tolerate, but not without limit. He will distinguish between harmless perversions and those which tend actually to deny or stultify the fundamental values. Towards the first he will be tolerant. There can be no compromise with the second.

Yet it is those regions which develop the extremes of a rampant materialism or an aberrant spirituality that in fact interest Huxley most of all. Writing of Burma and Malaya, of Indonesia and Japan, where he finds less to provoke him into philosophic reflection, he indulges in the evocation of setting which is one of the functions of the ordinary travel writer, and this makes more amiable reading than the descriptions of India and the United States which not only occupy the larger part of the book, but also grip the attention much more intensely because they represent the great dilemma which, for Huxley, this journey brought to the surface.

In India he saw religiosity in its most exaggerated forms. He was often disgusted with the worldiness of men who claimed to be saintly;

in Bombay, in Benares, in Calcutta, he was appalled by the magnitude and intensity of human misery in this land where spirituality was held in such high repute; it was only when he could get away from both crowds and gurus, in the splendid and fantastic cities of the Rajputs, in the deserted perfection of Fatehpur Sikri, that he felt at an ease reflected in the evocative passages of architectural description he could write about such places. Hindu religion he found, as he said, 'too high . . . for my taste'.

Philosophies, like pheasants, can be hung too long. Most of our highest systems have been pendant for at least two thousand years. I am plebeian enough to prefer my spiritual nourishment fresh.

Yet he detects occasionally, and in Gandhi especially, the almost invisible lineaments of genuine saintliness, and when he describes Indian political occasions with their erratic combination of frenzy and casualness, he makes clear his admiration for those Indians who struggle for independence. He doubts if Indian rulers will be any better than British, but he agrees that the mere fact of their being Indians will be an improvement worth seeking.

Huxley's strictures on religion are understandable as a projection of his experience of India, and particularly interesting when one realizes how near he was in time to the acceptance of an orientalized philosophy of existence. At this moment, however, it was from a bold Greco-Renaissance stance that he looked upon Asia, as 'one who believes that man is here on earth to adventure, to know, to try all things, to advance . . . towards some quite unattainable goal of perfection'. It is essentially a Godwinian attitude, proper to a follower of Peacock, and reinforced with that rhetoric of high experience which at times intoxicates shy and studious writers like Pater and Huxley. One expects the 'hard gem-like flame' to start burning.

From this viewpoint, and also from the viewpoint of shocked compassion, Huxley concludes that 'Religion is a luxury which India, in its present condition, cannot possibly afford'. And, in a tone which suggests that he has decided against Calamy the dialogue that ended *Those Barren Leaves*, he declares: 'The Other World—the world of metaphysics and religion—can never possibly be as interesting as this world.' He even takes up, against Hindu 'spirituality', the defence of western materialism, and when he leaves India it is with the sense of relief familiar to many travellers. 'For India is depressing as no other country I have ever known. One breathes in it, not air, but dust and hopelessness.'

There are further ironies for those who know what Huxley's later books will bring, for it is on this journey that Huxley first makes the literary acquaintance of Henry Ford, whose *My Life and Work* he finds in a ship's library between Java and Borneo. His astonished approval of what he reads suggests to him the relativity of all viewpoints.

> In these seas, and to one fresh from India and Indian 'spirituality', Indian dirt and religion, Ford seems a greater man than Buddha. In Europe, on the other hand, and still more, no doubt, in America, the Way of Gautama has all the appearance of the way of Salvation. One is all for religion until one visits a really religious country. There, one is all for drains, machinery and the minimum wage. To travel is to discover that everybody is wrong.

India and America between them set Huxley on a philosophic course that would leave him to the end of his life trying to reconcile the spiritual and the material elements in human existence. America astonished him with social paradoxes far more gigantic than anything he had observed in Europe. He found 'the Rome of Cato and the Rome of Heliogabalus' co-existing in an ambiance of generous extravagance and unprecedented vitality. He was appalled but fascinated, all the way from Los Angeles to New York, and much that he saw of American popular culture found its way, with Henry Ford's philosophy, into *Brave New World*. Of the elements of American life that were to attract and hold him on his return in 1937 there is no hint in *Jesting Pilate*. In that book India and America represent the Scylla and Charybdis of the spirit; the wise man sails between.

4

The effect of Huxley's world journey was almost immediately perceptible in the changing character of his essays. From his early evocative travel sketches, from those first splendid excursions into the exposition of the visual arts which appeared in *Along the Road*, he turned now, with a seriousness he was never to abandon, to the elaboration of social, political and moral themes. In *Proper Studies* he sought to establish a rational political system; in *Do What You Will* to create a philosophy of life that would combine the vitalism of Lawrence with the moderation of the Greeks.

Proper Studies, which Huxley later regarded as one of his least valuable books, was an attempt to break out of the Utopian-anti-Utopian pattern which for the greater part of his life dominated his expression of political theory. India and America had shaken his faith in democracy, and he developed an aristocratic philosophy which his critics at times interpreted as a kind of fascism for intellectuals.

Actually, having encountered them in Italy, Huxley had little use for the Fascists; his references to them in 'Little Mexican' and 'Green Tunnels' make that clear. True, he went to an Italian social philosopher for inspiration, but Vilfredo Pareto, who died shortly after Mussolini assumed power, was hardly a proto-Fascist. He was the originator of the doctrine of the 'circulation of élites'. He believed that, though it is quite possible for democrats to gain political victories, this does not mean that democracy can ever triumph, for the structure of power is always oligarchic and all that happens when it changes hands, whether by election or revolution, is that one ruling clique replaces another.

In developing the ideas he borrows from Pareto, Huxley rejects the Utopian outlook because it assumes the existence of beings who are essentially unhuman; even 'our democratic social institutions have been evolved in order to fit the entirely fabulous human nature of the eighteenth-century philosophers.' Huxley virtually denies the equality of men. Adapting Jung's doctrine of 'Psychological Types', he contends that human intelligences and abilities differ both in kind and in degree of excellence. No two men are similar; no two men are exactly equal, except in their basic rights.

Proper Studies is a jejune and unsatisfying book because it is a book that marks time. Huxley has felt the need to turn his mind to serious matters, but he has not found a personal direction, and in these miscellaneous essays on psychology, education, eugenics and politics he is rarely his own man, relying on other writers for his theories. There was a certain eccentricity about Huxley's choice of masters; Pareto is a good example. He was not a first-rate or even a very original thinker, but he had a central idea that helped to crystallize the drift of Huxley's thought at the time, and so his importance was exaggerated. The pattern was to be repeated; Huxley continually reinforced his own thoughts with the authority of men who intellectually and as writers were often his inferiors, and so over the years we watch a strange procession of gurus which includes Pareto, W. H. Sheldon, F. M. Alexander, Gerald Heard, and even, at the end, the American medium Eileen Garrett and the Canadian expert in psychedelic drugs, Humphrey Osmond. Observing them, one senses a Peacockian intelligence at work, selecting each to personify a special idea that had been added to Huxley's eclectic philosophy, until in the end one suspects that, instead of being the pupil, Huxley is really, in life as in his novels, the puppet-master, and that his apparent deference to his teachers conceals the fact that he is annexing them rather than accepting their suzerainty.

Certainly Pareto was utilized in *Proper Studies* to support the conclusions to which Huxley's experience had led him by 1927. The most important of them is the idea that men cannot live without leaders, and, since pure democracy is impossible, we must create a new aristocracy. Needless to say—as Mr. Scogan has already suggested in *Crome Yellow*—it is to be an aristocracy of the mind which will rule without reward. There was really no need to have brought in Pareto to prove this point; Plato had already developed it a long time before.

Huxley soon repudiated, by implication at least, the aristocratic pretensions of *Proper Studies*. In *Point Counter Point* he made the spokesman for leadership the megalomaniac Anglo-Fascist Everard Webley. In *Brave New World* he developed the chapter on eugenics from *Proper Studies* into a grotesque system of breeding élites in the laboratory. He realized that in trying to avoid an egalitarian Utopia he had created in *Proper Studies* the sketch of an élitist one.

Do What You Will did not appear until 1929, a year after *Point Counter Point*. While some of the essays were written before the novel was begun, it is likely that most of them were produced afterwards, for in March 1928, the month *Point Counter Point* was completed, Lawrence was encouraging Huxley to 'do a book on the great orthodox perverts', which is what *Do What You Will*, with its essays on Pascal and Saint Francis, Swift and Wordsworth, actually became. But the essays sprang so largely from ideas that were in Huxley's mind while the novel was being written that there is good reason to consider them before discussing *Point Counter Point*.

In *Do What You Will*, Huxley avoids the 'funny dry-mindedness' which Lawrence detected in *Proper Studies* by abandoning the formal plan of a book that attempts to discuss systematically all the aspects of the human condition. Instead, having assumed the philosophic stance of vitalism modified by moderation, he adopts the critical rather than the expository form; taking a Jansenist like Pascal, a Satanist like Baudelaire, a misanthrope like Swift, a political mythologist like Marx, a bland pantheist like Wordsworth, he leads us to his own viewpoint by examining theirs.

The result is a book whose underlying philosophy genuinely avoids the assumptions of Utopia (positive or negative) and pleads the cause of a vitalist humanism that would enable men to live in the moderate enjoyment of the present as in the past they had done only in 'the days of remote and pagan antiquity'.

Do What You Will opens with an essay, 'The One and the Many', in which–assuming that we can sensibly consider religion only in terms of human psychology–Huxley assesses the merits of monotheistic and polytheistic creeds. Monotheism he sees as a religion of the desert, flourishing in Islam and Judaism and extended in Protestant Christianity (for Catholicism has made its appropriate compromises with polytheism). Glancing over history, he observes that its most arid and materialistic times have been those when monotheism was in the ascendant; its richest times those in which–either openly or in some disguised form like the worship of the saints or the Trinity–men have in effect been polytheists. Yet–and here Huxley gives expression to his moderationist creed–the sense of unity has to exist within the sense of diversity. Only a new religion can save man from the 'dark and stinking gulf' into which modern civilization is leading him; it must be a religion whose morality will always have as its primary aim the enhancement of life. But such a religion will recognize that life is diverse and therefore needs many Gods or expressions. Yet, for all his multiplicity, man is individually a unity and in this way the one will exist beside the many.

The writers and teachers who are the subjects of individual essays in *Do What You Will* are chosen because in differing ways they deny the cult of life-enhancement.

Even less in literature than in the visual arts was Huxley a critic who proceeded primarily from the aesthetic viewpoint. The kind of close textual study which we associate with the New Critics was as uninteresting to him as it was to his contemporary George Orwell. His inclination was to take the aesthetic value of a work as accepted–to grant without argument for example that Baudelaire is the greatest modern poet or that Swift is a magnificent writer somewhat spoilt by scatological inclinations–and to proceed by arguments that combine the moral, the psychological and the historical. It is a way of penetrating to the heart of a work and the mind of its creator that can be as revealing as any close analysis.

What gives the best of these essays their special bite is the fact that Huxley partially shares the preoccupations of the writers or historical figures whom he criticizes. Precisely because he had recorded so splendidly the ennui which descended on the survivors of the Great War, he was able to appreciate Baudelaire, that high priest of spleen;

his novelist's awareness of the mutability of personality made him understand the processes by which a Satanist and a Godist lived within the same poet.

With regard to the essay on Swift, it is as well to remember a criticism of Huxley which the Marxist John Strachey published when *Do What You Will* appeared. 'Huxley's findings are always the same,' he asserted. 'Go where you will, do what you will, you will never escape from the smell of ordure and decay.' And, indeed, *Do What You Will*, with its essays on Swift, Baudelaire and Pascal, parallels its glorification of life with a generous savouring of the corruption that is part of life's process. The essay on Swift, like Orwell's essay on the same author, owes its special interest to the fact that Huxley is discussing a writer whom he resembles in his inclination to deal savagely with his characters and to present—as he did in *Point Counter Point*—an almost unrelievedly pessimistic view of human nature. It is not the negation of Swift's view that really stirs him; it is the special morbidity with which Swift presents it, laying so much stress on the process of excretion as a symbol of the evils of the flesh. But Huxley becomes so concerned over this aspect of Swift precisely because he himself is addicted in a somewhat different manner to the symbolism of decay. The symptoms of disease, often described in brutal detail, the disgusting signs of ageing, the gratuitous insult of death, all find a prominent place in his novels.

Just as Swift's scatological predilections can doubtless be traced, as Huxley suggests, to some trauma of his early life, so one can find the sources of Huxley's morbidity in his recurrent ocular disease and in the deaths that overshadowed his adolescence. Of the effect of such physical and ultimately psychological wounds Huxley himself warns us at this period, when he writes in *Proper Studies* on the poet Leopardi.

> When the microcosm is sick, the macrocosm is liable to be infected with its diseases. A bilious philosopher's opinion of the world can only be accepted with a pinch of salt, of Epsom salt by preference. When we have discounted his pains and antidoted his dyspeptic self-poisoning, his philosophy generally assumes a new aspect. Leopardi was one of those sick unhappy thinkers who inoculate the universe with their own maladies. Himself half blind and hard of hearing, he put out the eyes of the world and made it deaf to the cries of man. Suffering, he filled the world with his own pain. Most of the bitter and gloomy things he said about the cosmos were really said about himself. Most, but not all. . . .

These are passionate words, born of the fellow feeling of one half-blind man for another, of one sharp critic of the world for another, and there is a truth in them which applies to their writer as much as his subject. Huxley was scarred by early experience of sickness, death and emotional deprivation; we should never forget this in considering his work, never ignore an underlying community it provides with the very writers he attacked for their anti-vitalism. Given the obsessive quality of his visions of suffering and death, the only ultimate way of escape was a Buddhistic mysticism that regarded existence as Maya, the great illusion, and to this attitude, which rejected the vitalism expressed in *Do What You Will*, he eventually came. Even when he wrote this book there was a shallowness, almost a frivolity, about his defence of the vitalist position, as if he were conscious of whistling in the face of death: it emerges in the defence of inconsistency which recurs in *Do What You Will* and which seems incongruous with Huxley's resolute rationality, particularly when it is as weakly argued as in his essay on Pascal.

> For me, the pleasures of living and understanding have come to outweigh the pleasures, the very real pleasures (for the consciousness of being a man of principle and system is extremely satisfying to the vanity) of pretending to be consistent. I prefer to be dangerously free and alive to being safely mummified. Therefore I indulge my inconsistencies. I try to be sincerely myself–that is to say, I try to be sincerely all the numerous people who live inside my skin and take their turn at being the master of my fate.

It is, nevertheless, the long essay on Pascal that is the most impressive section of *Do What You Will*. It is an excellent study of the Jansenist mentality, of its strange combination of the rational and the mystical. But it also touches very close to Huxley's subconscious development at this time. Once again, as in his early story of Raymond Lully, Huxley is dealing with a convert and a conversion, and it is obvious that he partially identifies with Pascal at the same time as he repudiates his philosophy. It is particularly significant that in speaking of Pascal he uses the intensely personal image of darkness, and associates it with mystical experience as a divine fire and common life as a feeble dawn–that of the half blind.

> With Pascal, as with all other mystics, ecstasy was only a very occasional state. So far as we know, indeed, he had only one experience of its joys. Only once was he touched with the divine fires. His daily, his chronic revelation was of darkness, and the source of that revelation was not the God of Life; it was Death.

After a moonless night the dawn is a kind of decadence. Darkness is limitless and empty; light comes, filling the void, peopling infinity with small irrelevancies, setting bounds to the indefinite. The deepest, most utter darkness, is death's; in the dark idea of death we come as near to a realization of infinity as it is possible for finite beings to come. Pascal early made the acquaintance of death. Through all the later years of his brief existence he lived surrounded by the bottomless obscurities of death. Those metaphysical gulfs which were said to have accompanied him wherever he went were openings into the pit of death. All his meditations on the infinities of littleness and greatness, on the infinite distance between body and mind and the infinitely more infinite distance between mind and charity, were inspired by death, were rationalizations of his sense of death. Death even prompted some of his mathematical speculations; for if it is true, in Pascal's words, that 'Même les propositions géométriques deviennent sentiments,' the converse is no less certain. Sentiments are rationalized as geometrical propositions. When Pascal speculated on the mathematical infinite, he was speculating on that unplumbed darkness with which death had surrounded him. Pascal's thoughts become intelligible only on condition that we look at them against this background of darkness. A man who has realized infinity, not intellectually, but with his whole being, realized it in the intimate and terrifying realization of death, inhabits a different universe from that which is the home of the man to whom death and infinity are only names.

These are profoundly true words in so far as they refer to Pascal; they are also words written with feeling because, like Huxley's remarks on Leopardi, they say much about himself. It is out of his own experience that he talks of darkness, out of his own reflections (already expressed in Cardan's meditations on death in *Those Barren Leaves*) that he understands a man obsessed with death.

In spite of all its invocations of the cult of life, the feeling of the unanswerable presence of death hangs over the essay on Pascal. It becomes evident that Huxley's interest in mysticism has not declined so much as the anti-religious sentiments of *Jesting Pilate* might lead one to suppose. He now equates the mystic and the artist as men who have experiences which are undoubtedly psychological facts; it is not the reality of the mystical experience that he doubts, but merely the mystic's belief that this experience means that he is in direct communication with deity. 'Which, of course, he may be. Or may not. We are not in a position to affirm or deny.' Soon, like Pascal, Huxley would affirm.

But it is not the essay on Pascal itself that lingers most mordantly in the mind after one has read *Do What You Will*; it is Huxley's description of the festival of the Holy Face of Lucca, that extraordinary artifact which Huxley declared to be 'the strangest, the most impressive thing of its kind I have ever seen'.

Imagine [he continues] a huge wooden Christ, larger than life, not naked, as in later representations of the Crucifixion, but dressed in a long tunic, formally fluted with stiff Byzantine folds. The face is not the face of a dead, or dying, or even suffering man. It is the face of a man still violently alive, and the expression of its strong features is stern, is fierce, is even rather sinister. From the dark sockets of polished cedar wood two yellowish tawny eyes, made, apparently, of some precious stone, or perhaps of glass, stare out, slightly squinting, with an unsleeping balefulness. Such is the Holy Face.

As those who have seen the Holy Face will know, there is a strongly subjective factor in Huxley's reaction to it. It is indeed the stern-faced Christ of the Judgement, the Christ Pantocrator of the Byzantines, that is portrayed, but the emphasis on its balefulness suggests that Huxley was stirred with an unusual intensity, and he admits to having stood for hours watching the worshippers and, presumably, the face. At the climactic point of the essay he sets the face in a cave of illumination within darkness;

The church is dark; but in the midst of darkness is a little island of candlelight. Oh, comfort! But from the heart of the comforting light, incongruously jewelled, the dark face stares with squinting eyes, appalling, balefully mysterious.

It is true that in the essay Huxley places himself outside the drama, plays the observer, compares the worshippers hurrying out to the sunlight with those like Pascal to whom 'the metaphysical horror of the world' is like an ever-present and mysteriously hostile Holy Face. It is the thirst for life, he tells us, that sends the people out of the hush and darkness of the church into the sun and noise of the fairground outside.

It is life itself; and I, for one, have more confidence in the rightness of life than in that of any individual man, even if the man be Pascal.

Which is a strange ending, since it is not really Pascal that is in question, but the reality that lies behind Huxley's reaction to the Holy Face.

And here we cannot ignore a curious pattern of echoes. When Huxley places the Holy Face in a cave of light within darkness, he

recreates an image he had used at least twice before, at crucial moments
in *Crome Yellow* and in *Those Barren Leaves*. It is when Denis is in the
gardens of Crome and sees Anne's face preternaturally illuminated in a
cave of light that he loses his chance with her; it is when Francis Chelifer
sees Barbara's face at an evening party, similarly illuminated by a
chance-lit match, that his disastrous passion for her begins. Both Anne
and Barbara can be regarded as standing, like Myra Viveash, for that
Circean principle which, offering the false image of life, is in fact life-
denying, and yet unavoidable. In the same way, despite the rather feeble
statement of vitalism with which Huxley leads us out into the noise and
the sunlight, we cannot forget that the Face is still there, in its cave of
light within darkness; what the Face recalls us to is the Essential Horror,
decay and death, from which, as *Point Counter Point* had already shown
by the time this essay was published, Huxley, as a man in this world and
conscious of its reality, could not escape.

5

Early in his career Huxley had rejected 'Realismus' as an aim in writing;
when he found himself named as a classicist he as firmly rejected that
label.

> I have never had the smallest ambition to be a Classic of any kind,
> whether Neo, Palaeo, Proto or Eo. Not at any price. For, to begin
> with, I have a taste for the lively, the mixed and the incomplete in
> art, preferring it to the universal and the chemically pure. In the
> second place, I regard the classical discipline, with its insistence on
> elimination, concentration, simplification, as being, for all the formal
> difficulties it imposes on the writer, essentially an escape from . . .
> actual reality. (*Music at Night*)

This statement of position is important in considering the most
elaborate of Huxley's novels. *Point Counter Point* attempts to find a
formally satisfying framework within which life can, with a semblance
of its chaos and death, with an acknowledgement of its gratuitousness,
be convincingly portrayed. It is a novel without an ordinary linear plot
and without a hero. It begins with the collapsing extra-marital relationship between Walter Bidlake and Marjorie Carling, but both these
characters have receded from our attention when the novel ends, with
the death by shooting of the Satanist Spandrell followed by the sordid
anticlimax of Burlap, the saintly editor, taking his first shared bath with

Beatrice, the middle-aged literary virgin. There is no single relationship, no single fate that can be regarded as providing the core of *Point Counter Point*; even Philip Quarles, the journal-keeping novelist who acts as a one-man chorus, only enters the novel after the action has proceeded for several chapters, and he is not present for the dramatic finale. Time flows through the novel in a regular, unbroken current with few flash-backs and most of those disguised as memories, but it is not the chronological structure that is important. The main patterns are created in the balancing of themes, in the elaborate interlacing of view-points and in parallelisms of action. Plot and character in the ordinary novelistic sense are relatively unimportant. No character in the short space of time covered by the action of *Point Counter Point* has time to develop under our eyes; its inhabitants stand before us as what their pasts have made them, and the interplay of their wills and of external fate creates the tragic-pathetic design of the book. For both tragic and pathetic it is. Everard Webley and his killer, Spandrell, die in the classic manner from the tragic inner flaws that impel them to their fates. But little Phil, the child of Quarles and his wife Elinor, who dies horrifyingly from meningitis, is pathetic in the most excruciating way; his death is wholly gratuitous and unrelated to his character or to anything he has done in this life. It is that child's death which gives the novel its special horror. Neither Huxley's wife Maria nor his friend Lawrence could accept that horror, and Lawrence expressed his ambivalent reaction to the novel when he wrote to Huxley: 'I have read *Point Counter Point* with a heart sinking through my boot-soles and a rising admiration.'

Point Counter Point is indeed a strange book to have been written by a man who at this period was presenting himself in his essays as a devotee of life worship, and Lawrence caught its essential pessimism when he continued:

> I do think that art has to reveal the palpitating moment or the state of man as it is. And I think you do that, terribly. But what a moment! and what a state! if you can only palpitate to murder, suicide and rape, in their various degrees—and you state plainly that it is so—*caro*, however are we going to live through the days?

But there seems no doubt that here art was speaking more faithfully than exposition, and that the sombre death-oriented picture presented in *Point Counter Point* in fact represented Huxley's vision more accurately than the positive life-worshipping view of life he tried to present in

Do What You Will; the Holy Face balefully haunted him. Lawrence regarded *Point Counter Point* as evidence that Huxley was on the edge of insanity; not long after completing it he did in fact enter the deep and stubborn depression that led to conversion and to that startlingly different book, *Eyeless in Gaza*.

There is little external record of the state of mind in which Huxley began and completed *Point Counter Point*. He was, by nature, reticent about such matters, and his works themselves are usually the best evidence of the mood in which he wrote them. But in his letters he does tell something about the way in which he planned and executed the novel as an actual construction. In October 1926, in the early stages of composition, he told his father:

> I am very busy preparing for and doing bits of an ambitious novel, the aim of which will be to show a piece of life, not only from a good many individual points of view, but also under its various aspects, such as scientific, emotional, economic, political, aesthetic etc. The same person is simultaneously a mass of atoms, a physiology, a mind, an object with a shape that can be painted, a cog in the economic machine, a voter, a lover etc., etc. I shall try to imply at any rate the existence of the other categories of existence behind the ordinary categories employed in judging everyday emotional life. It will be difficult, but interesting.

In part, this represents an attempt to carry further into fiction the aspects of discontinuity of personality which he had already studied in 'Two or Three Graces'; we all have many facets, and usually the consistency between them is not evident.

One way in which Huxley attempts to show the divergence between the various aspects of human life, as he explains later in one of the essays of *Music at Night*, is by juxtaposing 'two accounts of the same human event, one in terms of pure science, the other in terms of religion, aesthetics, passion, even common sense: their discord will set up the most disquieting reverberations in the mind.' In this way a curious double process is set going. We are amazed that the merely physical can have such splendid mental and spiritual emanations; we are appalled that the human will should operate by such sordid mechanisms. A typical example occurs at the beginning of *Point Counter Point*. Marjorie Carling is expecting Walter Bidlake's child:

> Six months from now her baby would be born. Something that had been a single cell, a cluster of cells, a little sac of tissue, a kind of worm, a potential fish with gills, stirred in her womb and would one

day become a man–a grown man, suffering and enjoying, loving and hating, thinking, remembering, imagining. And what had been a blob of jelly within her body would invent a god and worship; what had been a kind of fish would create and, having created, would become the battle-ground of disputing good and evil; what had blindly lived in her as a parasitic worm would look at the stars, would listen to music, would read poetry. A thing would grow into a person, a tiny lump of stuff would become a human body, a human mind. The astounding process of creation was going on within her; but Marjorie was conscious only of sickness and lassitude; the mystery for her meant nothing but fatigue and ugliness and a chronic anxiety about the future, pain of the mind as well as discomfort of the body.

There is an even more effective juxtaposition at the concert at Tantamount House when the music of Bach is doubly described, as a series of physical happenings in the ear caused by men vibrating cylinders of air in tubes and scraping lambs' intestines, and as a sublime pattern weaving truths otherwise inexplicable. The passage serves a triple purpose. It mocks both the inadequacies of scientific description and the excesses of our claims for art; it also shocks us into considering the mysterious relationships that exist between the material and the spiritual. Without Huxley's later career, such a revelation might be dismissed as cynical, intended merely to denigrate in our minds all thought of the higher aspects of existence; looking forward to *The Perennial Philosophy* we can see in it an anticipation of the attitude which would regard the phenomenal and the spiritual as both existing in their fulness, separate yet linked inextricably.

Juxtaposition of this kind is only one of the many forms of relationship which Huxley uses in a novel that sets out to present in microcosm the educated world from which–if one accepts the theories propounded in *Proper Studies*–the leaders of society must be drawn. Art delineates more sharply than political theory, and it is not a reassuring picture Huxley creates, from the viewpoint of the Platonic political theorist at least, for we observe that these people–as their sexual aberrations show –are as scarred emotionally as any class can be. The worlds of art and science and politics are represented; the ages of man from the babe within the womb to the dying septuagenarian; the social classes from the scientist of proletarian origin to the decrepit landowning marquess; and a whole range of views of existence from Illidge's Marxist materialism to Carling's sentimental Catholicism and from Rampion's Lawrencian vitalism to Spandrell's Baudelairian Satanism.

In its scope *Point Counter Point* resembles that vast social chronicle, *Les Hommes de bonne volonté*, but Jules Romains did not begin to publish his novel until four years later. If any strong influence was at work in the writing of *Point Counter Point*, apart from the abiding Peacockism of the early Huxley, it came from André Gide, whose *Les Faux-Monnayeurs* had appeared in 1926 and had been read and praised by Huxley almost immediately after publication.

There are striking differences between Gide's novel and Huxley's. Homosexuality, which dominates *Les Faux-Monnayeurs*, makes no appearance in *Point Counter Point*, and this modifies the types of characters; Huxley does not present anything resembling that intriguing but appalling gallery of *enfants terribles* who in Gide's novel are the agents for the shadowy counterfeiters. But the resemblances are equally striking, in detail as well as in general form. In each novel a young zoologist is a leading character—Vincent Molinier in *Les Faux-Monnayeurs* and Illidge in *Point Counter Point;* the triangle in which Vincent deserts Laura (who has left her husband for him) for the degenerate aristocratic Lady Griffith is similar to that in which Walter Bidlake deserts Marjorie for Lucy Tantamount; in each novel there is a novelist who is part of the action of the novel and yet at the same time is chorus-commentator. Both novels are concerned with the counterfeit currency of intellectual and artistic life which is symbolized by Gide's fake coins of gilded glass.

The deepest resemblance is to be found in the way each novel builds up a structure of linked parallels that goes far beyond the mere juxta-position of the scientific attitude with the artistic or the more broadly human view. Gide concentrates largely on discovering variations of counterfeiting, divergences between the actual and the ideal which are eventually resolved through art—in this case the mirror novel which Edouard is writing within the novel on the same subject.

In Huxley's case the parallels—and the contrasts—are of many kinds. Three people die, and all at the moment of death become insensate matter, but the ways they die differ, and this is perhaps important: one is a child dying in delirium, one is a man clubbed to death and barely aware of it, and one is a man going consciously to the death he has engineered, with the sublime tones of Beethoven's A minor Quartet ringing in his ears. Five seductions feature in the novel—Walter's original seduction of Marjorie, his provoked near-rape of Lucy, Spandrell's Satanic corruption of the wretched little Harriet, Burlap's sanctimonious corruption of Beatrice, and the ludicrous affair of old

Sidney Quarles with the typist Gladys, while John Bidlake's remembered affairs with women now turned into respectable matrons move in the background; all the relationships reflect upon each other, and are meant to be judged against the touchstone of the vital, healthy relationship of Rampion and his wife Mary.

The pattern of contrast and parallelism runs through every aspect of the novel. Spandrell's Satanism, Burlap's sentimental worship of Saint Francis and Carling's sanctimonious obsession with Catholic ritual and hagiography are seen as various perversions of a religion centred in a personal God, and are contrasted with Rampion's agnostic cult of the balanced life. Everard Webley's British variant of fascism is contrasted with Illidge's communism and Spandrell's nihilism; the violence that unites them appears when Webley is killed by the two others. Against the limitations of a scientist's outlook, which sees only facts and figures, are set the aridities of a narrowly literary outlook like that of Philip Quarles who is capable of writing and thinking but not of feeling and acting, and the selfishness of John Bidlake who is tender in painting and brutal in human relationships. Such juxtapositions proliferate through *Point Counter Point*, and, if Huxley does not reconcile them internally through a built-in device like Edouard's novel in *Les Faux-Monnayeurs*, they are nevertheless harmonized by a pattern of interlocking themes which Huxley analogically models on music. Quarles, Huxley's spokesman, develops the idea in his journal.

A theme is stated, then developed, pushed out of shape, imperceptibly deformed, until, though still recognizably the same, it has become quite different. In sets of variations the process is carried a step further. Those incredible Diabelli variations, for example. The whole range of thought and feeling, yet all in organic relation to a ridiculous little waltz tune. Get this into a novel. How? The abrupt transitions are easy enough. All you need is a sufficiency of characters and parallel, contrapuntal plots. While Jones is murdering his wife, Smith is wheeling the perambulator in the park. You alternate the themes. More interesting, the modulations and variations are also more difficult. A novelist modulates by reduplicating situations and characters. He shows several people falling in love, or dying, or praying in different ways – dissimilars solving the same problem. Or, *vice versa*, similar people confronted with dissimilar problems. In this way you can modulate through all the aspects of your theme, you can write variations in any number of different moods.

How Huxley carries out his modulations and variations in *Point*

Counter Point, we have already seen; we have observed some of the themes that unite them into definite patterns. But above themes and variations rises the general structure of the novel, which one can recognize as having its musical form, based on four movements. The first movement embraces the action of the first evening and night—the concert at Tantamount House where we are introduced to the world of *Point Counter Point* and to most of its inhabitants, and the subsequent gathering at Sbisa's restaurant where the outsiders, Spandrell and Rampion, appear to present their respective death-oriented and life-oriented philosophies. The next movement is ironic allegro, the illusion of happiness, dominated by Walter's success with Lucy and the return of Quarles and Elinor from India to a happy reunion with their child. In the third movement the music grows sombre with old Bidlake's sickness, Lucy's defection, and the threat of a break between Quarles and Elinor, who is attracted to Webley. The last movement is dominated by death.

This musical structure is deepened by the part music itself plays in the action of the novel. Bach's Suite in B minor for Flute and Strings is the occasion for the Proustian gathering at the beginning of the novel, which ends with the *Heiliger Dankgesang* from Beethoven's A minor quartet, played, as he awaits the killers who will come to avenge Webley's murder, by Spandrell to Rampion in the vain hope that it will prove the reality of the existence of God. What the two pieces are meant to demonstrate is that an ideal order does exist, at least in the mind, with which man has contact by means of art and in which the disorders of actual life are reconciled. To this extent, it is Spandrell who is right and Rampion, rejecting the evidence of the music in favour of a creed based on the mystique of life as it is, who is wrong.

Point Counter Point is the most experimental of Huxley's early novels, involving a departure from the linear pattern of its predecessors which I shall further consider in dealing with the chronological dislocations of *Eyeless in Gaza*. On the whole, the experiment is successful, for the very complexities of the maze-like plot provide a constant stimulation to the attention; one becomes quickly sensitive to the shifts of theme and mood in which the action moves forward to the dark ironies of its end.

If we wish to plunge deeper into the significance of *Point Counter Point*, it can best be done by isolating the more important characters and assessing their function in terms of thematic structure. Like all its predecessors, *Point Counter Point* is in part a *roman à clef*. Burlap, it was agreed by everyone, including the aggrieved original, was modelled on

John Middleton Murry. Rampion and Mary, the proletarian's son married to the lapsed aristocrat, took most of their features from Lawrence and Frieda. For Spandrell's characteristics, Huxley turned to both literary history and fiction; he is derived from Baudelaire with a touch of Dostoevsky's Stavrogin. John Bidlake is Augustus John spiked with Renoir. Lord Edward Tantamount resembles J. S. Haldane, the father of J. B. S. Haldane and Naomi Mitchison, in whose house Huxley had often stayed when he was a boy. And the novelist himself distributes his own personality among at least two characters. Walter Bidlake is an expression of a continuing persona, the artist as a young man, who begins with Denis Stone in *Crome Yellow* and ends with Sebastian Barnack in *Time Must Have a Stop;* Philip Quarles, his name echoing that of one of Huxley's beloved seventeenth-century melancholic poets (author of the lugubrious *A Feast of Worms*, 1620), is Huxley as what he critically feared he was at this time becoming, the literary man already crippled physically (his half blindness paralleling Philip's lameness) and well on the way to being crippled mentally by his bookish interests, which have reinforced the prison of reserve whence even the experience of India has not liberated him.

By no means all of these characters are sufficiently liberated from their originals to emerge as convincing figures of fiction. Lawrence angrily condemned Rampion as a boring 'gas-bag', and Huxley himself later admitted that 'Rampion is just some of Lawrence's notions on legs.' The trouble is not that Rampion is a bad portrait of Lawrence; it is rather that he is not a convincing character in his own right. He is too didactic, too obviously there in order to express a special point of view. Huxley had a difficult task, of course, since Rampion's vitalism strikes out against the general current of the novel, which sets darkly towards death, but he did not solve the problem by making Rampion a kind of glib Socrates who has achieved a wholeness of life, of which he boasts relentlessly to the unregenerate. He is, in a sense, the equivalent in *Point Counter Point* of Scogan and Cardan in earlier novels, but he is the first of the great Huxleian talkers to present a positive point of view, and in this way he is the predecessor of Miller, Propter and the other mystic-moralist gurus who appear in the later novels.

Even in his role as a proletarian who has climbed into the déclassé ranks of Bohemia, Rampion is not nearly so authentic as Illidge, who lives convincingly by his weaknesses and inconsistencies, by the social bitterness that an appeal to snobbery can so easily dissolve, by the theoretical violence which gives way to fearful squeamishness when he is shamed by Spandrell into taking part in the murder of Webley, by the furtive loyalty which makes him send money to his mother. It is from this complex, unattractive being that we hear a criticism of the world of the rich that is far more authentic than Rampion-Lawrence's pseudo-philosophical rantings. 'Neighbourliness is the touchstone that shows up the rich,' Illidge remarks. 'The rich haven't got any neighbours.' And as he continues, a window opens into another world, as it opened when Gumbril listened to the ex-carter talking at Hyde Park Corner; it is almost as if the eye of an Orwell seeking to become one with the workers had suddenly opened in Huxley's vision.

> When my mother had to go out, Mrs. Cradock from next door on the right kept an eye on us children. And my mother did the same for Mrs. Cradock when it was her turn to go out. And when somebody had broken a leg, or lost his job, people helped with money and food. And how well I remember, as a little boy, being sent running round the village after the nurse, because young Mrs. Foster from next door on the left had suddenly been taken with birth pains before she expected! When you live on less than four pounds a week, you've damned well got to behave like a Christian and love your neighbour. To begin with, you can't get away from him; he's practically in your back-yard. There can be no refined and philosophical ignoring of his existence. You must either hate or love, and on the whole you'd better make a shift to love, because you may need his help in emergencies and he may need yours—so urgently, very often, that there can be no question of refusing to give it. And since you *must* give, since, if you're a human being, you can't help giving, it's better to make an effort to like the person you've anyhow got to give to.

At the end of this speech one feels an unwilling respect for Illidge, but, discontinuity of personality being what it is, the excellence of his sentiments at this moment does not prevent him from uttering immediately afterwards a vitriolic attack on Lucy Tantamount or—before the night is ended—from feeling all his servility warmed into life when she honours him with a friendly smile.

Illidge's fellow scientist, Lord Tantamount, is an example of the rich man who has found the one way out of the solitude of pointless gregariousness that is possible for a man of his class: he has accepted dedication to a cause larger than himself and—like Darwin at Down—lives engrossed in the cause of science. By nature he is a better man than Illidge, lacking his viciousness, sharing his generosity, but his attentions are devoted to the life of experimental biology by which he hopes to reconcile his passions for music and science by proving, quantitatively and mathematically, the truth of Claude Bernard's concept of a 'universal concert of things' in which the life of every animal is related to 'the total life of the universe'. Such a proposition can never be proved quantitatively, any more than Tantamount's elder brother, the Marquess of Gattenden, can find a mathematical proof of the existence of God, and Tantamount thus emerges as a classical example of Huxley's thesis of the limitations of the scientific approach. It is significant that he balances his daughter Lucy's rather cold promiscuity with an almost childlike sexual indifference, and that, like Shearwater in *Antic Hay*, he is a noted cuckold. Even Tantamount's experiments, as he tries to induce the tail-buds of newts to grow into legs, seem singularly academic. Ironically, his really sound ideas on the waste of invaluable materials through our ways of disposing of sewage and corpses have become the Peacockian crotchets that arouse either laughter or exasperation in those he encounters on his rare expeditions outside the laboratory.

Both Illidge and Lord Tantamount, with the mental habits and the limitations of the science they serve, project expanding echoes into the Utopian setting of *Brave New World*. Walter Bidlake, on the other hand, looks backward rather than forward, for his adventures in *Point Counter Point* remind one of Gumbril's frustrated quest in *Antic Hay*. He encounters his Emily in Marjorie Carling, and goes through that idyll of the country cottage which Gumbril never attained, only to encounter disillusionment when innocence reveals itself as priggishness, and to fall at this point under the spell of Myra Viveash's Circean counterpart, Lucy Tantamount.

The character in *Point Counter Point* who is really important in terms of his creator's development during the crucial period between this novel and *Eyeless in Gaza* is Philip Quarles. Quarles has done the trip to the East and has been shaken by it; Quarles has begun to feel imprisoned in the limitations which his literary life has imposed upon him; Quarles, shaken by Rampion's example, begins to wonder whether the vocation of seeking truth is in itself enough. As this character, revealed to us with a strange reticence and clumsiness, records in his diary the nature of his dilemma there is one passage we can almost take as a statement of the problem which at this time more strongly than ever Huxley himself was feeling the need to face and solve.

Till quite recently, I must confess, I took learning and philosophy and science—all the activities that are magniloquently lumped under

the title of 'The Search for Truth'–very seriously. I regarded the
Search for Truth as the highest of human tasks and the Searchers as
the noblest of men. But in the last year or so I have begun to see that
this famous Search for Truth is just an amusement, a distraction like
any other, a rather refined and elaborate substitute for genuine
living, and that Truth-Searchers become just as silly, infantile, and
corrupt in their way as the boozers, the pure aesthetes, the business
men, the Good-Timers in theirs. I also perceived that the pursuit of
Truth is just a polite name for the intellectual's favourite pastime of
substituting simple and therefore false abstractions for the living
complexities of reality. But seeking Truth is much easier than learning
the art of integral living. . . . Shall I ever have the strength of mind to
break myself of these indolent habits of intellectualism and devote my
energies to the more serious and difficult task of living integrally? . . .

Though, unlike Quarles, Huxley went beyond the Lawrencian vitalism
which Rampion preached, from this point it was the task of living
integrally that he was to follow, and in this sense the meditations of
Quarles can be taken as a clue to the movements in his creator's thought.

Yet it is not Quarles, any more than Rampion, whose character
remains most strongly in the memory after reading *Point Counter Point*.
By far the most memorable character is Spandrell, an inverted transcendentalist who has sought to supplant orthodox good by orthodox evil,
but, as Rampion detects, has never quite destroyed the child within
himself in the games of corruption which he follows with a sickening
realization that whatever thrill they bring is mean and impermanent.
Spandrell is the saint inverted; it is not surprising that his last moments
are obsessed by the desire to convince himself, by convincing Rampion,
that God exists. But he is so skilfully portrayed that his poses of evil are
shot through with glimpses of an essential decency; when he decides to
kill, it is a potential monster of violence, the quasi-fascist Webley, that
he chooses as his victim, afterwards atoning for his act by a virtual self-
execution, when he dies at the hands of Webley's followers whom he
has provoked into shooting him. Petty and tawdry as so much of
Spandrell's life turns out to be, there is still a latent nobility about the
man, and a ruined charm that lingers in the mind. And understandably.
For Spandrell, like Baudelaire and Swift, represented that other side of
Huxley from which he could never rid himself, the self that knew darkness and despaired of man. More than any other character, Spandrell
projects the true spirit of *Point Counter Point*, its pessimism that cannot
abandon hope, its brutality that yearns for tenderness, its sense of
despairing finality.

PART III

CHAPTER SEVEN

Destructive Encounters

I

Transitions, in history or in human lives, are rarely abrupt or clearly defined, and it is not the dark and dramatic satire of *Point Counter Point* that marks Huxley's abandonment of his preoccupations with the hinterland of Bohemia and the Monde in the immediate post-war years so much as his last volume of stories, *Brief Candles*, which appeared in the spring of 1930.

Brief Candles consists of three shorter stories and a novella, 'After the Fireworks'. The most persistent theme is the destructive encounter between the generations. The presence of that conflict is itself nothing new in Huxley's work. The theme is strong in earlier stories, especially 'Happily Ever After'. It is muted in *Crome Yellow*, *Antic Hay* and *Those Barren Leaves*. Henry Wimbush and Gumbril Senior may be dottily eccentric, but they are genially portrayed; Scogan and Cardan may at times seem tedious elderly bores, but usually they have some philosophic point to make that interests the reader and presumably the younger characters, who in general listen to them with respect. It is in the portrayal of women past their prime, like Priscilla Wimbush and Mrs. Aldwinkle, that malice becomes evident in these earlier novels, and it can be interpreted more plausibly as an example of Huxley's chronic misogyny than of hostility towards an elder generation. Generally speaking, in the first three novels, it is mainly among his own contemporaries, the men and women spoilt by direct or indirect participation in the war and growing up in its shadow, that Huxley is inclined to find his more unpleasant characters. In *Point Counter Point* the criticism of the older generation has sharpened. In developing the character of John Bidlake, Huxley makes rather brutally the point that a selfishness acceptable in a young man of charm and talent is no longer so in an ageing artist whose best work lies in the past. And in the elder

Quarles, viewed with contempt by his own son, we have the young ne'er-do-well grown old, and trapped in a sordid generation-cum-caste situation by his abduction of a young typist.

When, after *Point Counter Point*, the theme of the generations is persistently repeated in *Brief Candles*, it seems clear that Huxley's preoccupation is connected with his own growing sense of passing out of youth. He was thirty-five when he collected the stories in *Brief Candles*, and that, as Cardan told Calamy, is the first of the great climacterics. He was conscious of advancing middle age, conscious also that this advance was accompanied by fundamental changes in the self who had written his first four novels. It must have been obvious to him, even as he completed it, that he could never write another dark masterpiece like *Point Counter Point*, and we may see 'After the Fireworks', the most important piece in *Brief Candles*, as Huxley's farewell to the literary life as he had experienced it up to this time, the life of the novelist as distinct from the teacher who, with *Brave New World*, finally assumes the ascendancy.

'Chawdron', the first story in *Brief Candles*, is interesting for the various anticipations of Huxley's future writing which it brings together. Chawdron himself, the ruthless financier hero, is the prototype of Joe Stoyte, the crude entrepreneur who dominates *After Many a Summer*, and 'the Fairy', his tawdry little secretary with her spiritual airs, anticipates the promiscuous but pietistic Virginia Maunciple, who is Joe Stoyte's young mistress. But while Virginia holds Joe Stoyte by her physical charms, 'the Fairy' holds Chawdron by her power of deceiving herself into fake mystical states. Huxley treads at last those marginal lands of the spiritual life inhabited by the genuine mystics of his later novels, but also by the victims of possession and false spirituality portrayed in *Grey Eminence* and *The Devils of Loudun*.

'Chawdron' is constructed in the Conradian manner, as a dialogue taking place at the time of Chawdron's death between the anonymous narrator and a failed writer named Tilney–a kind of grand might-have-been like Cardan–who has written a single masterpiece. It is the book that passes as Chawdron's autobiography; the canny old financier succeeded in suppressing the evidence of its real authorship so effectively that Tilney has in fact no monument to his own talents. In any case, he wrote it mainly for money, to support his love affair with Sybil, a 'pale-eyed, pale-haired ghost' of Huxley's Circean type. The shadowy Sybil ends a drug-addict, and in her degeneration anticipates Mary Amberley, the mistress of Anthony Beavis in *Eyeless in Gaza*. More than that, Sybil's addiction marks the beginning of a growing interest in drugs, and their effects on the human personality and human perceptions, that remains with Huxley from this point to his death, eventually changing in its direction, like his interests in mysticism and in Utopias, from negative to positive.[1]

If 'Chawdron' looks forward to Huxley's later works, 'The Rest Cure' returns to one of the strands of *Antic Hay*, for Moira Tarwin adventuring in Italy is an elaboration of Rosie Shearwater adventuring in London; both are wives of scientists, and both find disillusionment in what they imagine is romance. While Rosie's experiences tend to the farcical, Moira's have a hysterical intensity that is bound to end in tragedy. She exemplifies the fact–which Huxley observed mingling with the English residents in Italy–that: 'One of the pleasures or dangers of foreign travel is that you lose your class-consciousness.'

With Moira it is more than a loss of class-consciousness; she lacks the experience that enables her to judge character with ease, and she is so ready for a change from the detested John Tarwin that she falls easily for the cheap charms of the small-hotel-keeper's son, Tonino. As Moira becomes impassioned, Tonino's interest cools. There is a final scene in which, after he has gone, Moira misses her handbag and thinks he has stolen it. Believing that he has made love to her merely for her money, she shoots herself. Then comes a last sardonic twist in the manner of Maupassant. As the servants arrange the bed to lay her out, the bag falls to ground; it had lodged between the bed and the wall.

This bitter exemplary tale is the best of the shorter stories in *Brief Candles*. 'The Claxtons', which follows it, is an excessive attack on the sandal-wearing vegetarian cultists who were regarded as fair game by English satirists in the 1930s; it is also a depressing study of the way a human will can be destroyed. The plot centres on the struggle of wills between Martha Claxton and her sullen, wilful and unattractive

---

[1] Shortly after publishing 'Chawdron', Huxley was to write a play, *The World of Light* (published in 1931 and produced in 1933), which concerns another aspect of possession, the phenomenon commonly described as spiritualism. Like Henry James, William Godwin, Charles Lamb and other writers who should have known better, Huxley had a persistent illusion that he was a good playwright, but *The World of Light*, like his other works for the theatre, is a very mediocre piece of writing, and is of lingering interest only because, while the pretensions of the medium in the play to communicate with the dead are proved to be false, it is later shown that he did make true revelations through his powers of telepathy. In later years the interest in parapsychology was to become an important part of Huxley's general philosophic approach.

daughter Sylvia. Sylvia is finally made tractable by the kindness of her aunt Judith, who reveals to her a life that seems rich in experience after the austerities of home, and when she returns to the country cottage where the Claxtons pursue their lives as minor artists, she is vulnerable, her rebellion breaks down, and she becomes the dull tool of her mother's will. The real interest of 'The Claxtons' lies in its revelation of the shedding of Lawrence's influence. For Herbert and Martha Claxton are the other side of the Rampions–a rich girl marrying a poor man, setting out to live the balanced life of creativity and spiritual fulfilment, and in this case ending in hypocrisy and moral tyranny. This is only one of the ironic allusions to Lawrence in *Brief Candles;* Moira's surrender to the lower-class Tonino reminds one of *Lady Chatterley's Lover*, while in 'After the Fireworks' one of the characters claims attention, like Lady Chatterley herself, for an affair with a gamekeeper.

'After the Fireworks' exists on quite a different level of complexity from the shorter stories. Like 'Uncle Spencer' and 'Two or Three Graces', it is a novella that deserves the greater attention it would have gained from separate publication, and, like them, it differs from Huxley's larger novels (with the exception of *Eyeless in Gaza*) in presenting an intensive psychological study of one human being in a special predicament.

The hint from which 'After the Fireworks' developed came from Huxley's reading of Chateaubriand's letters.

When he was sixty [Huxley told a correspondent] a very young girl at a watering place came and threw herself at his head. He wrote her a most exquisite letter, which is extant. And there the matter ended, even though she did invade his house one evening. With my usual sadism, I thought it would be amusing to give it the cruel ending. And as one couldn't use Chateaubriand himself–that monstrous pride and loneliness and, underneath the burning imagination, that emotional aridity would have been impracticable to handle–I made the hero one of those people (they have always fascinated me and provoked a certain envy) who know how to shirk natural consequences and get something for nothing, give Nemesis the slip.

There is more in the story than this summary suggests, and the final impression it leaves is not that the hero has given 'Nemesis the slip'; to the contrary, in fact. Miles Fanning is a successful novelist who has specialized in romantic stories of liberated young women. An elegantly ageing man, he contrives to give an impression of unworn vitality that conceals his real condition. It is his curious fate to be entrapped in one of the situations he loves to invent in fiction.

Pamela Tarn–her very name that of a heroine in cheaply romantic fiction–writes to Fanning, and then waylays him in Rome. She is twenty-one, and juvenile for her age; Miles is charmed with her prettiness and her evident adoration. He starts out with a kind of avuncular patronage, but both he and Pamela are the victims of their delusions; she is deceived by the air of the romantic man of letters which he projects, and he by the manner of a character out of one of his novels which she has assumed.

It soon becomes evident that Pamela intends to follow the routine of a Fanning novel and be seduced by the writer-hero. Realizing this, Fanning debates flight, but Pamela frustrates his plans of secret departure. She becomes his mistress, and the experience on both sides is a shedding of illusion, a learning, through sheer physical experience, what a love affair between a vain, ageing man and a sentimental, immature girl actually means.

Pamela's first lesson comes when she realizes that life with a romantic writer is not romantic; he is so absorbed with fictional people while he is at work that the real ones have little meaning for him. Here, seen by the victim, is the problem of the atrophy of human feelings that Philip Quarles in *Point Counter Point* viewed as a writer.

But it is–typically–in sickness with its grotesque reminders of physical decay, that Huxley teaches his characters the ultimate lesson of the folly of romantic expectations. In the spring of 1929 Huxley had suffered from an acute liver ailment and had visited the great spa at Montecatini with its '750 hotels and pensions'. He was fascinated by the macabre comedy of the scene, the parade of 'the obese, the bilious, the gluttons', including 'a high percentage of priests, who flock thither in black swarms to drink off the effects of the proverbial clerical overeating'. The final scenes of 'After the Fireworks' take place in this grim but ludicrous setting, for Fanning is jaundiced because of a chill on the liver brought on by sexual excesses with Pamela which his ageing body has not been able to sustain. As the story ends, Pamela is about to leave him for a younger man. Romance in real life is an illusion.

'After the Fireworks' marks Huxley's rejection of the role of the novelist as artist, his farewell to the dilettantish pursuit of pure art and pure knowledge. For Fanning, though he is not recognizably a self-portrait, represents Huxley's inclination to become immersed in aesthetic and scholarly interests. When he remarks: 'That's the definition of culture–knowing and thinking about things that have absolutely nothing to do with us,' he is expressing an attitude Huxley now wishes to repudiate. Yet, while it is a final rejecting look at the past, 'After the Fireworks' is also, in a curiously inverted way, prophetic of the future. For Fanning's *past* in some ways anticipates Huxley's *future;* he has played with drugs, though less fatally than Sybil in 'Chawdron'; he has been 'quite perversely preoccupied with mystical experiences and ecstasies and private universes'. And, of more immediate interest at this stage in Huxley's development, it is Fanning who sees that link between Plato and 'Henry Ford and the machines', which will be developed in *Brave New World*.

2

Other events, as well as the publication of *Brief Candles*, mark the years of 1930 and 1931 as a climacteric period in Huxley's life. The spring of 1930 was clouded by the death of Lawrence. For at least two years Huxley had been painfully aware of the deterioration in his friend's health, though he had been amazed at the brightness with which the spirit's flame burnt in that body wasted by sickness. In January 1930, when he was living at Suresnes, Huxley learnt that Lawrence had entered a sanatorium at Vence, and towards the end of February he and Maria set off to visit him. They arrived to find him struggling with death. Huxley was present when Lawrence slipped into the last morphine sleep from which he never awoke.

> He gave one [Huxley told Eugene Saxton] the impression that he was living by sheer force of will and by nothing else. But the dissolution of the body was breaking down the will. . . . He was really, I think, the most extraordinary and impressive human being I have ever known.

Immediately, at Frieda Lawrence's invitation, Huxley began to collect Lawrence's letters and prepare them for publication. During 1930 and 1931 this was one of the tasks that most occupied his mind, and the very process of encountering in the letters aspects of his friend of which he was unaware led him to revise his views both of Lawrence and of the vitalism and primitivism which were essential to his beliefs. That process reached its conclusion during Huxley's visit to Mexico in 1933.

Meanwhile, in Europe, Huxley and Maria had drawn their Twenties

to a geographical as well as a temporal end by abandoning the hinterland of the Italian Riviera, where his first four novels had all been
written, and moving to France: at Sanary, near Bandol on the Côte
d'Azur, they found a villa which reminded Huxley of the house of
Bouvard et Pécuchet; 'a museum piece' as he told Robert Nichols, '–it
seems almost a crime to alter and refurnish it.' Until their abandonment
of Europe for the United States in 1937, the house at Sanary became
their headquarters.

Here Huxley marked another break with the past by collecting his
last volume of verse, *The Cicadas,* whose publication in 1931 was the
virtual end of his career as a poet. His production of verse had been
diminishing for a number of years, and the majority of the poems that
make up *The Cicadas* had already appeared two years before in a smaller
collection entitled *Arabia Infelix;* even the title poem, 'The Cicadas',
belonged to that collection.

The earliest of these poems, 'Theatre of Varieties', dates from 1920,
and the group of poems about the Roman emperors Nero and Caligula,
which first appeared in *Those Barren Leaves* as the work of Francis
Chelifer, must have been written before the completion of that novel
in 1924. Of the two most important poems, 'Arabia Infelix' was
published initially in 1926, and 'The Cicadas' in 1928. Most of the other
poems were first published either in *Arabia Infelix* or in *The Cicadas,* but
it is hard to date their composition; up to 1920 Huxley discussed his
poems freely in his letters, but after that time he rarely even referred to
them, a sign that his interest in poetry as an art was declining even
when his poetic craftsmanship was becoming most accomplished.

Accomplishment, indeed, is the neutral quality that most distinguishes
Huxley's later poems; they are smoother, more precise and economical
than his earlier work, and, like everything he wrote, they make interesting statements. But they show the failure of development that occurs
when a writer remains merely a craftsman, as Huxley did in poetry.
There is no experimenting in form; the sonnet, the quatrain, the
couplet, all in regular iambics, are Huxley's usual moulds. There is none
of the complex use of allusiveness and parody which Eliot and Pound
developed so effectively. And though, in imagery and at times in tone,
Huxley is clearly influenced by the symbolists, he is not–as they were–
seeking to establish his meaning by suggestion and indirection. He is,
as much as Dryden, a poet of logical statement.

Much has been made of Huxley's French models, and there is no
doubt that superficial characteristics were derived from the symbolists,

from Laforgue, from Rimbaud, and from Baudelaire, a translation of whose poem on Lesbians, 'Femmes Damnées', appeared in *Arabia Infelix*. But the poems themselves as they emerge after the absorption of these influences are curiously English and even Victorian in their overt concern with the moral life of the author. In the group of sonnets about storms and tides that appears in *The Cicadas* one is left in no doubt that Huxley was Matthew Arnold's grand-nephew. For in few writers of the 1920s can one find such faithful echoes of Arnold as the final lines from the sonnet 'Mediterranean', which begins by evoking the gemlike sapphire that brims the tideless Tyrrhenian, and continues:

> *The ebb is mine. Life to its lowest neap*
> *Withdrawn reveals that black and hideous shoal*
> *Where I lie stranded. Oh deliver me*
> *From this defiling death! Moon of the soul,*
> *Call back the tide that ran so strong and deep,*
> *Call back the shining jewel of the sea.*

In a companion sonnet, 'Tide', Huxley envisages the tide for ever out, the sea retired past recall, and admonishes himself to a stoic resistance to despair.

> *There is a firm consenting to disaster,*
> *Proud resignation to accepted pain.*
> *Pain quickens him who makes himself its master,*
> *And quickening battle crowns both loss and gain.*
> *But to this silting of the soul, who gives*
> *Consent is no more man, no longer lives.*

This is not great or highly original poetry, but it is honest. Huxley is too conscientious to affect modernism for its own sake, to experiment without the creative passion that would give it meaning. He finds conventional verse, at this stage, a concise and effective way of expressing, through a mixture of metaphor and argument, his own mental condition. In the poems contained in *Cicadas* the storms that already ruffled the inner sea of his mind on the eve of his conversion are recorded, and there is an intense personal relevance to almost every poem, sometimes lightly disguised ('Arabia Infelix') and sometimes very directly stated ('The Cicadas').

'Arabia Infelix', probably inspired by watching the bare hot sands of the Yemeni desert from the boat to India in 1926, is a lyrical evocation of that arid land.

Parched, parched are the hills, and dumb
That thundering voice of the ravine;
Round the dead springs the birds are seen
No more, no more at evening come.

When the rain does come fleetingly to the dry hills of Arabia, the land
awakens only briefly and in agony, for the cloud

Came laden with a gift of dew,
But with it dropped the lightning's flame;

A flame that rent the crags apart,
But rending made a road between
For water to the mountain's heart,
That left a scar, but left it green.

Faithless the cloud and fugitive;
An empty heaven nor burns, nor wets;
At peace, the barren land regrets
Those agonies that made it live.

It is a striking image, and its ultimate meaning lies in the creator's heart,
but we are left in doubt whether the cloud means love or creativity or
mystical insight. This perfectly achieved ambiguity makes 'Arabia
Infelix' one of Huxley's most successful poems.

'The Cicadas', because it is more explicit, is at once a lesser poem and
a more interesting personal document. For here the dilemma of death-
orientation and life-orientation which was plaguing Huxley by 1928 is
clearly stated and linked with his characteristic preoccupations regarding
darkness and sight. The tone, Arnoldian to begin with, shifts by the end
into a Wordsworthian key.

Huxley envisages himself standing in the Italian night. The first words
of the poem echo back through his manhood into the blindness of
adolescence.

Sightless, I breathe and touch; this night of pines
Is needly, resinous and rough with bark.
Through every crevice in the tangible dark
The moonlessness above it all but shines.

Everything is still, but the stillness is that of continuous sound – the harsh
and endless ringing of the cicadas.

> *I hear them sing, who in the double night*
> *Of clouds and branches fancied that I went*
> *Through my own spirit's dark discouragement,*
> *Deprived of inward as of outward sight:*
>
> *Who, seeking, even as here in the wild wood,*
> *A lamp to beckon through my tangled fate,*
> *Found only darkness and, disconsolate,*
> *Mourned the lost purpose and the vanished good.*
>
> *Now in my empty heart the crickets' shout*
> *Re-echoing denies and still denies*
> *With stubborn folly all my learned doubt,*
> *In madness more than I in reason wise.*

The madness of life that inspires the cicadas reawakens the poet's imagination, and, though he realizes that man's fate is still a moonless and 'labyrinthine night', from the knowledge of life's wonder he has learnt the value of desire that makes all experience new.

> *Clueless we go; but I have heard thy voice,*
> *Divine Unreason! harping in the leaves,*
> *And grieve no more; for wisdom never grieves,*
> *And thou hast taught me wisdom; I rejoice.*

The idea of sound as regenerative harks back to the time of Huxley's blindness, when music and the human voice took on special importance because they compensated for the loss of sight; sound in the darkness—like the 'music at night' which provides the title for Huxley's next book of essays—becomes a metaphor for enlightenment, though the enlightenment of 'The Cicadas' is not that which Huxley ultimately sought.

A complete study of Huxley's poems in relation to the development of his philosophic attitudes has never been made, and there is no room here to do more than hint at the importance of the elements of spiritual autobiography hidden under the bland and polished surface of these verses. The later poems—those written between 1929 and the publication of *The Cicadas* in 1931—are especially suggestive of the onset of deep and painful spiritual searching. Even more significant than the two Arnoldian sonnets in which the image of the ebbing tide is used to project an almost existentialist attitude of courageous hopelessness is 'The Moor', in which Iago, elevated as a model of orthodox Christian

virtues, is shown being received into heaven. A more interesting fate—
anticipating that of the later, mystical Huxley—awaits Othello.

> *Turning back meanwhile*
> *From outer darkness, Othello and his bride*
> *Perceive the globe of heaven like one small lamp*
> *Burning alone at midnight in the abyss*
> *Of some cathedral cavern; pause, and then*
> *With face once more averted, hand in hand,*
> *Explore the unseen treasures of the dark.*

3

If any vision runs more persistently than others through Huxley's works,
from *Crome Yellow* in 1921 down to *Island* in 1962, it is that of Utopia,
the world where a kind of perfection has been attained, change has
come to a stop in a temporal parody of eternity. As a young man he
saw Utopia as Hell on earth; as an old man he saw it as the earthly
paradise. The difference between the two sides of the vision derives
from a change in Huxley's views of human potentialities. For the
greater part of his life he believed that only a tiny minority was capable
of the highest thought or—in later years—of spiritual enlightenment, yet,
apart from the brief period when he wrote *Proper Studies*, he distrusted
the idea of a world which the élite planned for mankind as a whole. In
his final years he believed that he had discovered the way, through
mystical discipline and the intelligent use of drugs, to give every man
an equal chance of an enlightened existence, and so a Utopia based on
a balance of the physical and spiritual, the temporal and eternal,
seemed possible to him; such was the vision he gave concrete form in
Island.

Huxley's preoccupations with Utopias belong to a wider movement,
for many writers in the earlier twentieth century were turning away
from the facilely benign Utopias of the Renaissance and the nineteenth
century. Some followed the example of Samuel Butler in *Erewhon* by
creating negative Utopias, pictures of a future which, by reason of some
flaw in human capabilities, has turned out to be the opposite of the
ideal worlds that early socialists and early writers of science romance
conceived. Even the most distinguished of the science romancers, H. G.
Wells, balanced his positive Utopia *Men Like Gods* with the terrifyingly
negative vision of *When the Sleeper Wakes*. Years before Huxley wrote
Brave New World, E. M. Forster ('The Machine Stops') and Karel

Čapek (*R.U.R.*) already portrayed in varying ways the withering of man's spiritual life and even of his physical capacities when he becomes too reliant on a machine-oriented world, and in 1924 there had appeared the first of the three great anti-Utopias of the twentieth century, Evgeny Zamiatin's *We*.

While *We* had a profound influence on the third of the key anti-Utopian novels, *1984*, its influence on *Brave New World* is obviously—if it exists—less profound and direct, despite the many striking resemblances between the two novels.

Both Huxley and Zamiatin see Utopia as a possible, even a probable outcome of twentieth-century technological developments, especially of the refinement of techniques in psychological suggestion. Both assume that in the process of creating Utopia man's outlook on life will be radically altered, since the stability necessary to maintain society unchanged will mean the elimination of the idea of freedom and the knowledge of the past, and the reduction of culture to a pattern of mechanical enjoyments. Both envisage the economic structure of Utopia as collectivist, and see its political structure as hierarchical, a pyramid topped by a tiny group of guardians who rule through effective police systems and conditioning techniques. They foresee the destruction of the very ideas of individuality and privacy, of passionate personal relationships, of any association outside the state. Both make happiness the goal of their Utopias, and equate it with non-freedom. Both use a passionless sexual promiscuity, based on the theory that each belongs to all, to break down any true intimacy between persons. The individual becomes an atom in the body of the state and nothing more. Even the rebellions in the two novels are alike, for in each case the hero —D.503 in *We* and Bernard Marx in *Brave New World*—is physically and mentally an atavistic throwback, and both heroes are tempted to rebellion by contact with men who have escaped the conditioning hand of the state: the hairy people who live outside the protective green wall of the Utopian city in *We*, the primitives of the New Mexican reservation in *Brave New World*. Needless to say, both rebellions fail; the unitary world utopian state continues on its course.

Striking as the resemblances may be, it is hard to prove that Huxley was influenced by Zamiatin at the time he wrote *Brave New World*. Unlike Orwell, he never admitted such an influence. And though, given Huxley's omnivorous reading habits, it seems unlikely that he failed to read *We* during the seven years between its publication and that of *Brave New World*, this appears to have affected only secondary details of his book. The essential outline of *Brave New World* was sketched already in *Crome Yellow*, and while it is true that *We* was written in 1920, and was secretly circulated as a forbidden text in Soviet Russia, it is improbable that Huxley saw a copy of it or even learnt of its existence before he conceived the character of Mr. Scogan and filled his mind with Utopian ideas.

The concept of Utopia, implicitly rejected in *Crome Yellow*, haunted Huxley as he watched the advance of the applied sciences and particularly of physiology and psychology. Utopia, he realized, was not entirely an impossible abstraction. Perhaps it cannot be made with men as they are. But science can change – if not men themselves – at least their attitudes and reactions, and then Utopia becomes feasible as a society in which men cease to be individuals and become merely the components of a social collectivity.

Utopia, of course, is a matter of imposing a pattern, of subordinating human life to a discipline of abstraction analogous to geometry. 'A mind impregnated with music', said Huxley in *Beyond the Mexique Bay*, 'will always tend to impose a pattern on the temporal flux.' But it seemed evident to him that any human attempt to impose an ideal order on Nature or on men would be perverted by man's limitations. So, for all his love of order in geometry and architecture and music, he distrusted it in political or social planning.

Brave New World marks a fundamental change in Huxley's use of the novel; it is no longer fiction intended to describe and satirize. The satirical element remains, but the primary function is now to exhort. Like Orwell's *1984*, *Brave New World* was deliberately devised as a cautionary tale. The earlier novels may have been didactic in part, as *Point Counter Point* clearly was whenever Rampion held the field; *Brave New World* is the first that will be didactic in total intent. This function of the novel, quite apart from any entertainment value it may have as a piece of futurist fantasy, is clearly stated in the description which Huxley gave his father in August 1931: he saw it as

a comic, or at least satirical, novel about the Future, showing the appallingness (at any rate by our standards) of Utopia and adumbrating the effects on thought and feeling of such quite possible biological inventions as the production of children in bottles (with consequent abolition of the family and all the Freudian 'complexes' for which family relationships are responsible), the prolongation of youth, the devising of some harmless but effective substitute for alcohol, cocaine, opium etc: – and also the effects of such sociological reforms on Pavlovian conditions of all children from birth and before birth, universal peace, security and stability.

The shift to the openly didactic novel had been presaged by the shift in direction of Huxley's essays. The experience of India and the influence of Lawrence had between them awakened a dormant sense of social responsibility, and from now to the end of his life Huxley was to remain concerned with the fundamental social issues of peace and freedom and the preservation of the environment; even after his conversion to mystical religion he did not retreat out of social responsibility, as many self-styled mystics have done, but remained—even if he did not long continue a political activist—intensely concerned with the plight of man in his temporal existence.

Music at Night, the volume of essays which in 1931 followed the vitalist manifesto of *Do What You Will*, can be read with particular profit as a kind of notebook for *Brave New World*. It discusses a whole series of possibilities which Huxley sees as latent in the European-American world of the late 1920s, and which will form part of the fabric of *Brave New World*: the cult of perpetual youth, the problem of leisure, the perils of Fordism to the human psyche, the possible development of eugenics as a means of shaping the man of the future, the implications of the attempt to make man primarily a consumer, and the perils to freedom of a dogmatic egalitarianism. A reading of the relevant essays shows that, though *Brave New World* is projected on to the screen of the future, it is derived almost entirely from tendencies which Huxley observed with alarm and distrust in the world around him.

Music at Night is less definite in its expression than *Brave New World*, for Huxley often presents his possibilities neutrally, with the suggestion that men in the future may use them either for good or for ill. This is the case in his discussion of the ideal drug, which in his essay, 'Wanted, a New Pleasure', he presents as a possible benefit to mankind. He suggests endowing a band of research workers to find 'the ideal intoxicant.'

> If we could sniff or swallow something that would, for five or six hours each day, abolish our solitude as individuals, atone us with our fellows in a glowing exaltation of affection and make life in all its aspects seem not only worth living, but divinely beautiful and significant, and if this heavenly, world-transfiguring drug were of such a kind that we could wake up next morning with a clear head and an undamaged constitution—then, it seems to me, all our

problems (and not merely the one small problem of discovering a novel pleasure) would be wholly solved and earth become paradise.

This ideal drug will be used both negatively and positively in Huxley's novels; in *Brave New World* it provides a conditioning technique and its effect is therefore negative and life-constricting, but in *Island* (written in 1962 after Huxley had experimented with LSD) it is used in a positive Utopia as part of a technique of mental liberation.

Music at Night includes several essays which develop a theory of literature that reflects Huxley's changing practice. In 'Tragedy and the Whole Truth' he draws the opposition between two types of literature: that which, like Shakespearian tragedy, acts quickly and intensely on our feelings by isolating the dramatic elements in life, and the Wholly Truthful literature, represented by writers like Proust and Dostoevsky and Lawrence, which is 'chemically impure' and mild in its catharsis because it is based on 'the pattern of acceptance and resignation', on taking life as it is. Huxley grants that we need both kinds of literature, but it is clear that he is most attracted to Whole Truthism. In 'Art and the Obvious' he points out how high art has retreated completely from certain areas of life because popular art has vulgarized them. But these aspects of life do exist.

> And since they exist, they should be faced, fought with, and reduced to artistic order. By pretending that certain things are not there, which in fact *are* there, much of the most accomplished modern art is condemning itself to incompleteness, to sterility, to premature decrepitude and death.

Vulgarity in literature lies not in the content, as Huxley points out in the essay which ends *Music at Night*, but in a pretentiousness unrelated to real life. He illustrates this with a brilliant comparison between Dostoevsky and Dickens, between the death of the child Ilusha in *The Brothers Karamazov* and the death of Little Nell. Why is the first moving and the second not? It is, Huxley suggests, because Dickens isolates in a cloud of emotion the suffering and the innocence of Nell, while Dostoevsky evokes vividly the factual details of everything that happens around Ilusha's deathbed, and so relates it constantly to 'the actual realities of human life'.

These discussions of literary form are as closely related to *Brave New World* as are the speculations regarding scientific and social developments, for they draw one's attention to one of the principal reasons why this is still the most widely read of Huxley's books. It is a fantasy of the future and a satire on the present. And in both roles it carries conviction because of the expert and convincing handling of detail to create a plausible world. It is England six hundred years ahead, and Huxley has been wise enough not to change it beyond recognition. It is the country we know and a different world, and this paradox sustains our attention.

As we have seen, *Brave New World* projects happiness as the principal goal of Utopia and equates it with non-freedom. The society of the future is a parody of Plato's republic, with a small group of World Controllers ruling five castes of subjects, divided not merely socially but biologically, since they have been conditioned to their future tasks in the bottles where they were bred. To preserve happiness, the World Controllers throw away everything that might provoke either thought or passion.

> The world's stable now [says Mustapha Mond, Controller for England]. People are happy; they get what they want, and they never want what they can't get. They're well off; they're safe; they're never ill; they're not afraid of death; they're blissfully ignorant of passion and old age; they're plagued with no mothers or fathers; they've got no wives, or children, or lovers to feel strongly about; they're so conditioned that they practically can't help behaving as they ought to behave.

The most striking difference between *Brave New World* and *1984*, with which it has so often been compared, is the absence of violence and overt repression.

> In the end [says Mond] the Controllers realized that force was no good. The slower but infinitely surer methods of ectogenesis, neo-Pavlovian conditions, and hypnopaedia. . . .'

Men are so conditioned from the time the spermatozoon enters the egg in the Hatchery that there is little likelihood of their breaking into rebellion; if they do become discontented there are always drugs to waft them into the heavens of restorative illusion. Thus the Controllers are able to govern with a softly firm hand; the police use whiffs of anaesthetic instead of truncheons, and those over-brilliant individuals who do not fit the established pattern are allowed to indulge their heretical notions in the intellectual quarantine of exile.

The daily lives of the conditioned inhabitants of the brave new world are passed in a carefully regulated pattern of production and consumption. Since it was found that too much leisure created restlessness, scientists are discouraged from devising labour-saving inventions, and the working day is followed by gregarious pleasures so organized that elaborate machinery is required and maximum consumption is encouraged. Complete freedom of sexual behaviour, plus the availability of soma, provide releases from all ordinary frustrations. The abolition of viviparous birth has made families and all other permanent attachments unnecessary; individuals have become merely cells, each occupying his special position in the carefully differentiated fabric of society.

All this would not make a novel of its own; Utopian fiction that merely describes a futuristic society is notoriously tedious. Huxley brings his to life by showing the perils of any attempt at a perfect society. The higher castes of the community, the Alphas and the Betas, cannot be as closely conditioned as the worker castes, because their tasks involve intelligence and the occasional need to use judgement; and even the best conditioning is not foolproof. So we get sports like the stunted Bernard Marx who has a heretical longing for solitude, like the pneumatic Lenina Crowne who is inclined to remain a little too constant in her attachments, like Helmholtz Watson who secretly writes forbidden poems about the self instead of slogans for the state.

Bernard is already suspected of disaffection and threatened with exile to Iceland, but the crisis in the life of all these three misfits in Utopia is provoked–like crises in Huxley's own life–by a journey into unfamiliarity. Bernard takes Lenina on a trip to the reservation for primitive people in New Mexico. For Lenina the first sight of dirt and disease is traumatic, but Bernard is rewarded by the discovery of a woman from Utopia who was lost years ago and has since lived and brought up her child among the Indians. The young man–John–is not only a savage; he has also, accidentally, acquired a copy of Shakespeare which, with the mixed heathen and Christian cults of the Indians, has enriched his language and shaped his outlook. In our sense he is far more 'cultured', if not more 'civilized', than the utopians.

Bernard brings the savage back to London, where he creates a sensation by his baroque behaviour and Elizabethan speech. On Bernard and Helmholtz he has the effect of crystallizing their sense of difference from the society to which they have been bred. Lenina, who is merely a Beta Plus and therefore not so inclined to intellectual rebellion, lapses into an old-fashioned infatuation for the savage, who meanwhile has conceived a romantic attachment to her. There is an extraordinarily comic scene of crossed purposes, in which the savage declares his love in resounding Shakespearian terms, whereupon Lenina, reacting in the only way she knows, unzips her garments and advances upon him in all her pneumatic nakedness, and the savage, shouting Elizabethan curses, drives her from him.

The rebellion, slight as it is, fails. The three young men, Bernard, Helmholtz and the savage, after creating a minor riot by interrupting a distribution of soma, are brought before Mustapha Mond. There is a Peacockian interlude in which each of the four characteristically reacts to the situation, and then Bernard and Helmholtz are exiled to join those who have shown themselves unreliable in the past (the real intellectual élite of the brave new world). The savage is forbidden to join them, because Mond wants to continue the experiment of subjecting him to 'civilization'. Since he cannot go anywhere else, the savage tries to establish a hermitage in the Surrey countryside of Huxley's youth, but Utopia's equivalents of newshounds discover him, and the fervent pleasure-seekers of the brave new world, hearing that he is flogging himself like a New Mexican penitent, descend on him in their helicopters. Lenina is among them. There is a great orgy in which the savage first whips and then possesses her. The next day, revolted by Utopia and his surrender to its seductions, he hangs himself.

In thematic terms, *Brave New World* opposes the scientific-industrialist ideal of Mustapha Mond (and, by derivation, of Henry Ford) to the primitivist vitalism of Lawrence, the acceptance of life with all its joys and miseries, as it exists. A decade later Huxley criticized himself for having failed to add a third possibility, that of the decentralized, libertarian society, where industry is minimized and man is liberated to pursue the life of time by the illumination of eternity. Yet it is difficult to see how the novel could have been changed to include this third possibility. The anti-individualist tendencies latent in our society have to be opposed by the poetic primitivism of the savage, who alone, since he is the only character conscious of the nature of tragedy, can embody the tragic possibilities of man's future.

One is tempted to consider *Brave New World*, because it is a Utopian fantasy, as an exceptional work that stands outside the general pattern of Aldous Huxley's fiction. In reality, its function is to close the sequence of the earlier novels. The central characters belong clearly in the Huxleian succession. Bernard is a latter-day Gumbril who has to inflate himself perpetually in order to feel equal to others, and who can only fulfil himself in exceptional circumstances. Helmholtz is a Calamy, an expert amorist who has lost his taste for sensual delights and longs for something more elevated and intelligent. The savage is a more acceptable vehicle for the Lawrencian viewpoint than the excessively didactic Rampion. And Mustapha Mond, with his orotund delivery, is a Scogan or a Cardan who has at last made good. As for the world of the novel, it is the Bohemia of *Antic Hay* and *Point Counter Point*, carried to its logical end, its pleasures sanctified and its personal irresponsibilities institutionalized so that the freedom of the libertine is revealed as the most insidious of slaveries. There can be no doubt of the continuity between *Brave New World* and the earlier novels. It is the direction of the journey that has changed.

PART IV

CHAPTER EIGHT

Gotama and the Corpse

I

In *Beyond the Mexique Bay* one image stands out with such peculiar intensity, that I have always believed the experience it describes was for Huxley the most significant of the journey which the book narrates. Huxley and Maria had left England at the end of January 1933, on the cruise ship *Britannic*, bound for the West Indies. After the days on the Atlantic in the company of elderly people as determined to behave like children as the inhabitants of *Brave New World*, Huxley was depressed by his first view of the Caribbean islands: not merely by their poverty and their air of colonial dependency, but even more by an atmosphere that revived the negative feelings of his Asian travels.

> It was six years since I had been in a hot country, and I had forgotten how unspeakably melancholy the tropics can be, how hopeless, somehow, and how completely resigned to hopelessness.

In Bridgetown, Barbados, he and Maria went out one evening to dine indigenously, and found themselves in a restaurant owned by a white man who described himself as 'The Friend of the Poor'; he was the Napoleon of the island's business world, owning stores, a bus-line, an undertaking establishment. The Friend of the Poor invited them to visit his store in Speightstown, and they drove out along the seashore, past the tiny shacks and the corrugated iron chapels echoing with hymns. It was in the shop at Speightstown that Huxley's epiphany waited.

> In a back room behind the shop, lit by a dim oil lamp, a very old negress was sitting, with her hat on, of course, cleaning flying-fish. Snick, snick – off went the long fins, the tail, the head; another snick, out came the guts and, with a little manipulation, the backbone. The fish was dropped in a basket. An incredibly beautiful, pale brown

girl was sitting beside her, sewing. The door behind them was open
on to the sea. There was nothing specially curious or remarkable
about the scene; but for some reason it held, and in my memory still
holds for me a quality of extra-ordinary alienness and unfamiliarity,
of being immeasurably remote. Nothing I ever saw and–since our
fantasies are *ours* and so are always nearer, however extravagant, than
the intuitions that reach our minds from without–nothing certainly
I ever imagined was so far away as that little room at Speightstown.
And the girl, so beautiful, with her face shining in the lamplight, as
though it were illumined from within, the old negress, under her
battered hat, busy with black hands among the silvery fish–they
were the inhabitants, it seemed, of another universe.

Beyond the Mexique Bay is a curiously mask-like book. In some ways
it is more animated than *Jesting Pilate*; it contains more sharply described
episodes, more travelling hardships, especially when Huxley journeys
on muleback over the coastal sierra of Mexico, and at least one genuine
adventure, when the travellers fly from Guatemala to the Mayan ruin
of Copán and are arrested by Honduran militia. Yet one always feels
that the writer is not revealing fully what goes on in his thoughts, that
the long passages of generalized reflections on sights and experiences
really conceal deep and inarticulate movements of the mind, which one
glimpses occasionally, as one sees a real eye through the hole in a mask.
The magical sense of the alien conveyed in the description of the old
negress and the beautiful mulatto girl is a glance of that real eye,
though what it means does not become evident, perhaps even to
Huxley, until he struggles in solitude with the inner results of his
travels.

Continuing with the *Britannic* from Barbados, the Huxleys visited
Trinidad, Venezuela and Panama, and finally, at Kingston, Jamaica,
abandoned the ship and took a Norwegian banana boat to Belize on
the mainland. From British Honduras, which provoked reflections on
the consequences of the decline of the fashion for mahogany, Huxley
proceeded to Guatemala, and there, among sympathetic baroque
architecture and disturbing scenic magnificences, the journey he had
planned, the journey into the heart of primitivism, began. The inner
journey had begun, of course, in Speightstown, as unlikely a place as
the beginnings of inner journeys usually are.

Huxley's portrayal of Guatemalan Indian villages like Chichicasten-
ango, where Christian and pagan cults continue side by side, and of the
great Mayan ruins, are capable and evocative, though he is too

objective to be a completely effective travel writer. His descriptions of the Mexican hills, for instance, are much more vivid and credible in *Eyeless in Gaza*, when he feels justified in intensifying the effects for fictional purposes, than they are in *Beyond the Mexique Bay*, where his narrative tends to be flatly factual and his reflections have to provide the baroque flourishes that bring the book to life in the mind.

At times the reflections are excessive; they disturb the book's proportions. The history of disunity and conflict between the Five Republics of Central America becomes the excuse for nearly forty pages of thoughts on the psychological and spiritual causes of war, leading up to the suggestion that peace conferences arranged on a political basis are useless, and that to cope with the fundamental issues we need a World Psychological Congress. The sight of coffee plantations sets off a train of musings on the irrationality of our economic system as evidenced in the coffee slump. Taking out his palette for an interlude of painting at Antigua, Huxley despairingly dilates on the inverse relation between dramatic landscapes and good landscape pictures. One wonders at the virtually automatic reaction, the mental tic; almost any excuse, no matter how apparently trivial, may set the fertile Huxley mind on its speculating path, relating the remote particularities of Central American villages to the general themes of human existence.

The most constant preoccupation of all is with primitivism. Even today, in an age of transistor radios and modern roads, of motor transport and networks of air services, one still encounters in the villages of Mexico and Guatemala a way of life that has not changed greatly (except perhaps to get steadily poorer) since the Spanish rule ended a hundred and fifty years ago and which still contains notable elements derived from the Aztec or the Maya past. When Huxley was there nearly forty years ago, many of the areas now easily accessible could be reached only on muleback. Riding up and down the hills, descending and ascending the steep slopes of the barrancas that sliced across the countryside, sleeping on boards in primitive houses, Huxley found whatever vestiges he may have retained of Wordsworthian nature worship slipping away from him.

Nature worship is a product of good communications. In the seventeenth century all sensible men disliked nature. . . . Untamed, nature seems not so much divine as sinister, alarming and, above all, exasperatingly obstructive.

Towards the Indians his attitude was ambivalent. He found their predicament interesting as a problem in cultural history. They were indeed primitives, ready at any chance to turn back to the worship of their sinister ancestral gods, but they had been four hundred years in contact with Europeans, and their primitivism often expressed itself in terms of western culture. Huxley found fascinating the hybridism evident in Indo-Christian religious ceremonials and ecclesiastical art. But in Guatemala, and again in Mexico which he reached by another coasting banana boat, he developed a mounting and irrational dislike of the Indians as human beings. 'Frankly, try how I may,' he noted in Guatemala, 'I cannot very much like primitive people. They make me feel uncomfortable. "La bêtise n'est pas mon fort." '

The fact was that Huxley found Indian and mestizo Guatemala and Mexico so far removed from his own idea of good living, so utterly alien and incomprehensible, that he was impelled to reject them at sight. There was an active resistance to comprehension; in no other way is it possible to explain the essential falsehood of this description of the Zapotec village of Miahuatlan, on the way to Oaxaca.

> The scene, as it reveals itself to the wandering spectator, is typical– a standard Southern Mexican back-cloth. At the centre of things lies the great desert of a glaring plaza, with tortoise-eyed Indian women sitting in the dust, each with her three pimientos, her nine bananas, her half-dozen of tomatoes, arranged in geometrical patterns on the ground before her. Above the market towers the vast church, hopelessly dilapidated and shored up against irremediable collapse by a precarious structure of poles and beams. Along streets of half-ruined houses the donkeys come and go, flapping their ears; bare feet move noiselessly through the dust, and under enormous hats, under close-drawn shawls one catches the reptilian glitter of Indian eyes. . . .
>
> Here, in Miahuatlan . . . there was and there still is just the deep-rooted weed of primitive human life. If you happen to be a primitive human being, it must be quite a pleasant place to live in. But if you happen to have come within sniffing distance of the transcendental lilies, how unspeakably depressing.

The most significant point about this passage is the repeated likening of Indian eyes to those of lower forms of life–tortoises and reptiles in general. That 'reptilian glitter' has become something of a cliché in describing Mexican Indians, but, though I have travelled among the Zapotecs in the area Huxley discusses, I have never been able to see in their eyes anything more unusual than those varying degrees of warmth and hardness one encounters in any other dark-eyed people.

But such descriptions are useful to observers who find the Indian way of life so alien that they do not wish to enquire deeply into it. I do not criticize Huxley's desire to retain the lilies of western culture, and I agree when he says, later on, 'The attempt to return to primitiveness is both impractical and, I believe, wrong.' But it remains true that, if he had looked a little more deeply into Miahuatlan life, he would have found that its Indians were not in fact caught in a circle of 'day-to-day animal living'. The Zapotecs, even today, have a high consciousness of their long tradition, a rich ceremonial life, and a piety which, though it may interpret the spiritual life differently from the way Huxley was on the point of adopting, nevertheless raises their existence into something much higher and more meaningful than the merely animal.

Yet it was not as a civilized snob or in a spirit of racial superiority that Huxley spoke. He was in the process of shaking free from Lawrence, under whose influence he had imagined that it was possible to enjoy the best of the world of the primitive, of innocence and blood, and also the best of the world of intellect and spirit. Sailing across the Gulf away from Mexico towards the United States, he re-read *The Plumed Serpent* and found its message forced and unconvincing. He concluded that we cannot have the virtues of both primitiveness and civilization; civilization, meaning spirit and intellect, exacts the price of abandoning the advantages 'of intuitions, of emotional spontaneity, of sensuality still innocent of all self-consciousness'. Lawrence had tried to give up civilization and take those primitive virtues back again. But, as the absence of conviction in *The Plumed Serpent* showed, he had failed. Mexico liberated Huxley from the gospel according to Lawrence, but it merely freed him for the acceptance of another faith.

2

Often, when we look retrospectively at a writer's career, some remark which seemed insignificant when it was written takes on an unpremeditated importance. It is so with one paragraph from the early pages of *Beyond the Mexique Bay*:

... sooner or later even the most highly civilized and emancipated person comes to a mental frontier which he cannot pass–comes to it, of course, unaware, and does not realize his inability to go further; for it is of the essence of these inward barriers that they never reveal their presence, unless, as the result of some fortunate or unfortunate conjunction of circumstances, we are shaken out of our second nature and transported violently to the other side of what is thenceforward perceived to have been an arbitrary definition of our freedom.

Nothing in *Beyond the Mexique Bay* gave any special importance to the statement, yet we know now that the period in Mexico was also the beginning of the long crisis that both delayed the completion of *Eyeless in Gaza* by several years and transformed it from the 'picaresque novel of the intellect and emotions—a mixture between *Gil Blas*, *Bouvard et Pécuchet* and *Le Rouge et le Noir*' which Huxley originally projected in 1930, into the novel of questing, testing and conversion it actually became.

The inner lives of men as reticent as Huxley are difficult to penetrate unless they leave revealing confessions. Huxley did not. Like Tolstoy, he refrained from writing any formal account of his conversion, and even his published letters give only hints of what was happening in his mind between the two crucial dates in his literary life, when *Point Counter Point* and *Eyeless in Gaza* respectively were completed.

Yet *Eyeless in Gaza* is the account of a conversion obviously similar to his own, and by comparing this novel with Tolstoy's *Resurrection* we can to a degree compare the spiritual crises which the two men underwent. Tolstoy, for all his political radicalism and his stubborn anti-clericalism, accepted a traditional morality, a Christian frame of dogma. Huxley found any individual religion too limiting for his sceptical type of mind. In 1933, when his inner perturbations were obviously moving towards crisis, he still insisted to Naomi Mitchison: 'I have never more passionately felt the need for using reason *jusqu'au bout*.' And, though he rejected the kind of determinist thinking which in the nineteenth century became known as rationalism, there is no doubt that even in the development of a mystical religion he saw himself acting according to the laws of reason, proceeding empirically and—in the purest of scientific traditions—with an endlessly open mind.

At the same time he came very close to Tolstoy's central doctrine; if he did not believe that 'the Kingdom of God is within you', he did conclude that only by an inward path could unitive knowledge of the Divine Ground be attained. Like Tolstoy he understood that this knowledge was possible as a condition of the harmonization of every aspect of living, and this realization led him along parallel ways to Tolstoy in the acceptance of pacifism, anarchistic politics, and decentralist economics.

There were some aspects of political Tolstoyanism which Huxley did not accept. Unlike Tolstoy and William Morris, he would not reject totally the achievements of modern technology; he recognized that electricity and the internal combustion engine, used responsibly, could facilitate the break-up of the great cities and of concentrated industry. Nor, intellectual by breeding and inclination that he was, did he feel the urge which the landowner Tolstoy experienced to identify with the peasants. Rather than going to the people, in the old Russian sense of accepting their way of life, Huxley foresaw—and finally developed in *Island*—a society in which the people would enjoy the best of a culture normally reserved for an élite determined by education and opportunity.

Central to these changes in Huxley's viewpoint, to his acceptance of a definite political vision and a clear moral purpose, was the fruition of a tendency that had always been running in opposition to the main direction of his novels. That direction was pessimistic and iconoclastic; the semi-conversion of Calamy in *Those Barren Leaves* is so weakly conceived that it merely underlines the general message of decay and hopelessness the novel projects. Deeply concerned with displaying the amorality of modern man, the early books gave little scope for the development of a positive morality. The dark negation of *Point Counter Point*'s ending was their logical conclusion.

Up to this point Huxley was following the customary progress of the black satirists—Swift in the past, Céline in our own day. Every satirist begins with a vision of innocence and flays the world that does not realize it. His peril is misanthropy that makes impossible the return to love; this happened to both Swift and Céline, and turned their lives into lonely prisons of mounting insanity. Huxley, who had never entirely lost the vision of innocence, was saved from that ending, and in this he resembled Dostoevsky who, no matter how fiery his denunciation of the intellectual and moral perversions of his time, had always room in his imagination for the Myshkins and the Alyoshas, those crippled apostles of love.

Retrospectively, we have seen, one can trace from Huxley's very beginning the fascination with the process of conversion. One is also aware, even in Huxley's earliest works, of a longing to withdraw into solitude which complements his fascination with the gregarious life, a longing typically expressed in the essay describing a visit to the abbey of Montesenario which he wrote, as far as one can judge, just before he set to work on *Those Barren Leaves*.

The solitude was as profound as the shadowy gulf beneath us; it stretched to the misty horizons and up into the topless sky. Here at the heart of it, I thought, a man might begin to understand something about that part of his being which does not reveal itself in the quotidian commerce of life; which the social contacts do not draw forth, spark-like, from the sleeping flint that is an untried spirit; that part of him, of whose very existence he is only made aware in solitude and silence. And if there happens to be no silence in his life, if he is never solitary, then he may go down to his grave without a knowledge of its existence, much less an understanding of its nature or realization of its potentialities.

The experiences that lead to conversion are those of darkness as well as light, and it was necessary for Huxley to go through the night of *Point Counter Point*, with its deep and apparently hopeless involvement in meaningless suffering and death, to begin the search for light. That had been the experience of the Buddha, and in his essay on *Vulgarity in Literature*, first published in 1930, Huxley made a specific reference to an experience of Buddha's shortly to be mirrored exactly in his own life.

> . . . Prince Gotama, more than two thousand years before, had also discovered the vulgarity of living. The sight of a corpse rotting by the roadside had set him thinking. It was his first introduction to death. . . .
> What with making their way and enjoying what they have won, heroes have no time to think. But the sons of heroes—ah, they have all the necessary leisure. The future Buddha belonged to the generation which has time. He saw the corpse, he smelt it vulgarly stinking, he thought. The echoes of his meditations still reverberate, rich with an accumulated wealth of harmonics, like the memory of the organ's final chord pulsing back and forth under the vaulting of a cathedral.

A year later, beside the road leading down from the mountains to Miahuatlan, Huxley saw a corpse lying by the roadside. In *Beyond the Mexique Bay* he described the incident with a curious offhandedness, noting the frequency of vendettas, the inclination of the Indians to violence when drunk, but saying nothing of his own reaction. Indeed, the sense of the overbearing presence of mortality which every traveller to Mexico experiences on his first visit is hardly evoked anywhere in *Beyond the Mexique Bay*. Yet it emerges in the Mexican chapters of *Eyeless in Gaza*. In the meantime Huxley had obviously come to terms with the memory of that corpse by the Mexican roadside.

Scattered through the books which Huxley published after *Point Counter Point* there are positive signs of a renewed interest in mysticism, a growing desire for some philosophy that would enable one to live without the sense of inner discontinuity, to cope with the knowledge of solitude and death. 'Goethe's advice is sound,' he says in one of the notes to the anthology, *Texts and Pretexts*, which he published in 1932; 'the best way to be happy is to try to live out of personal separateness, in the all.' And he also says: 'The *all* feeling is brief and occasional; but this is not to say that a metaphysical system based upon it must necessarily be untrue.' Writing on El Greco in *Music at Night*, he shows an obviously engaged interest in the spiritual life of this extraordinary painter, and remarks: '. . . though the light is good, though it is satisfying to be able to place the things that surround one in the categories of an ordered and comprehensible system, it is also good to find oneself sometimes in the dark. . . .' And here 'the dark' means the mystical experience, which in these early years of the Thirties begins to return to his writing as something whose reality he accepts, but of whose meaning he is still unwilling to hazard any certain opinion. He had been immersing himself again in the works of the mystics when he wrote in 1930:

> For the literature of mysticism, which is a literature about the inexpressible, is for the most part misty indeed–a London fog, but coloured pink. It is only in the work of the very best mystical writers that the fog lifts–to reveal what? A strange alternation of light and darkness: light to the limits of the possibly illuminable and after the darkness of paradox and incomprehensibility, or the yet deeper, the absolute night of silence.

Huxley had experienced the night of blindness; the night of silence was yet unknown to him. But it is significant, in view of his sustained scepticism, that at the same time he should also say: 'Mystical religion is the ideal religion for doubters–those ultimate schismatics who have separated themselves from all belief.'

Yet the causes of spiritual revolution within human beings are so complex that we cannot see either the experience of Mexico as the land of death or the renewed interest in mystical experience as the prime cause of Huxley's crisis. There were obviously other causes, some unknown to Huxley himself. The bare facts–and there is not much else to go on outside the evidence contained in *Eyeless in Gaza*–tell us that Huxley returned to Europe depressed by the situation produced there by the rise of Nazism, by, as he told Naomi Mitchison, 'the awful sense of invisible vermin of hate, anger crawling about looking for blood to suck'. He finished *Beyond the Mexique Bay* before the end of the year and then began work on *Eyeless in Gaza*, whose original plan he described in December 1932 as that of a novel about the progress of a character who achieves material, mental and emotional freedom, and then finds it a 'rather awful vacuum'. The theme is indicative of his own mood at the time, of the sense of disastrous emptiness that often precedes profound spiritual changes.

1934 and 1935 were the two most unhappy and unproductive years of Huxley's life. He began to withdraw from other people, with the feeling that human contacts sapped his physical and psychological energy, and in the autumn of 1934 he experienced chronic depression and an insomnia which virtually disabled him as a writer. He tried Yoga exercises and gardening without effect; in October 1935 he returned to London and placed himself in the hands of the Australian therapist, F. M. Alexander, a well-known writer on the control of the self, who had treated such distinguished figures as Bernard Shaw and Stafford Cripps; under Alexander's care Huxley recovered and was able to end the long agony of writing *Eyeless in Gaza*.

Alexander was more than a therapist in the ordinary sense. For Huxley, he was something of a guru. By a process of 're-conditioning' he revealed to him those continuities between all aspects of living, physical and mental, moral and spiritual, that he had long sought, and introduced him to effective techniques of meditation. By the end of 1935 Huxley had virtually accepted not only the reality but also the truth of mystical experiences, though it was not for some time afterwards that he began to systematize his thoughts on the subject. For the time being, however, the search for social peace seemed even more urgent than the search for inner peace, and in the autumn of 1935 Huxley abandoned his lifelong political neutrality to become an active pacifist.

Most changes in one's view of existence come from a combination of many inner and outer factors. And there is no doubt that Huxley was helped on his way not only by F. M. Alexander, but also by Gerald Heard, a fellow pacifist and a student of oriental philosophy whom Huxley had met in 1929. Heard was a man of interests almost as encyclopaedic as Huxley's own, with a knack for making scientific and philosophic problems comprehensible to laymen which many people remember from the days of his brilliant BBC talks in the 1930's. From 1933 onwards he was an increasingly important influence on Huxley's life and thought.

Eyeless in Gaza, the product of those years of moral and mental agony, could not fail to reflect a great deal of Huxley's own experiences. It became a manifesto in fiction of his changed philosophy. But still – unlike his later novels—it stands in its own right as a work of fiction, and as such I now propose to consider it.

3

There is none among Huxley's books that so sharply confronts the critic with the need to illuminate what the imagination builds upon the autobiographical. Superficially, it is easy to dismiss *Eyeless in Gaza* as no more than autobiography transmuted into effective didactic fiction. One intention of the novel is obviously to transmit a message; the message is implied in the epigraph, which extends the phrase used in the title to Milton's complete line from *Samson Agonistes*—'Eyeless in Gaza at the Mill with slaves'. *Eyeless in Gaza* is not merely a novel about the blind receiving inner sight; it is also a novel about liberation from a slavery that bears the look as well as the name of freedom. We have seen how Huxley originally contemplated a novel which would deal with illusory freedoms leading to a spiritual vacuum; in *Eyeless in Gaza* he demonstrates how external forces and the acquisition of internal disciplines can together lead to the real liberation, inevitably a metaphysical one. At this point, Huxley is showing a development which resembles that of T. S. Eliot rather than that of the young writers who by 1936 had already been accepted as typical of the 1930s. While the typical 'men of the Thirties'—Day Lewis and Spender and (for the time being) Auden—felt a political anger and called for a political solution, Huxley in his earlier novels, like Eliot in *The Waste Land*, was experiencing a metaphysical malaise, and thus it was not surprising that, like the later Eliot, he found all the questions of life leading him towards a metaphysical answer.

This answer has its basis in Huxley's experience, and on this level we may accept the identity which many critics have sought to establish between Huxley and the anti-heroic hero, Anthony Beavis. It is obvious that in those obscure years from 1933 to 1935 Huxley did go through an experience analogous to that of Beavis: the entry into a night of the soul, with a terrifying sense of the emptiness and futility of his life, work and thoughts up to this point; the passage through that night with the help of the Virgils whom fate had planted along his way; the emergence into a philosophic equilibrium, a Middle Way of the spirit, that has its manifestation in the right action of pacifist propaganda. Moreover, there is much in Anthony's childhood and his years at preparatory school and university that echoes Huxley's real life.

Yet as soon as one goes more deeply in search of autobiographical parallels, one enters the forest of ambiguities which awaits anyone who attempts to disentangle the motives and the impulses that inspire the imaginative writer. For Anthony, with his 'detachment' – the opposite of the mystic's 'non-attachment' – is not Huxley so much as an extension of the fictional persona which goes through many transformations after its first appearance in Denis Stone, and now, in Anthony, has become so experienced and hardened by disillusionment and indurated guilt that in a mood of total emotional non-commitment he has embarked on an affair with Helen Ledwidge (daughter of his former mistress Mary Amberley). An absurd incident, the falling of a dog from an aeroplane, acts upon him like the corpse that Buddha saw beside the roadside in Nepal; from this point his conversion begins, and Denis Stone, Gumbril, Chelifer, move towards fulfilment.

Even those experiences which Anthony shares with the Huxley of the Thirties have been altered to suit the mysterious imperatives of the art of fiction and the theme of regeneration. Anthony, like Huxley, goes to Mexico and travels through landscapes with which his creator was familiar, yet what happens in those landscapes is quite different from anything Huxley encountered. Similarly, though the author and his hero return from Mexico to a period of mental readjustment that will end in both becoming pacifist propagandists, their experiences as war-resisters are also different.

The same applies to the lesser characters in whom critics have been inclined to find resemblances to people in real life. John Beavis, Anthony's father, seemed so much like a malicious portrait of Leonard Huxley, that Aldous's stepmother, Rosalind Huxley, felt impelled to write him in protest. Huxley's reply was a salutary demonstration of the way a fictional character comes into being.

The most repulsive of the many displeasing features of John Beavis is the way in which, after demonstrating a poetically inconsolable grief for his wife, he is able to respond to the flattering admiration of a young female disciple. At the height of his passing sorrow he is haunted by the lines from Henry King's 'Exequy':

> *Till age, or grief, or sickness must*
> *Marry my body to that dust*
> *It so much loves; and fill the room*
> *My heart keeps empty in thy tomb.*
> *Stay for me there; I will not fail*
> *To meet thee in that hollow vale.*

This poem had long fascinated Huxley; he had already used it in *Antic Hay*, during the grotesque play in the nightclub, when the father of the Monster whose mother has died giving birth to him cries out: 'Margaret! Margaret! Wait for me there: I shall not fail to meet you in the narrow [sic] vale'. There seemed to be an association in Huxley's mind – possibly of true feeling opposed to sentimentality–between King's poem and Coventry Patmore's 'Tired Memory', for Huxley told his stepmother that he wrote a story about a character Patmore's poem suggested and later incorporated the idea into the characterization of John Beavis.

Following a principle which I have always used [he adds]–that the only way of rendering simultaneously the subjective feeling of a person and the objective judgement of other people upon that person is to mingle tragedy with a certain element of extravagance–I introduced the element of philology. This was based upon descriptions given by Frieda Lawrence of her first husband, who was a philologist. Treated in a different manner, the character yet has a strong resemblance to the parson in D. H. Lawrence's *Virgin and the Gypsy*, a figure who was actually derived from the same source. After that it became necessary to fix the personage in time, as the inhabitants of a certain epoch. And here, I am afraid quite unjustifiably, I made use of mannerisms and phrases some of which were recognizably father's. I had not thought that they would prove recognizable to others and I am most distressed to find that they should have been.

Here Huxley appears disingenuous; Rosalind was by no means the only member of the Huxley circle who recognized Leonard Huxley in John Beavis, and there is no doubt of the close resemblance between the Swiss holidays of the Beavis family and those of the Huxleys, or of the atmosphere of faded agnosticism which the real and the fictional families share.

Eyeless in Gaza opens on the 30th of August, 1933, the crucial turning day of Anthony's life; he is engaged in the Proustian pastime of looking through a pile of photographs that remind him of incidents from the past–photographs of his mother, dead a generation ago, of Mary Amberley his first mistress, of himself in the grotesque boy's garb of the Edwardian age, of family holidays at Rosenlaui, of a forgotten girl named Gladys. Huxley does nothing so crude as to draw the action of the novel directly out of the memories evoked by these photographs, but *Eyeless in Gaza* is built up on the rearrangement of fractured time, and is essentially–if not explicitly–a recollective work. Furthermore, in Anthony's mind the snapshots become the images of inner discontinuity. 'Somewhere in the mind a lunatic shuffled a pack of snapshots and dealt them out at random.'

Thus the real chronological action of the novel actually begins in Chapter 4, when young Anthony is going down with his father and his uncle James to the village where his mother will be buried. The scene is partly autobiographical; for Anthony the death of his mother was the same kind of traumatic experience as the death of Julia Huxley for Aldous, but there the resemblance ends, for Maisie Beavis obviously had little in common with Julia Huxley. This day is more than the end of childhood; it also foreshadows the beginning of manhood, for at the funeral is the newly married Mary Amberley, nine immeasurable years older than Anthony. Ten years later, when Anthony meets her at Oxford and the nine years' difference has telescoped with time, she takes Anthony as her lover and–cultured immoralist that she is–'civilizes' him.

When Anthony first impinges on the reader's consciousness in Chapter I he is the unregenerate man who has sought detachment from emotional entanglements and has become Helen Ledwidge's lover on the implied understanding that there will be no commitment on either side. This conception of freedom he combines with a development of the idea of discontinuity which Huxley had discussed in his essays of the 1920s; Anthony believes that man's existence consists of a series of unrelated states of mind and, in a rather more systematic way than Huxley in *Proper Studies*, he is writing a survey of social relationships based on this philosophy.

The ultimate aim of the novel, in thematic terms, is to disprove this theory, and to replace it by a concept of interconnection not merely between all the human faculties–physical, emotional, intellectual and spiritual–but also between all the acts and experiences of a man's life. Nothing is wholly accidental, will be the ultimate conclusion; we are all–though Huxley does not at this point use the word–constrained in what the Buddhist would call a karmic chain, for our actions condition our later existence. No incident can be separated from another, any more than man can be separated from man. Separation is indeed the human condition, yet 'that which men come finally to demand of themselves, is the realization of union between beings who would be nothing if they were not separate. . . .' In this paradox, at the end of the novel, Huxley returns to that line of Fulke Greville which had haunted him since he first used it in *Limbo* and which had formed part of the epigraph to *Point Counter Point*:

> Born under one law, to another bound.

For the solution lies in the presence, beyond the phenomenal world, of a spiritual dimension in which unification becomes possible.

The structure of *Eyeless in Gaza* is used to facilitate this change in perception in the reader, as it takes place in Anthony himself. When we begin the book, it reads almost like a Dadaist exercise in dislocation. Chapter I takes place on the 30th August 1933, Chapter II is an extract from Anthony's diary on the 4th April 1934, Chapter III takes us back to 30th August 1933, though there is no obvious continuity with Chapter I, Chapter IV is set in 1902, Chapter V in 1926, and so on throughout the 54 chapters of the book, with no two contiguous chapters in consecutive relationship. At first it seems as though Huxley were giving practical form to Anthony's theory of discontinuity, as though the destruction of sequential time in the novel implied an acceptance of separation within man and between men.

As we proceed, however, we realize that Huxley's purpose in fracturing the time sequence is not in fact the Dadaist one of dislocation for its own sake; rather, it resembles the purpose of the Cubists, who fracture a three-dimensional scene in order to re-arrange its components two-dimensionally and enhance their relationship by forcing us to see them in a new arrangement.

Time is in fact reconstructed so that there is a multiple progression. The novel can be divided into six related groups of chapters, as follows:

1. 6th November 1902 to January 1904. Chapters 4, 6, 9, 15.
2. June 1912 to July 1914. Chapters 10, 16, 19, 27, 30, 33, 36, 43, 48, 52.
3. December 1926 to April 1928. Chapters 5, 11, 14, 18, 20, 22, 24, 34, 39, 45. (One day, 8th December 1926, is divided between Chapters 5, 11, 14, 18, 20, and 22.)
4. May 1931. Chapters 25 and 29.
5. August 1933 to February 1934. Chapters 1, 3, 8, 12, 21, 26, 31, 37, 41, 47, 49, 51, 53. (One day, 30th August 1933, is divided between Chapters 1, 3, 8 and 12.)
6. April 1934 to February 1935. Chapters 2, 7, 13, 17, 23, 28, 32, 35, 38, 40, 42, 44, 46, 50, 54.

Within each of these sequences time runs consecutively, and the last chapter in sequence 6 takes place on the last date in the book, so that in fact one does have six series of events intertwined in such a way that past and present constantly reflect and illuminate each other, showing not merely how past shapes present, but also how both are drawn by the lodestone of the future. Each of the sequences, moreover, presents a crucial episode or period in Anthony's life.

Sequence 1 relates to the great crisis of childhood, the death and burial of Anthony's mother, but it also contains the seeds of the future. Anthony first sees at the funeral Mary Amberley, carrying in her womb the child who will become Helen Ledwidge. He returns to school and is immersed in the companionship of boys who will play a crucial part in his mature years: the dashing gamesman Mark Staithes, the pathetic Goggler Ledwidge with his truss and his auto-erotic fantasies, the scrupulous, stuttering Brian Foxe, who is Anthony's closest friend. These years are clouded by his father's remarriage to the unsympathetic Pauline, an event that increases Anthony's sense of self-defending isolation.

Sequence 2 shifts to Oxford and young manhood, with Anthony the omnivorous Huxleian erudite, ready out of snobbery to play the clown among the aristocratic hearties he despises, and to neglect his real friends, Brian Foxe and Mark Staithes, in the process. Neglect eventually leads to betrayal. Brian, whom Huxley admitted he modelled partly on his brother Trevenen, is a mother-dominated Edwardian puritan, and when he falls in love with the daughter of the Rev. Thursley (one of Huxley's most biting anticlerical portraits) he finds scruples fighting against desires, so that he can neither have any physical relationship with Joan out of marriage nor accept his mother's offer of the money to sanctify their union. In bitterness Joan confides in Anthony, and Mary, who has become his demanding mistress, challenges him to seduce the girl. In a scene reminiscent of Myra Viveash's ultimatum to Gumbril, she threatens not to see Anthony again; he surrenders and finds Joan a willing victim. Brian, they decide, must be told, and Anthony meets his friend in the Lake District with the intention of confessing. He delays so long that Joan writes to Brian under the impression Anthony has already told him. Brian commits suicide by jumping down a precipice. Already, in the death of the savage in *Brave New World*, Huxley had used the actual method by which his brother Trevenen had killed himself, and now he changed it. But the appearance in two successive novels of suicide motivated by a pure or puritanical feeling towards a beloved girl shows how strongly the memory of Trevenen's suicide still affected Huxley. For Anthony, Brian's suicide becomes the source of enduring guilt, and increases his fear of emotional involvements.

One of the results of Brian's death is that Anthony parts from Mary, and does not see her again for many years. When he does, in sequence 3, we are again in the world of Huxley's early novels, for six of the chapters concern a single day in 1926. In the first Helen Amberley (later to become Helen Ledwidge) is introduced, stealing goods from shops to fulfil a boast to her timid and respectable sister, the future memsahib Joyce. In the second, Anthony decides to attend the party to which Mary has unexpectedly invited him. The party, occupying three chapters, is a Proustian set piece, a diminished version of the great musical soireé in the beginning of *Point Counter Point*, in which the social landscape of that period is revived like an old theatre set, with the actors posturing before it almost as if they had come out of the past novels. Mary, as rapacious for company as Mrs. Aldwinkle or Lucy Tantamount, rules the circle as a desperately ageing Circe whose charms have begun to lose their magic so that she is obliged to content herself with the gigolo services of the decayed aristocrat, Gerry Watchett. Mark Staithes has become a practising cynic like Spandrell, except that his nihilism has taken a political turn. He is now a Communist who seeks revolution for his own sake; and bears a considerable resemblance to Garine, the hero of Malraux's novel, *Les Conquérants*, which Huxley had admired greatly. For the first time, in the person of the trivial and repellent Beppo Bowles, Huxley introduces homosexuality as an aspect of the degeneration of the times.

There are two innocents in this situation. The false innocent is Hugh Ledwidge, now a theoretical ethnologist at the British Museum, given to romanticizing women for whom he has no real desire. Helen is the subject of one of his ethereal fantasies; she is the true innocent, a lighter Irene, liable to be swept on any wind of fancy or emotion, so that it is not long before Gerry Watchett has contrived to seduce her. As her mother's life is collapsing into drug addiction and chronic debt through Gerry's depredations, she has an abortion in Paris, and, on the rebound from her lover's brutality, marries Hugh, only to discover the meaninglessness of his sentimental attachment.

The two brief chapters of sequence 4, five years later, show Helen at the stage of cynical disillusionment with her marriage.

> But Hugh didn't want her to be a good wife [she reflects], didn't want her, so far as she could see, to be anything. A divine presence in a place divine. But the place was his letters; she was present, so far as he was concerned, only at the other end of the postal system. He didn't even want her in bed – or at any rate not much, not in any ordinary way.

At this point, in 1931, Helen meets Anthony again, and the situation which existed between him and her mother in 1912 is reversed, for it is now she who finds that the gulf of years which seemed to part them in 1926 has closed. By 1933, at the beginning of sequence 5, their relationship is near to its end. Physical passion is all that holds them together, and for Helen this bond is broken traumatically with the falling of the dog. The same event (which echoes grotesquely Brian's falling to his death) awakens in Anthony a tenderness for her that he had tried in the interests of his emotional freedom to ignore.

Anthony is now afflicted by the sense of inner vacuum which was the destination of Huxley's first plan for *Eyeless in Gaza*. He realizes that his freedom has become a slavery. But he has no idea how to liberate himself, and in this mood he accepts Mark's invitation to join him in a quixotic trip to take part in a Mexican revolution.

Mark propounds the existentialist or absurdist view that man gives his life meaning by his own actions, and that we prove that meaning by facing extreme situations. 'Death', he says, 'is the one thing we haven't succeeded in vulgarizing" Not only does Mark resemble Malraux's Garine; the journey into Mexico, superficially modelled on Huxley's own journey, in fact takes on the atmosphere of the progress into evil which Malraux portrays in *La Voie Royale*, and the expedition ends in a jungle hut with Mark's gangrened leg in the same way as that in *La Voie Royale* ended in a jungle hut with Perken's gangrened leg. But, whereas Perken died, Mark lives because of Anthony's fortunate meeting with Miller the doctor-anthropologist, who saws off the injured man's leg before an audience of Indian children.

Miller's arrival means for Mark a prolonged physical existence which he accepts with an ill grace and a bitter verse from Rochester; for Anthony it means a renewed spiritual life. Miller, who has learnt as an anthropologist that pacifist methods work admirably with primitive peoples, seems to have been based partly on Theodore Pennell, a doctor who in the 1890's used non-violent techniques effectively in his dealings with American Indians; it is also evident from his first remarks to Anthony, whom he criticizes for bad posture and diagnoses as a victim of chronic constipation, that he contains much of F. M. Alexander. Maria Huxley's words in describing Alexander's achievement might be used to describe Miller's effect on Anthony: 'He has brought out, actively, all we, Aldous's best friends, know never came out either in the novels or with strangers.' By liberating potentialities, Miller has not created a new Anthony; he has merely brought into the light an Anthony whom fear, guilt, and a detachment that is really the most insidious form of attachment, have so long concealed.

While Anthony has been undergoing this existentialist pilgrimage, Helen has been following a parallel course on a lower level. She has left Hugh, and has known real love for the first time with a German Communist refugee, Ekki Giesebrecht. Because of her happiness, she imagines that in Communism she has found the true faith, but when Ekki is kidnapped and taken to death in a Nazi torture chamber, she realizes the hollowness of the doctrine to which she remains faithful in deference to Ekki's memory.

In sequence 6 it is the changed Anthony that we encounter, grave yet joyful in a way he has never been before. He is now an active pacifist, and working for the movement headed by Purchas (a minor character modelled on the preacher and war-resister Dick Sheppard). Anthony is sustained by a sense of the unity of all being that Miller has planted firmly in his consciousness, and as the novel ends we see him setting out to address a gathering which he knows will be his great testing time, since a gang of patriotic thugs has threatened to attack him there. What he fears most is that under attack he will show his fear, but he goes into a long meditation on the evil of separation, the good of union, and realizes that he is committed to his enemies as much as to his friends. Thinking on Fulke Greville's statement of man's condition, he perceives in a different way the human predicament which he–and Huxley–had once chosen to regard as either a bad joke of destiny or a sign of life's pointlessness. Now he sees the point of the paradox 'that one demands of oneself the achievement of the impossible', and that the impossible is achieved when meditation has brought one to peace, conceived first as darkness, then as light. At the culmination of what from every point of view is his most significant novel, Huxley has reached the point where the dark of refuge, of blindness, passes over into the light of an ecstasy not yet achieved perhaps, but metaphorically conceived. 'For now there is only the darkness expanding and deepening, deepening into light; there is only this final peace, this consciousness of being no more separate, this illumination.'

Rearranged in this way, *Eyeless in Gaza* becomes a chronological tale of conversion against a social background in which the desperate futilities of the Twenties merge into the equally desperate searchings for faith of the Thirties. But the temporal dislocation of the novel as we first read it has its reasons. It displays, as no chronological record could do without elaborate flashbacks, the constant interplay between what we are and what we have been, the way in which every choice reflects a multitude of choices made by or for us in the past. What seemed to Anthony a discontinuity is revealed to be a unity, and the 'intermittences of the heart' are shown to be not accidental, but manifestations of a pattern which chronologically minded man does not comprehend until, as the structure of *Eyeless in Gaza* urges him to do, he steps out of time. The novel assumes an organic rather than a mechanical form.

Impressive as one finds the structural ingenuity of *Eyeless in Gaza*, this is not the only quality that makes it especially memorable among Huxley's novels. Anthony is far more elaborately developed than any previous Huxley character, and the experiment of making a single life the centre of a major novel has resulted in a psychological complexity Huxley had not achieved before in fiction and would never repeat. At the same time, Huxley breaks out of the confines of the Twenties; by extending action and memory over more than thirty years he dispels that feeling of brittle contemporaneity which one sensed in the earlier novels, and even, curiously, in *Brave New World*, whose Future was so recognizably a caricature of Today. To psychological and temporal depths he adds a thematic breadth which is shown especially in the counterpointing of the various attitudes to life which the book develops. The brutal rapacity of Gerry Watchett is balanced by the gentle rapacity, disguised as love, of Mrs. Foxe. To Hugh Ledwidge's museum-bound ethnology, which liberates him from actuality to become the author of a nauseating novel of spiritualized love, is opposed Miller's arduous field anthropology, a true science of man rooted in human experience, not in abstractions. To Brian's self-torturing moralism is opposed Anthony's detached amoralism, and we know that neither is right. To the Communism which Mark and Helen in turn realize is not enough, is opposed the active pacifism of Miller and Anthony. To the tyrannical transcendental religion of the Rev. Thursley is opposed a liberating and universalist mysticism. More than any other of Huxley's novels *Eyeless in Gaza* fitted his requirements for a literature of the Whole Truth.

The attitudes Huxley expressed were unpopular among the fashionable critics of the 1930's, and *Eyeless in Gaza* was condemned for its content even more than for its form. Some of the defects these critics denounced were there in reality. The orating elder had been acceptable when he was an amusing reprobate like Scogan or Cardan; even Mustapha Mond's cynical irony had been tolerable. But Miller is both boring and improbable, a didactic preacher drawn from the evangelical novels of a past age and only lightly disguised. With the dubious exception of Calamy, he is the first of Huxley's exemplary characters, dedicated not only to witnessing the truth in their lives, but also to expounding it. Anthony's conversion in turn is rendered implausible by his relationship with this chance-found and unlikely guru. Most unconvincing is the final chapter, with Anthony's long meditation and his departure for the testing encounter with his enemies. 'Dispassionately, and with a serene lucidity, he thought of what was in store for him. Whatever it might be, he knew that all would be well.'

The difficulty of this facile passage, a difficulty to be repeated in *Time Must Have a Stop*, is that of rendering a meditational experience in words that leave in the reader's mind the slightest impression of the reality. In *Eyeless in Gaza* Huxley falls into the very error of which he often accused the scientists: of trying to convey human experience in abstract terms.

> Unity beyond the turmoil of separations and divisions. Goodness beyond the possibility of evil. But always the fact of separation persists, always evil remains the very condition of life and being. There must be no relaxation of the opening pressure. But even for the best of us, the consummation is still immeasurably remote.

What do such phrases actually tell us in terms of real knowledge? Little. It is only at the end of several pages, by using the image of a double cone, that Huxley finally achieves a little of that substance which the metaphysical poets once succeeded in conferring on the insubstantial.

> Cone reversed from the broken and shifting light of the surface; cone reversed and descending to a point of concentrated darkness; thence, in another cone, expanding and expanding through the darkness towards, yes! some other light, steady, untroubled, as utterly calm as the darkness out of which it emerges. Cone reversed into cone upright. Passage from wide stormy light to the still focus of darkness; and thence, beyond the focus, through widening darkness into another light.

Yet, while they remind one of Huxley's passion for the serene geometries of Piero della Francesca, there is still a curiously mechanical quality about those cones and focuses, as if the way to God lay through Euclid, as it had seemed to Guido in 'Young Archimedes'.

Apart from literary effectiveness, this was a strange way for a writer who had been regarded for a decade as one of the banner-bearers of the *avant-garde* to end a novel that appeared in July, 1936, the month of the Spanish Civil War. It called all Huxley's values into public question, and intensified that division between him and the literary vanguard which had already become evident on the publication two months before of his pacifist pamphlet, *What Are You Going to Do About It?*

CHAPTER NINE

New Worlds of the Mind

I

In the end, when it is expressed definitively in *The Perennial Philosophy* and *Time Must Have a Stop*, one thinks of Huxley's change of heart as predominantly religious in nature. But, to understand his complete evolution, we have to understand how far in its beginning it was a political conversion as well. Huxley wrote or edited at least four predominantly political pieces – *What Are You Going to Do About It?* (1936), *An Encyclopedia of Pacifism* (1937), *Ends and Means* (1937) and *Grey Eminence* (1941) – before he turned in 1945 to his first non-fictional work concerned entirely with mystical religion, *The Perennial Philosophy*.

The impression that political disillusionment played a greater part in Huxley's malaise than in Anthony Beavis's is confirmed by the references Huxley makes, in the final pages of *Ends and Means*, to his abandonment of 'the philosophy of meaninglessness', which he remarks that he and most of his contemporaries in the 1920's had adopted as 'essentially an instrument of liberation'. As a justification for sexual freedom, for rebellion against the political and economic status quo, it had been effective. By the Thirties, however, a reaction set in, 'away from the easy-going philosophy of general meaninglessness towards 'the hard, ferocious theologies of nationalistic and revolutionary idolatry'. These theologies, which Huxley saw younger writers accepting without criticism, resulted in the concept of meaningful communities (nations or classes according to whether one were Fascist or Communist) existing within a meaningless universe, and from this situation, Huxley believed, came the negative impulses towards rearmament and economic nationalism which were making general war increasingly probable. 'It was the manifestly poisonous nature of the fruits that forced me to consider the philosophical tree on which they had grown.'

In practical terms, Huxley was concerned with means to avoid war and with devising a social order that would give minimal encouragement to the urge to power or the emotion of bellicosity. That he turned towards pacifism with an anarchistic orientation was the natural result of his temperament and his background.

The leaders of resurgent pacifism in England during the 1930's were not the generation who came to manhood during that decade (though many of these joined the movement and provided a continuity with the larger nuclear disarmament movements of the Fifties). They were, rather, men of the Twenties, many of whom had direct experience of the First World War. Among Huxley's associates, when he became one of the sponsors of the Peace Pledge Union which Dick Sheppard founded in 1936, were not only resisters to World War I like Bertrand Russell, but also former soldiers and poets like Siegfried Sassoon, Edmund Blunden, Osbert Sitwell, and Max Plowman. The Peace Pledge Union never became the mass organization its founders expected to create after the success of the great Peace Ballot which collected eleven and a half million signatures in support of the League of Nations, and when the war came in 1939 only a minority of the hundred thousand members which the Peace Pledge Union had gathered by the middle of 1936 actually took their pledges seriously enough to become conscientious objectors. But, for Huxley, who had approved of war resisters in 1918 and had made Richard Greenow, the hero of his first novella, a conscientious objector, the Peace Pledge Union provided a possible basis for the moral-political revolution which he envisaged.

His concern for pacifism became active in 1935. During the summer he attended the peace congress which the veteran French pacifist Henri Barbusse organized. By November he and Gerald Heard were discussing ways of organizing a really effective pacifist movement. 'The only hope', he wrote at this time to the Argentinian writer Victoria Ocampo, 'lies in the pacifists being better disciplined than the militarists and prepared to put up with as great hardships and dangers with a courage equal to theirs. Not easy. But I suppose nothing of any value is easy.'

With Heard, Huxley devised some curious schemes for halting the threat of world war, such as cornering the Canadian nickel supplies to keep them out of Nazi hands, but in practice his support for the Peace Pledge Union was mainly demonstrated in writing and speaking. A tall, stooping figure, gesturing with the tentative motions of the hands which he had acquired during his blindness, he was one of the leading personalities at the Albert Hall pacifist rally of November 1936. His pamphlet, *What Are You Going to Do About It?*, sold at threepence, was the Peace Pledge Union's first publication, and later he edited and largely wrote a 120-page sixpenny handbook, *An Encyclopedia of Pacifism*, which the Union published in the summer of 1937.

Both these booklets rely to a great extent on earlier books like Richard Gregg's *The Power of Non-Violence* and Bart de Ligt's *Conquest of Violence*. Huxley urges his fellow believers to create a movement as disciplined as those of their Fascist and Communist rivals and as dedicated as the *satyagraha* movement which had achieved such dramatic results under Gandhi's leadership in South Africa and India. He argues that, 'though mainly preventive, pacifism is also . . . a technique of conflict, a way of fighting without the use of violence.'

Preventive pacifism Huxley sees as the pursuit of any and every means that averts war. Combative pacifism he sees as 'the strategy and tactics of non-violent resistance to violence', a technique which relies, he says with an assurance that seems rather naïve in the 1970's, 'on the fact that it is impossible to display the virtues of courage, patience, devotion and disinterestedness without evoking sooner or later a response from even the most ardent and highly trained practitioners of the militaristic technique'.

To prevent war, he urges the sincere offer, on the part of the powers that emerged enriched from the Versailles treaty, of such sacrifices as would equalize world resources, in return for a halting of the arms race. For this end pacifists must work immediately, since once war has started there will be little any group can do to end it. To carry on effective propaganda, he advocates an organization of dedicated people who accept not merely the responsibility for collecting funds and distributing literature, but also a pacifist discipline in their own lives; they should organize themselves in cells of five or ten people, meeting regularly for discussion and mutual help and criticism, and for spiritual exercises, so that their own lives will show the virtues of disinterestedness which they call upon the world to adopt.

The Peace Pledge Union, though it survived, never evolved either the organization or the dedication Huxley urged, and many of his fellow pacifists regarded *What Are You Going to Do About It?* as a speculative work remote from the realities of the time. From the non-pacifist Left, particularly after the outbreak of the Spanish Civil War, came a storm of criticism, ranging from Kingsley Martin's mild admonitions in the *Political Quarterly*, to Cecil Day Lewis's hostile rhetoric in *We're Not Going to Do Nothing* which was published as a special pamphlet by the Stalinist literary magazine, *Left Review*.

Huxley did not allow his pacifism to be deflected by the emotions aroused by the Civil War. In 1937 the *Left Review* circulated its celebrated questionnaire to British writers, asking 'Are you for, or against, the legal Government and the People of Republican Spain?' Huxley expressed his sympathy with the Government side, 'especially the Anarchists: for Anarchism seems to me much more likely to lead to desirable social change than highly centralized, dictatorial Communism.' But he added that in his view the real choice was not between two sides, both of which used violence, but between 'militarism and pacifism. To me, the necessity of pacifism seems absolutely clear.'

Huxley sent this answer in the summer of 1937 from San Cristobal in New Mexico. He had already ceased direct activity on behalf of the Peace Pledge Union. He had also given his critics a further excuse for attack by retreating from Europe at a time when it was felt by the Left that every intellectual should remain to take part in the struggle against Fascism.

The reasons for Huxley's abandonment of Europe were more complicated than his opponents, who accused him of desertion, can have appreciated. Ever since his return from Mexico in 1933 he had been depressed by the state of Europe, and as early as October in that year Gerald Heard, who eventually accompanied him across the Atlantic, had been urging him to 'clear out to some safe spot in South America or the Pacific islands before it is too late'. Maria dreaded the prospect of another war like that which had sent her into exile as a child, and, half consciously, Huxley himself appears to have welcomed the thought that a new setting would enable him to come to terms with his changed attitude towards existence. At first he intended to visit the United States for a year at most, during which he would lecture, complete a short book on desirable social changes, and see his son settled in an American university. But by the time that year had ended – in the middle of 1938 – Europe had become more threatening than ever and the United States had proved unexpectedly congenial. He remained and returned to Europe only as a visitor.

The three Huxleys, with Gerald Heard, sailed in April 1937 on the *Normandie*. From New York they travelled first to Duke University to meet the parapsychologist J. B. Rhine, whose experiments in telepathy and clairvoyance greatly interested Huxley. Thence, via New Orleans and Texas, they reached Taos in New Mexico, where Huxley accepted Frieda Lawrence's invitation to stay on her ranch at San Cristobal while he wrote his final pacifist work, *Ends and Means*. It took him the whole summer, from May to September.

Ends and Means expands the arguments of *What Are You Going to Do About It?* into a philosophy of individual and social life, a systematizing and updating of the earlier scheme of living he had put forward in *Proper Studies*. In some ways it duplicates that earlier work; the arguments on integrated education are very similar, and Huxley repeats, now with the support of W. H. Sheldon's theories of physiopsychological types, the contention put forward in *Proper Studies* and tacitly withdrawn in *Point Counter Point*, that men are unequal in their capabilities.

The most important difference between *Proper Studies* and *Ends and Means* is the positive religious ethic that emerges from the later book. As his title suggests, Huxley argues that we can never create satisfactory political institutions unless we use pure means, since all ends are conditioned by the way in which they are attained. Non-attachment is the path we should seek; at the end of it lies not merely the good society but also a serene outlook on life, and, if we are persistent and fortunate enough, an insight into 'the real nature of ultimate reality'.

As in the fictional Utopia of his last book, *Island*, Huxley is attempting to base a social vision on the insights of mysticism which, by definition, is non-institutional religion. But he considers last of all the things of the spirit. The early parts of *Ends and Means* are concerned with establishing the kind of society that will not produce recurrent wars, and that will also ensure the maximum practicable social justice (which Huxley characteristically does not equate with total egalitarianism).

In such a society as he envisages large-scale changes must proceed not by violence but by persuasion and consent. They must respect the conservatism natural to most men, and reduce the risk of opposition by adapting familiar institutions and accepted principles. There is an air of reformism about such arguments which Huxley's critics were not slow to detect, particularly as he was sharply critical of national planning which, in his view, would encourage international chaos.

It was towards what he called, in a letter of the time, 'anarchism in the sense in which Kropotkin uses the word' that he inclined when he considered the necessary structural changes in society. The state should be reduced in power and prestige, to help lessen nationalist emotions and other psychological causes of war. The emphasis should be on decentralization and self-government by small working groups. Huxley suggests that in industry twenty-five or thirty people is the practicable maximum, and in organizations with a more intellectual basis twelve; large factories can be organized by co-ordinating many small functional groups, within which the level of individual responsibility will be high.

Such a decentralist society would encourage the spread of voluntary associations to counter the atomization of modern industrial life, and particularly associations of dedicated activists, pledged to pursue socially useful ends and to create property-sharing communities which would act as the model cells of a society dominated by the ideal of non-attachment and cured of the obsession with money and power.

To ensure the effectiveness of such communities of militants there must be integrated education, aimed at making children self-reliant and able to resist the incessant external stimulation of the emotions with which the contemporary world surrounds its citizens. There must also be integrated training in bodily discipline, so as to produce a harmony between the physical and the psychological of the kind taught by F. M. Alexander.

But the greatest of all educational processes, Huxley now believes, is religion, by means of which 'human beings may train themselves, first, to make desirable changes in their own personalities and, at one remove, in society, and, in the second place, to heighten consciousness and so establish more adequate relations between themselves and the universe of which they are parts.' For that majority of human beings who do not seek 'enlightenment', the disciplines of meditation and ritual can still provide moral strength (though Huxley is doubtful how far this will work if the religion is centred on a transcendental deity). True religion, like art, can take us beyond science by revealing realities which cannot be measured; it can provide the synthesis that gives each scientific speciality its meaning in a universal view. It can, ultimately, lead to the ecstatic realization of unity with all being. But that realization, in turn, can only be attained by the practice of 'the primary virtues of the ethical system', which are 'love, compassion and understanding or intelligence'.

Ends and Means is a subtly contradictory book, for its tone projects a pessimism the book never states explicitly, but which undoubtedly derives from Huxley's saddened realization during the months when he wrote the book that it was unlikely to have any immediate influence in a world already bound for war. Today, having lived unscathed physically–though not psychologically–for a quarter of a century in the shadow of atomic holocaust, we tend to forget the peculiar inevitability that the prospect of world war had already taken in the minds of Europeans by the summer of 1937. Any vision of a better society published at that time was as much an act of desperation as of faith, and a realization of this fact may well have been partly responsible for the tentative feeling which *Ends and Means* leaves on the mind. But another reason for its failure to convince is the contradiction that emerges when one attempts to base even the simplest political organization on a discipline as solitary as that of mystical religion. It is possible to be a man in society and a mystic; but social responsibility does not follow necessarily from mystical insights. The Hindus wisely distinguish the karma yogi, who gains salvation through action, from those who follow the direct path of mystical experience. Ecstasy is not the only path to non-attachment.

2

In Huxley's later writing the essays and novels tend increasingly to echo each other; as the novels become more and more didactic, the essays become less concerned either with the aesthetics of literature or with experience merely observed. In these respects *The Olive Tree*, which appeared in 1936 a few months after *Eyeless in Gaza*, is a transitional collection. Along with recently written essays, it includes others that appeared ten years before; one has the feeling that Huxley, conscious that his future would be a great deal different from the years up to 1936, was deliberately tidying up his past.

There are many farewells in *The Olive Tree*. It includes, now published as an essay, the study of Lawrence which introduced *The Letters*. And if we can regard that as a Goodbye to Vitalism, we can fairly treat the long paper on *T. H. Huxley as a Literary Man*, first delivered as a Huxley Memorial Lecture at the Imperial College in 1932, as a last pious gesture to the scientific traditions of the family; it is a curiously evasive piece, in which Huxley contents himself with studying the functional qualities of his grandfather's prose and avoids the criticisms of the scientific attitude which had played so large a part in his writings from *Antic Hay* onwards.

Earlier pieces include a travel essay, 'In a Tunisian Oasis', and a study of the novels of Crébillon fils, both of which were written in the first years of the 1920's, and an essay on the painter Benjamin Robert

Haydon which served as an introduction when Haydon's Autobiography was republished in 1926.

Comparing these early essays with their successors in the same
volume, one realizes Huxley's attitudes had already changed by 1936.
Nowhere in his writings after 1929, for example, is there a travel essay of
the same quality as 'In a Tunisian Oasis'. Huxley ceased to be interested
in observing a place for its own sake, in fixing on paper the fugitive
impressions that register it in the mind as a special conjunction of man
and his environment. But that interest is still strong in 'In a Tunisian
Oasis', where the sense of a desert town feeling the first slight influences
from Europe is recorded as evocatively as the smell and feel of the
expeditions on which Huxley wanders with Arab children in the palm
groves and through the dark and tortuous passageways of the town.

Yet the division between the earlier and the later Huxley is no sharp
break. Some preoccupations are abandoned, others expanded, and it is
significant of an underlying philosophic continuity that Huxley should
criticize transcendentalist religion in the final pages of 'In a Tunisian
Oasis' and again, much more elaborately, in the long essay, 'Justifications', written a decade later.

Even here, however, the focus has shifted. In Tunis what depresses
Huxley is that the Arabs, once heirs of the enquiring tradition of
classical Greek science, are now ready to attribute everything that
happens to the will of God, and to leave fate 'to do things unassisted,
in its own way – that is to say, from the human point of view, the
worst way'. In 'Justifications' he shows how in Christianity the
acceptance of a transcendental God has worked in a rather different
way. Seeing God as a person, men were led to imitate him, and this,
as Huxley admits, 'has released a vast amount of energy directed towards
good ends'. Yet one of the dangers of regarding God as a person is
that we anthropomorphize, we attribute to Him the kind of negative
passions which we ourselves possess, such as pride, anger, jealousy,
hatred and even lust. From the shadows of British religious history,
Huxley unearths the example of the Rev. Henry Price, who declared
himself God and, in the community of Agapemone plundered his
followers of their possessions and seduced his female disciples by
divine prerogative. The point, Huxley implies, is not whether we
regard Price as sincere; it is that the idea of a personal, all-powerful
and hence unpredictable deity lends itself to such abuses, and to more
sinister ones, such as the justification of nationalism, beside which the
sexual peccadilloes of erring clergymen are of little importance.

With Benjamin Robert Haydon, that grandiose failure, Huxley discovered a haunting feeling of kinship. Haydon, modernized, had been the model for Casimir Lypiatt, the painter in *Antic Hay*, so fine in his conceptions and so lamentable in their execution; he appears again as a kind of distant presiding genius in 'The Tillotson Banquet'. Like Huxley, Haydon had suffered in childhood from an eye disease but persisted in pursuing his art despite this affliction. Yet—as Huxley often felt when he thought of his own limitations as a novelist—Haydon had really chosen the wrong art. As a painter he was ambitious but incompetent, and when he was popular it was for the wrong reasons—for his politics rather than his paintings. Essentially, as Huxley remarked, 'He was only interested in the literature of painting; he needed a subject to stimulate his imagination.' The sentence need only be slightly amended to illuminate Huxley's own peculiarities as a writer: 'He was interested only in the themes of writing; he needed a theory to stimulate his imagination.' For him the aesthetics of writing were, in themselves, as unimportant as the aesthetics of painting were for Haydon; the main difference was that Huxley was blessed with a natural literary eloquence, whereas Haydon's gift in painting was mediocre. It was as a writer that Haydon did excel, and of his literary—as distinct from his painterly—talents Huxley gives a description that might admirably fit himself. 'His special gifts were literary and discursive. His brain teemed with general ideas. He was an acute observer of character; he could talk, and he could write.'

It is less a personal than a literary affinity that becomes evident in 'Crébillon the Younger'. Crébillon occupied an equivocal place in *Antic Hay* as the favourite writer of the unpleasant Mercaptan, but in his essay Huxley turns to the real merits of Crébillon's school, whose virtue was to see things as they are, without romantic illusions. Huxley praises the 'scientific' attitude which Crébillon takes towards love, treating it as basically physiological, but accepting the feelings that go beyond the physical as subjective realities which may ennoble our pleasures. He also admires Crébillon's method as a novelist, with its preliminary process of 'intellectual digestion'.

> Crébillon is a characteristic eighteenth-century psychologist. With the dry intellectual precision of his age, he describes and comments on his characters, analyses their behaviour, draws conclusions, formulates generalizations. What a contemporary novelist would imply in twenty pages of description and talk, he expresses outright in two or three sentences that are an intellectual summing up of all the evidence.

The novelist who employs the older method gains in definition and clarity what he loses in realism, in life, in expansive implication and suggestion. There is much to be said for both methods of presentation; most of all, perhaps, for a combination of the two.

In his best writing, Huxley also approximated to that middle way; one has only to compare *Antic Hay* with Lawrence's *Women in Love*, whose London chapters concerned the same world and even some of the same people as Huxley's novel, or *Brave New World* with Orwell's *1984*, to see how much nearer, in the economy of his description and of such time-consuming techniques as the interior monologue, Huxley is to the eighteenth-century writers.

Despite the common threads that unite *The Olive Tree*, one is impressed by the lowered interest in literature and the much greater inclination to generalization in the later essays. The piece on Lawrence, written in 1931, is the last on a specific writer. The essays, after that date, are concerned with aspects of public culture that come within the same spectrum of interest as *Ends and Means*. Apart from 'Justifications', with its exposure of the moral risks presented by a transcendentalist religion, there are essays like 'Readers and Writers' and 'Words and Behaviour', which discuss the use of literature as propaganda, the breakdown of the common literary tradition of western civilization through the abandonment of the Bible and the classical authors, and the deliberate distortion and impoverishment of the language for political purposes, a theme that was to preoccupy Huxley for the rest of his life. Finally, there is the title essay, 'The Olive Tree', which terminates the book in a lyrical celebration of the olive as a symbol of peace and plenty. It leads to a discussion of the ecology of Provence, and dilates on the irony by which the rehabilitation of the Midi through the replanting of its ancient forests would destroy the peculiar beauty Cézanne drew from its ravaged hills. At this moment Huxley seems to stand poised in feeling between art in the desert and the recovery of the flourishing landscape of the Roman past. Such ambivalences will not long be characteristic of him; the logic of his intellectual development will drive him, as inexorably as it drove Tolstoy, to set the demands of life–organic and spiritual–above those of art.

3

'I have been re-reading *Martin Chuzzlewit* and the letters from America printed in the *Life of Dickens*,' Huxley wrote in 1925 to his brother Julian, who had suggested that he lecture 'for lucre' in the United States; 'the people – at any rate to judge from the specimens one meets here and from what they write – are just the same: the same interminable canting balderdash about high moral principles and ideals, couched in the same verbose, pseudo-philosophic, sham-scientific meaningless language, the same pretentiousness then as now.' This distaste for an American hypocrisy louder and more sanctimonious than its British counterpart, had been compounded in 1926 by his horror at the vulgarity of the actual American scene.

And yet, having reached America in 1937, he settled there with such decisiveness that one of the striking features of his life in the 1940's is the steady weakening of links with European friends. A completely new group of correspondents appears, and most of them are North Americans.

There were some aspects of American life that Huxley still regarded with revulsion tempered by pitying amusement. He never committed himself to the decisive symbolic step of accepting American citizenship. The oath he was required to take was repugnant to his pacifist beliefs, and so, after twenty-six years of life on the American continent, he died an Englishman, speaking still with an English accent and spending his last conscious hours on the consideration of the greatest of English poets.

Yet many features of American life pleased him. A generation ago Los Angeles was not only a much smaller city than today; it could also boast the clear atmosphere of a true desert climate, and Huxley found the quality of its light beneficial to his eyesight even before he began to use the Bates method of visual reconditioning. For a period he and Maria moved out to Llano on the very edge of the wilderness, and there Huxley would often walk contemplatively in the still emptiness of the desert.

He also found in the United States a greater variety of the kind of people whose interests coincided with his own, at a time when he was turning away from literature as art and towards that world of metaphysics, decentralist politics and the marginal sciences in which his later life was mainly lived. He could visit universities willing to follow lines of research – like Rhine's work in parapsychology – which no European academy would pursue. He could take a part in the foundation of an institution devoted to the study of mystical religion and Vedantism – the Trabuco College in which Gerald Heard became the leading guru. He could meet men working on those verges of science which orthodox savants regarded as beyond the pale of academic respectability. Even the writers who now became his friends–apart from Isherwood–were unlikely people like Anita Loos, the minute and irrepressible author of *Gentlemen Prefer Blondes*, and he found a great deal of congenial companionship among the Hollywood fraternity of actors and expatriate literati.

He even became absorbed occupationally in that milieu. One of the reasons for his slight output of substantial books in America–one every three or four years compared to one every year in the early Twenties–was that he spent much of his time, often fruitlessly, trying to produce film scripts. In 1938 he began a script on the life of Madame Curie; the film appeared in 1943 in another writer's version, but Huxley earned $15,000, Later he worked on scripts of *Pride and Prejudice* and *Jane Eyre* which were filmed, and by such work, and by writing for American magazines like *Esquire*, he was able to live reasonably well and to dispense a great deal of covert largesse at a time when the sales of his books were declining and his income from England had been reduced by devaluation.

In fact, he rarely did anything entirely for the money it earned. If he wrote for *Esquire*, it would be on a subject which interested him deeply, like hypnosis or the treatment of madness. His film adaptations of novels were meant, not only to make money, but also to establish a foothold in a medium which he saw could be used educationally to propagate the truths which he felt necessary for man's survival. Here he was moved by the same desire that made him spend so many fruitless months of his later years trying to turn his stories into plays through which his views might reach a new public. But his ideas for films on population and the life of Gandhi, and for cinematographic adaptations of *Brave New World* and *The Devils of Loudun*, came to nothing, possibly because most of the directors saw him in the same light as Walt Disney did when he found Huxley's outline for a film version of *Alice in Wonderland* too literary. It was ironical, at a time when Huxley had rejected in theory any aesthetic pretensions, that the habit of treating writing as an art should mark him off inalienably from the Philistines; in 1957 he was reduced to preparing the outline for an animated cartoon of *Don Quixote* to be played by Mr. Magoo.

In a way, Huxley's undistinguished but time-consuming involvement in the film industry was a manifestation of retreat from the literary world to which he had in the past belonged. It is not uncommon for writers, once they have established styles of life, thought and expression, to abandon the setting in which they have developed. Huxley's retreat in the 1920's, first for summers in Italy and later permanently to France, was the beginning of a journey into the solitude often desired by a writer who has found what he believes to be his true course. When Huxley saw that course in a way of thinking that seemed to contradict his early writings, it was appropriate that he should go half way round the world to establish a home among a strange people whom he regarded sometimes as admirable Houyhnhnms and often as detestable Yahoos, but rarely as common human beings.

In the one novel which Huxley wrote about the American present–*After Many a Summer*–it is certainly the Houyhnhnms and the Yahoos who predominate. The one credible human being is Huxley's ironic projection of a rejected self in the mother-dominated English scholar Jeremy Pordage, who has read the mystics and abandoned them for a world of curious literature and even more curious facts. And it is through the eyes of this weak and sniggering Gulliver that American life is seen in all its grotesque extravagance and mindless violence, personified in the death-obsessed millionaire, Joe Stoyte. Joe's descent into Yahoo negation is counterbalanced by the elevated preachings of Mr. Propter, but Propter's presentation of the Huxleian position is as dead and didactic as the preachings of Swift's talking horses. *After Many a Summer*, in fact, arouses the same reaction as *Paradise Lost* provoked in Blake: one wonders if Huxley is not still of the Devil's party without knowing it, so exuberantly are the lost depicted, so grey and empty seem the saved.

After Many a Summer can best be charted as two interconnecting worlds that unite in the point of childhood when Joe Stoyte and Mr. Propter are at school together. They have followed wildly separate courses, Joe ruthlessly pursuing money to compensate for his juvenile insecurity, and Propter adopting an academic career that leads him to a philosophy of non-attachment. Yet the two men remain linked by obscure affections complicated by Joe's secret admiration for Propter's integrity and Propter's compassion for Joe's ignorance. When Propter buys a few acres of land in a Californian valley to live a life as physically detached from the world of American capitalism as self-subsistence will make him, Joe buys the hills above and builds there a great concrete stronghold resembling William Randolph Hearst's fake castle of San Simeon. With the architecture of the Middle Ages, Joe Stoyte acquires their terrors; he lives surrounded by armed guards, with drawbridges and portcullises kept in working order to frustrate kidnappers and

bandits, while in his mind, trained since childhood in the rigid Sande-
manian doctrines of election and hellfire, the idea of death is as constantly present as in that of a medieval man living in daily fear of
plague and Dantesque inferno.

The world of Joe Stoyte and his castle is the world of damnation;
the world of Propter in his little house among orange trees whose
fruit hang like lamps in darkness is the world of salvation. Each moves
according to its own modality, so that even in manner *After Many a
Summer* is divided into a number of mutually irreconcilable currents.
Life in the castle is perverted Peacock, *Nightmare Abbey* revised by the
Marquis de Sade; interpolated is the story of the eighteenth-century
fifth Earl of Gonister, which Jeremy Pordage finds among the Hauberk
papers and reads to Dr. Obispo, in much the same way as Henry
Wimbush reads the history of Sir Hercules Lapith to the assembled
company in *Crome Yellow*. But, whereas Sir Hercules is pathetic,
Gonister is Gothically diabolic; he has discovered the elixir of longevity
in the guts of carp. There is a robust eighteenth-century obscenity
about him, but his experiments have the proper Peacockian eccentricity,
and at the very end of the novel, when the world of Joe Stoyte and the
world of Gonister come together, we are in the neighbourhood of
Melincourt and its mockery of Lord Monboddo's fantasies of human
links with the apes. In achieving immortality in the secret caves below
his family house Lord Gonister has devolved into an ape, as filthy and
despicable as a Swiftian Yahoo.

There is a great deal of vigorous satire in these sequences of *After
Many a Summer*, satire more savage than any Huxley ever wrote except
when, in *Ape and Essence*, he returned to the simian comparison, and
once more revealed with Swiftian ferocity the defects of Yahoo
humanity. Despite the compassion he avows through the lips of
Propter, Huxley is as merciless as Dante in his portrayal of those whose
attachments damn them. None of his previous characters has been
quite so emphatically the villain as Dr. Obispo, a black priest of scientific
detachment, exploiting the fears of Joe Stoyte and the lusts of Virginia
Maunciple with a ruthless objectivity. Virginia herself is a twentieth-
century Lenina, a girl conditioned by the materialist concepts of her
time; her religion is a formality powerless to save her from animal
desire. Jeremy Pordage has deliberately turned away from enlightenment to follow the false lights of learning, and is as much the prisoner
of attachment as the great works of art which, ripped from their
contexts, gleam from the walls of the castle as mute comments on the

baseness of its life. Pete Boone, Obispo's laboratory assistant, is the victim of romanticism, which induces him to fight in Spain for an ideological cause; still relatively unformed, he is the one inhabitant of the castle who appears to respond to Propter's teaching, but his chivalrous love for Virginia proves his undoing, for he is shot by the ferociously jealous Joe Stoyte. The murder enables Obispo to confirm his ascendancy by blackmail over both Stoyte and Virginia, and together they set off for England where they find the fifth Earl in his cellar. Joe is willing to accept the apish condition in return for the promise of immortality.

Superficially, *After Many a Summer* can be seen, like Evelyn Waugh's *The Loved One*, as a satire on the American fear of death and the cults of youth and longevity. At a deeper level it is a fable illuminating the difference between survival and eternity. Joe, achieving conditional survival on a diet of carps' guts, illustrates the futility of attempting to find within time the true way of life; it is a modern version of the myth of Tithonus to whom the gods gave immortality but not the gift of eternal youth. Propter, following a life of non-attachment, demonstrates that it is in eternity, which is other than time and distinct from immortality, that we achieve enlightenment.

It is in the treatment of this theme that *After Many a Summer* disintegrates. We are not only subjected to Propter as a self-righteous preacher. We are also forced to follow him in interior monologues that read like unkempt essays. It is as if a very inferior Plato had been brought in to collaborate with Swift and Peacock, both in poor form. For the first time in Huxley's work we encounter an undeniable failure of literary art. The propagandist urge is similar in its effects whether it aims to advocate fascism or non-attachment; it demands the subordination of art to argument. And this is what happens in the sequences in *After Many a Summer* where Propter is at the centre of attention. The only question is whether, as with many artists when they turn to propaganda, Huxley's failure of art is the product of self-deceiving rationalization, or the result of a deliberate choice. The words of his mouthpiece leave us in little doubt. 'Art can be a lot of things,' says Mr. Propter, 'but in actual practice most of it is merely the mental equivalent of alcohol and cantharides.' He adds that 'the makers of imaginative literature have never forged an impersonal, uncontaminated language for the elucidation of immediate experiences.' Neither has Huxley, at least in *After Many a Summer*, a hybrid work which as fiction is inferior to his earlier novels and as the exposition of a philosophic doctrine is too cluttered with bad fiction to be effective.

However, just as the grotesque happenings in Joe Stoyte's castle are interesting as a fictional commentary on what we have been asked to admire as the American Way of Life, so the Propter sequences have a mundane interest when they develop the ideas of social organization already sketched out in *Ends and Means*. While working on *After Many a Summer* Aldous mentioned to Julian that he was 'collecting whatever information I can pick up in regard to the technique for giving a viable economic and social basis to philosophic anarchism – it being more and more clear that the present system of production necessarily involves centralization and dictatorship'. He had found an experiment in New York State that seemed to answer many of his questions: the School of Living at Suffern, founded by Ralph Borsodi, author of a number of books on rural renewal, and a fervent experimenter in the techniques of decentralization. When Mr. Propter lectures his friends on the desirability of developing power at no cost by means of solar accumulators, when he points out that mass production is economic in only about a third of the products we need and that the rest can be produced more efficiently and with greater moral benefit by power tools in small household workshops, he is echoing Borsodi's ideas. Propter as the community-maker, working away at his power lathes and putting up decent shacks for the transients from the Kansas dust bowl, is much more convincing than Propter the metaphysician, because Huxley is now telling us something concrete, and his fiction is always best precisely when it is concrete and sharply particular.

4

Throughout Huxley's later years, the dark and the light alternate. He is always aware of the black irony of ordinary human existence, and in this respect his vision is not markedly different from that of his early novels; it is in the portrayal of Mr. Propter rather than that of Joe Stoyte and Dr. Obispo that we encounter an author different from the novelist who wrote *Antic Hay* and *Point Counter Point*. *Eyeless in Gaza* represents an eventual triumph of light over darkness in the heart of a single person, Anthony Beavis; because this particular unity is abandoned in *After Many a Summer*, and Joe Stoyte remains the victim of the dark forces personified by Dr. Obispo, and kills Pete Boone before Propter's efforts at enlightenment can succeed, one can only accept this novel as, in the end, a triumph for darkness.

To write a work of fiction that would present only the Light, a Utopia that would balance *Brave New World* with a positive vision of the future, was in Huxley's mind by the time he had completed *After Many a Summer*. He envisaged it as a generalization of the proposals developed on a small scale by Propter; he saw its inspiration existing in men and women so trained in the disciplines of mystical religion that their moral life could not fail to be affected by the experience of intuitive unification with God.

He turned aside from this vision, at least temporarily, because of the realization that even mystical training is not proof against political activity involving the exercise of power. A study of the case of the Capuchin Father Joseph, the agent of Cardinal Richelieu in the Thirty Years' War, occupied him during 1940 and the early part of 1941; the result was the biography entitled *Grey Eminence*, a work of what Huxley termed 'religious psychology'.

The background to *Grey Eminence* lies in the disillusionment with political activity which had led Huxley to abandon pacifist activism before he left Britain for the United States in 1937. He reached the conclusion that any attempt to influence humanity outside a moral ambiance inspired by mystical religion was a futile palliative. He carried this attitude so far that in 1938, when his bookseller friend Jacob Zeitlin urged him to write an article protesting against the persecution of the Jews, he refused on the grounds that it would have no immediate ameliorative effect and would merely add to the sum of intemperance. 'It is useless', he argued, 'to treat smallpox by cutting out the individual pustules and stitching up the wounds.' A general change in 'habits of thought, feeling, action and belief' was necessary before people would abandon 'the habit of persecution'.

In the summer of 1939, he received a letter from Kingsley Martin asking about a community which he and Gerald Heard were rumoured to be founding. Huxley replied that he did not possess the necessary skills for such an enterprise, but that communities interested him because he had faith in very small associations but none in society as at present organized. He ended with a statement that was a kind of basic manifesto for *Grey Eminence*.

It is obvious now that the religious teachers were right and that nothing can be achieved on the exclusively political plane except palliation and the deflection of evils. So long as the majority of human beings choose to live like the *homme moyen sensuel*, in an 'unregenerate' state, society at large cannot do anything except stagger along from catastrophe to catastrophe. Religious people who think that they can go into politics and transform the world always end by going into politics and being transformed by the world (e.g. the Jesuits, Père Joseph, the Oxford Group). Religion can have no politics except the creation of small-scale societies of individuals outside and on the margin of the essentially unviable large-scale societies, whose nature dooms them to self-frustration and suicide.

Huxley's pessimism about large-scale social organization was intensified by the outbreak of war in 1939. Following the advice he had given to Julian in World War I, he did not return to England, but he followed events there with attention, adopting the fear then prevalent among pacifists: that the conditions of wartime would lead to democratic countries going the same totalitarian way as Germany. 'It certainly looks as though an age of tyranny were before us,' he wrote to E. S. P. Haynes in March 1940, and, after remarking that the only hope lay in a return to a decentralized society and the wider distribution of land and other property, he added gloomily that 'the probability of such reversal taking place seems almost infinitely small.' It was understandable, when war spread across Europe in the summer of 1940, that he should turn towards an earlier war that from 1618 to 1648 devastated a large part of continental Europe, and impoverished even those countries–like France–which it did not ravage.

Grey Eminence emerged as one of the best of Huxley's later books. While After Many a Summer had been marred as a novel by the introduction of unassimilated exposition, Grey Eminence was improved by the use of fictional techniques to illuminate psychologically the darknesses of Father Joseph's career. Born into the noblesse de robe as François Leclerc du Tremblay, inheriting through his mother the title of Baron de Maffliers, he at first attached himself to the French court. Almost immediately he was led by the example of his schoolfellow Pierre de Bérulle and the influence of the English mystic Benet of Canfield to accept a religious career and join the strict order of Capuchins. Following the example of Bérulle and Canfield, Father Joseph, as he was henceforward known, practised the disciplines of meditation to all appearances with success; his ecstasies were frequent and, in accordance with the spirit of the counter-reformation, often made publicly evident in the pulpit.

The Capuchin rule obliged Father Joseph to combine the active life of preaching and converting the heretics with an inward life of prayer and meditation; he not only became a leading figure in his own order,

organizing missions to Africa and the Near East, but was also instrumental in establishing a strict order of nuns, the Calvarians.

It was during the establishment of the Calvarians that Father Joseph
came in contact with Richelieu. Through his desire to spread the
Christian gospel by a last great crusade led by France, Father Joseph
performed a fatal act of transference by which he came to regard the
interests of the French crown as identical with those of God. This led
him to become entangled with the policies of Richelieu, who at the
time of their first meeting was a protégé of the powerful Queen
Mother, Marie de Médicis. Father Joseph played his part in the intrigues
by which Richelieu successfully established influence over Louis XIII
after Marie de Médicis was thrust from power. When the time came to
destroy the political power of the Huguenots through the reduction of
La Rochelle, Father Joseph incongruously combined the spiritual
leadership of the campaign with the organization of a network of
spying and systematic corruption that helped materially to weaken the
resistance of the Protestants. All one can say for Father Joseph on this
occasion is that, once La Rochelle had fallen and the power of the
Huguenots had been broken, he refused to countenance forcible
conversion; to his equal credit, Richelieu supported this refusal.

The political neutralization of the Protestants, with its assurance of
the internal unity of France, was the prelude to Richelieu's campaign
to destroy the continental hegemony of the Hapsburgs, who, ruling in
Spain, Austria, the Netherlands, and much of Italy, with the prestige
of the Holy Roman Empire at their command, came near to encircling
France in a ring of military power. To break that ring Richelieu did not
scruple to support the German Lutheran princes and the Protestant
king of Sweden, Gustavus Adolphus, against the Catholic Emperor.
Father Joseph rationalized this and the other anomalies of France's role
in the war in Germany on the grounds that all was necessary to
strengthen his country's position as the chosen instrument for the
spread of Christianity. To that end, even while he remained a practising
contemplative convinced of the reality of his mystical experiences, he
employed the most amoral political methods. It was largely his
influence that prolonged the war, to the devastation of Germany and
Bohemia and the impoverishment of the French peasantry. Father
Joseph died hated by his countrymen, his efforts at saintliness negated
by his political acts.

The biographical sections of *Grey Eminence*, in which Huxley analyses
Father Joseph's character, examines the development of his vocation,

and traces his gradual entanglement in the web of action, are written with a fine combination of historical insight into seventeenth-century France (a time and place Huxley appears to have found especially appealing) and the kind of personal empathy that is possible when one has followed as an enquirer a path parallel to that pursued by one's subject. There are times indeed when this biography of a person in history seems to belong to the world of Huxleian fiction, for Father Joseph's relationships with his mother and the girl to whom he was unwillingly attracted in adolescence have much in common with the tormented puritanism of Brian Foxe, while the passionate intensity with which the priest later follows his ungodly political cause has the diabolical power with which Huxley sometimes endued those characters, like Spandrell and Obispo, who have accepted a satanic role. This adds to the interest Father Joseph arouses in the reader for, as Huxley ruefully recognized, weakness and evil among men lend themselves more easily to the purposes of art than goodness and perfection, and Tragedy, which arises out of such qualities, is always in the end more moving than the Whole Truth. This is why *Grey Eminence* and *The Devils of Loudun* have worn better than the other books which Huxley wrote after *Eyeless in Gaza*. Father Joseph, and Father Grandier in *The Devils of Loudun*, are tragic figures, drawn into evil and destroyed by their own flaws; the completeness with which Huxley enters into their living darknesses makes his accounts of them far more convincing than the artificial light with which he seems to illumine characters like Mr. Propter and Bruno Rontini of *Time Must Have a Stop*.

But *Grey Eminence* is by intention more than literary art, more even than objective history. For Huxley has by now ceased to be objective, except in the sense that the committed assume their point of view to be necessarily objective. He presents, in the earlier chapters of the book, a condensed history of mysticism which is a kind of prelude to *The Perennial Philosophy*. The emphasis is on experience of the reality of God; Huxley ignores the fact that the concept of God can be conceived and established only by reason, and that the experience of the mystics is demonstrably true only in so far as it follows and reinforces reason; outside reason, it can have only personal significance. This represents—and will continue to represent in Huxley's discussion of mysticism—a curious failure of self-recognition. For it is clear that when Huxley discusses the mystical tradition he is in fact rationalizing and systemizing a body of thought of which he himself does not speak with the authority of direct experience. Throughout *Grey Eminence* and such later works as *The Perennial Philosophy* and *The Devils of Loudun* he uses those very methods of analytical thinking and imaginative projection which he condemns in *Grey Eminence* when he says: 'where analysis and imagination are active the mind is unable to receive into itself the being of God.'

More disturbing than these inconsistencies is the way in which, in *Grey Eminence*, the former sceptic turns dogmatist. Rejecting, in intent if not in practice, the methods of art, Huxley appears also to have rejected the virtues as well as the vices of science, and particularly its insistence on the theoretical and tentative rather than the dogmatic and assured. It is disconcerting to find him affronting the reader with such statements (strangely devoid of saintly humility) as: 'For the radical and permanent transformation of personality only one effective method has been discovered–that of the mystics'; and, a little later, insisting that mysticism is 'the only proved method of transforming personality'; and afterwards telling us that 'Society can never be greatly improved until such time as most of its members choose to become theocentric saints.' It is, of course, intellectual presumption to use the word 'proved' for any of these statements. Like the libertarian paradise of the anarchists, Huxley's theocentric Eden has the supreme appeal that it has never been tried, hence never proved, and for this reason it is more attractive to the idealist than those systems which have demonstrably failed to be other than imperfect. But this does not mean that the Huxleian attempt to transform natural man is any truer or more likely to succeed than the anarchist attempt to liberate natural man.

CHAPTER TEN

The Perennial Philosophy

I

Those who are converted to a religious or a philosophic point of view, if the conversion has any depth, are likely to go through a phase of pride and dogmatism, and to end in humility. One observed this with Graham Greene and his conversion to Catholicism: how dogma gave way to compassion, to a sense that judgement was not in man's hands. The same tendency was evident in Huxley, and by 1956, twenty years after the moral agony that had produced *Eyeless in Gaza*, he was to write of his claims to religious understanding with a humbleness which had hardly been evident either in *After Many a Summer* or in *Grey Eminence*. He had been asked to address one of the Californian Vedantist groups. He declined, and the reasons were significant:

> . . . I am not a religious person – in the sense that I am not a believer in metaphysical propositions, not a worshipper or performer of rituals, and not a joiner of churches – and therefore I don't feel qualified or inclined to tell people in general what to think or do. The only general advice I can give (apart from exploring individual cases on an ad hoc basis) is that people should use their common sense, act with common decency, cultivate love and extend and intensify their awareness – then ask themselves if they know a little more than they did about the Unknown God.

If anything especially characterizes Huxley's writings on mystical religion after the publication of *Grey Eminence*, it is the increasingly self-effacing withdrawal into the dual roles of the enquirer who shares with others the knowledge he has gained of religious truths, and the compassionate observer who watches among his fellow men the working out of that chain of choice and consequence which the Buddhists, to whose views Huxley drew increasingly closer in his later years, give the name of *karma*. The first stages of this development can be seen in the books which occupied him during the remaining years of World War II, the novel *Time Must Have a Stop* and those two treatises so different in intent but so curiously similar in approach, *The Art of Seeing* and *The Perennial Philosophy*.

After Huxley had finished work on *Grey Eminence* in 1941, he returned briefly to his idea of a Utopian novel, but the work that actually emerged from his thoughts during the summer of that year followed a very different course. If *After Many a Summer* was concerned with the fear of death, the novel that became *Time Must Have a Stop* was concerned rather with the fact of death in time seen against the background of life in eternity. Huxley started work on it in 1941 and did not complete it until the beginning of 1944; he wrote it—as his laconic references suggest—with difficulty, and it was not until the end of 1943 that he felt inclined to give even a brief description of its intent, when he wrote to his American editor, Cass Canfield, describing it as 'a piece of the *Comédie Humaine* that modulates into a version of the *Divina Commedia*'.

Both allusions are misleading guides to the real nature of *Time Must Have a Stop*. It begins indeed as human comedy in the sense that Huxley is once again presenting a satiric portrait of the follies and futilities of English upper-middle-class life at the end of the 1920's. But the tone is hardly that of Balzac; it is that of the Huxley of *Those Barren Leaves*, a gentler ironist than wrote *After Many a Summer*. And while the posthumous experiences of one of the two main characters provide a highly original element through a vein of supernatural fantasy quite new in Huxley's novels, the character of the vision is by no means that of the *Divine Comedy*; the Dantesque panorama of divine punishment and reward is replaced by a Buddhist drama of cause and effect based on Huxley's reading of the *Bardo Thödol*, or *Book of the Dead*, a Tibetan Mahayanist treatise on the art of dying.

The action of *Time Must Have a Stop* is relatively simple, classically condensed into brief spaces of time and restricted locales; the principal characters are all members of the Barnack family or linked with it by marriage or employment. In the dimension of time it tells the story of the death of Eustace Barnack, *bon vivant* and man of culture. But even death does not release Eustace from the circle of time, and in so far as the novel escapes from the temporal plane it is by the conversion of his nephew Sebastian Barnack.

In its setting, *Time Must Have a Stop* is an act of nostalgic reconstruction. It deals with the European scene from which Huxley had been absent for more than six years before he completed the novel. The opening scene lies in the Hampstead of 1929. The central and by far the larger part of the book is set in Florence a few days afterwards, its later chapters interspersed with glimpses of that realm beyond physical locality where Eustace Barnack experiences the travails of dying. The epilogue, fourteen years later, returns to London–the London of war-time which Huxley never saw.

Because *Time Must Have a Stop* ends with the conversion of Sebas-tian Barnack, one is tempted to compare it with *Eyeless in Gaza*. But Anthony Beavis's conversion is the very substance of *Eyeless in Gaza*, while we only encounter Sebastian as a spiritually transformed man in the brief epilogue to *Time Must Have a Stop*. It is true that his journey towards enlightenment passes, like that of Anthony, through seductions and betrayals which lead into the night of self-disgust, but the process by which he comes to his understanding of the philosophy of non-attachment lacks the inevitability one felt in Anthony's case; his conversion has even more the effect of an unassimilated after-thought than Calamy's retreat into the contemplative life at the end of *Those Barren Leaves*.

The body of the novel, on the other hand, has a distinct unity, and once one accepts the combination of supernatural fantasy with a modified realism in the description of temporal life, the whole story of Eustace's death and of the moral trap into which it leads Sebastian acquires a considerable plausibility.

In the world of time, to which the title so emphatically draws attention, men are damned by attachment to possessions, to careers, even to art and ideals, and the Barnack family, to whom we are introduced as the novel begins, seem all damned if not all silent. Sebas-tian, seventeen years old but so angelically young in appearance that women cannot resist petting him, is dedicated to poetry. His barrister father, John Barnack, is passionately devoted to socialist politics, and infects the lives of those around him with his abrasive secular puritanism. His wife left him long ago and is now dead, and Sebastian lives in the house of his aunt Alice Poulshot. There life is made wretched by Fred Poulshot's obsessive meanness, which forces his family to live in a singularly shabby gentility. Fred's brother-in-law Eustace Barnack is attacked by a much more invidious form of attachment, for to him wealth means not the money he can command, but the pleasures of body and mind it will buy him, and since Eustace is civilized in his tastes this means that he lives not merely a physically indulgent but also a culturally luxuriant life, which he defends with the eloquence of a second-rate Oscar Wilde. Eustace is a Cardan who has made good; he contrived to marry an elderly heiress who died a few years after the wedding and left him with the income necessary to indulge all his passions for pleasure and for art.

Since the evils of attachment are thematically so important, it is natural that two material objects should take on not only a symbolic but also an operative importance in the novel. One is the dinner suit which Sebastian obsessively desires because to possess it would be a sign of maturity and social position. His father refuses to buy one because to him it would be a symbol of class distinction. But Eustace promises to give Sebastian the suit when he stays with him for the summer holiday at his Florentine villa.

When the scene shifts to Italy, it is Eustace who is introduced, at the beginning of the last day of his life. It is a typically self-indulgent day, during which he visits his vulgar little mistress, lunches extravagantly, smokes the Romeo and Juliet cigars which he adores, and, with the proceeds of a successful gamble in foreign exchange, buys himself a couple of Degas drawings, one of which becomes the second material object of operational and symbolic importance. The break in the day's pattern is his visit to the bookshop of his remote Italian cousin, Bruno Rontini; Rontini is one of Huxley's saints, though fortunately not so prosaic as Mr. Propter, for he has a humorously aphoristic way of telling his unpleasant truths. Bruno sees destiny in Eustace's face, and tries telepathically to warn him that it is time to think of eternity. Eustace, trapped in his attachments, resists.

For Sebastian, who arrives that evening, the visit to Florence, which seems to promise so much, is the beginning of a degradation from which he will escape only long years afterwards into the light of spiritual understanding. He is fascinated by the artistic riches of Eustace's house, charmed by his uncle's kindness and humour, intrigued by the other members of the household, the blind and aged Mrs. Gamble who is Eustace's mother-in-law, with her craze for spiritualism, and her companion Veronica Thwale, a madonna-faced sexual experimenter. The evening seems to end idyllically, with Uncle Eustace not only renewing his promise of the dinner suit, but also offering Sebastian one of the Degas drawings to hang in his rooms at Oxford.

Then, late at night, when Sebastian is dozing from the unaccustomed effects of brandy, Eustace dies in the lavatory from a heart attack brought on by years of over-indulgence. Sebastian's grief, when he learns the news next morning, is not deep enough to eliminate his disappointment over the loss of his dinner suit, and he takes the drawing Eustace has promised him and hurries into Florence, where he sells it to the dealer Weyl for a third of its value, and then orders the suit.

But the estate Eustace enjoyed during his lifetime reverts by testament to his stepdaughter, and when she arrives with her accountant the disappearance of the drawing is immediately detected. Veronica Thwale diverts attention by suggesting that a gardener's child has taken it, and when Sebastian makes no denial, his degradation and its consequences begin. The child's family is accused, and in revenge poisons old Mrs. Gamble's dog. (The death of the dog, of course, echoes the dying dog in *Eyeless in Gaza* and, by arousing Sebastian's first guilt, presages his conversion.) Sebastian goes to Bruno about his predicament, and Bruno forces Weyl to give up the drawing. That night Veronica Thwale visits Sebastian to take his virginity as her prize; it is not the 'gay ethereal intoxication' of love he has imagined but, as the sexual act so often appears in Huxley's novels, 'a maniac struggling in the musky darkness with another maniac'. Next morning, going down to tell Bruno that everything has gone well, he arrives in time to see him being taken away by the Fascist police; Weyl has laid false accusations. The next day Sebastian leaves Florence, and we do not encounter him again until after his conversion, in which Bruno, exiled and dying in France, plays his appropriate role.

Meanwhile, chapter of fantasy alternating with chapter of 'real' life, Eustace goes through death as those he has left on earth follow their various pursuits, including the séances which Mrs. Gamble organizes to establish contact with him. The process he undergoes is a passage out of consciousness towards annihilation of the self, imaged in the clear light of the void to which he advances; the light is painful for his unprepared spirit, and time and again he rejects it until the self re-asserts itself, and at last, through a nightmare of death and copulation, Eustace realizes his reincarnation as child of the art dealer Weyl. He has chosen his parents according to the limitations of his past life. One of Huxley's few experimental pieces of writing, this series of chapters is also one of the rare modern attempts to render into fiction the process that may take place if consciousness does indeed persist after death. If not entirely convincing, it is certainly more plausible than the description of Anthony's meditation at the end of *Eyeless in Gaza*, and is so precisely because Eustace resists the light; this rejection fills his afterworld with the luxuriance of concrete images on which, rather than on the most beautiful of abstract concepts, literature is nourished.

Time Must Have a Stop is attractive–an adjective one can rarely apply to Huxley's fiction. It is so in part from the lyricism of adolescent frustration in the early chapters, dominated by the strange but compelling image of the little Primitive Methodist chapel near John Barnack's flat:

> And now here it confronted him [Sebastian muses], faithfully itself, the lower part of its façade suffused with the greenish gaslight of the street lamp in front of it, and the upper part growing dimmer and dimmer as it mounted from the light, until the last spiky pinnacles of Victorian brickwork hung there, opaquely black against the foggy darkness of the London sky. Bright little details and distinctions fading upwards into undifferentiated mystery; a topless darkness of the London sky. . . . Hideous, in the daytime, beyond belief. But an hour later, when the lamps were lit, as lovely and significant as anything he had ever seen.

The novel is attractive also from the iridescent light with which Huxley's nostalgia for Europe in the late years of the war bathed the Tuscan scene he had once known so well, a scene in which the parallel vision to that of the transfigured London chapel suddenly breaks in with its intimations of a higher order of consciousness as Sebastian and Eustace drive at night past Brunelleschi's masterpiece of Santa Maria del Fiore.

> Sebastian . . . saw great cliffs of marble and, above the cliffs, an enormous dome floating up into the sky and darkening, as it rose, from the faint lamplight that still lingered about its base into a mystery more impenetrable than the night itself. It was the transfiguration, not of a little squalor this time, but of a vast harmonious magnificence.
> 'Light first,' said Eustace, pointing a bloated finger that travelled upwards as he spoke, 'then darkness.'

Eustace, of course, is not only stating the two elements of the Huxleian cosmogony; he is also, unconsciously, foretelling the experience of supernatural light and darkness which that very night he will encounter.

Most of all, what distinguishes *Time Must Have a Stop* is the gentler attitude Huxley adopts towards his characters. These are not, for the most part, the grotesque damned, triumphed over by the one true saintly man, such as we encounter in *After Many a Summer*. There is indeed, only one character completely negative and therefore completely damned, and that is Veronica Thwale. In true Circean fashion, she is the constant temptress who holds Sebastian long under her spell by playing on his besetting sensuality. It is she who will force him to betray his dying wife as Myra Viveash forced Gumbril to betray Emily and Mary Amberley forced Anthony to betray Brian Foxe. But there is an unmitigated inhumanity about Veronica which even Myra and Mary lacked, and with Dr. Obispo she stands among Huxley's characters as a supreme example of what he will call in *The Perennial Philosophy* 'that literally diabolic wickedness which, together with sanctity, is one of the distinguishing marks of the human species'.

Eustace, the very type of that weak humanity which cannot take the ultimate step into non-attachment, is portrayed with exceptional sympathy. He is, indeed, gluttonous and gross, and this condition, which precipitates his death, is the price of his physical self-indulgence; karma operates in this life as well as after. At the same time, he is kind and thoughtful, good-natured, generous. His mind is closed to spiritual teachings, but open to intellectual matters and especially to aesthetic beauty. He has reached at least the lower steps of the staircase of understanding. For, as *The Perennial Philosophy* will argue: 'The poet, the nature lover, the aesthete are granted apprehensions of reality analogous to those vouchsafed to the selfless contemplative; but because they have not troubled to make themselves perfectly selfless, they are incapable of knowing the divine Beauty in its fulness, as it is in itself.' Such men, Huxley insists, are 'idolaters'; when Eustace refuses to enter the light, it is not because he is rejecting Nirvana like the Bodhisattvas to return and aid suffering beings, but because there are beauties of this earth he cannot leave behind.

Eustace's difficulty in accepting the mystical philosophy even when Bruno tries to instruct him is linked with his physique and his nature, for it is in *Time Must Have a Stop*, more than in any other of his novels, that Huxley puts to fictional use the theory of the correspondences between physical and psychological types he had learnt from W. H. Sheldon, whom he met in Chicago in 1937. Sheldon's three main types were the viscerotonic–self-indulgent, good-natured, gregarious and inclined to love art; the somatotonic–vigorous, heavily-boned, energetic, impulsive and domineering; the cerebrotonic–slightly built, delicate in health, hypersensitive, inclined to solitude, and intellectual. All three types are clearly represented in *Time Must Have a Stop*– Eustace as the viscerotonic, John Barnack as the somatotonic, and

Sebastian and Bruno Rontini as variations of the cerebrotonic. According to Sheldon's theory, as Huxley develops it, the cerebrotonics have less difficulty than the other types—who are more inclined to material attachments or to power—in attaining the unitive knowledge of the mystic.

The gentleness with which Huxley treats characters like Eustace and John Barnack has in fact a didactic rather than a fictional purpose. He is telling us that, no matter how generous and aesthetically sensitive Eustace may be, no matter how genuine John's ideals may be, these virtues avail little. Goodness, to amend Nurse Cavell, is not enough. It is goodness in addition to something more that we must gain if we are to reach spiritual fulfilment and, through enlightenment, influence even social and political life in a positive direction. And here we are forced to admit that, though the Epilogue which ends the novel with its glimpse of Sebastian fourteen years later may seem fictionally superfluous, it is didactically necessary. For it is here that Sebastian lays down his 'minimum working hypothesis', a manifesto of essential mystical beliefs which parallels in fiction the doctrines of *The Perennial Philosophy*.

> That there is a Godhead or Ground, which is the unmanifested principle of all manifestation.
> That the Ground is transcendent and immanent.
> That it is possible for human beings to love, know and, from virtually, to become actually identified with the Ground.
> That to achieve this unitive knowledge, to realize this supreme identity, is the final end and purpose of human existence.
> That there is a Law or Dharma, which must be obeyed, a Tao or Way, which must be followed, if men are to achieve their final end.
> That the more there is of I, me, mine, the less there is of the Ground; and that consequently the Tao is a Way of humility and compassion, the Dharma a Law of mortification and self-transcending awareness. . . .

It is fitting that Sebastian rather than Bruno should voice these principles, for he is the last form of that fictional persona which develops and changes from Denis Stone through Gumbril, Walter Bidlake and Chelifer, at first convinced of the world's meaninglessness as Huxley was; then—with Anthony—moves to conversion with his creator; and finally, with Sebastian, reaches the assurance of knowing what he is seeking even if he has not yet found it. The heavily reiterative common elements in this chameleon persona, including the weakness that makes him betray others and invariably leaves him at some time the prey to Circe and her degrading power, must mirror some traumatic experience in Huxley's past, real or hallucinatory, but I have found no clue to the particular source of this physio-psycho-logical parallelism; the spiritual parallels between the author and the changing persona, which in the end most interested Huxley, are amply documented.

2

Huxley lived almost twenty years after the publication of *Time Must Have a Stop*. In that time he wrote only three works of fiction, and two of them were brief novelle. It was as an expository writer that he now mainly functioned, producing occasionally the hybrid of biography, history and psychology already represented by *Grey Eminence*, but often contenting himself with the restatement of meta-physical or quasi-scientific ideas which he had found useful in his search for truth. Huxley was not an original philosopher, and he presented no spiritual or scientific insight others had not already offered, but he had the gift of clear and attractive exposition.

The Perennial Philosophy is one of Huxley's key books, not in the sense that it presents a new revelation, a seminal system, but in the more literal sense that it introduces us to the books and thinkers who influenced his later thoughts and his later novels. It is really an antho-logy of the mystics linked by explanatory commentary. Huxley makes no pretensions to being an adept; there is neither here nor anywhere in his writings the claim to have experienced once (as he granted to Pascal) the ecstasy that leads to the unitive knowledge of God. To a French correspondent he said, while he was working on the book, 'Quant à moi, je commence à pénétrer dans la fôret,' and by that he meant that he had reached the third age in Hindu counting, the stage when a man tries to understand 'nature, things and his own essence'; the fourth stage, that of the man who has detached himself from desire and lives in the eternity that can be seen even in temporal things, lay before him. The deliberate humility with which he approached his task is suggested in *The Perennial Philosophy* itself when, talking of the saints, he remarks: 'The rest of us are not yet in a spiritual position to do more than accept their findings on faith.'

It is necessary to stress this point so that the wrong kind of impor-tance shall not be attached to *The Perennial Philosophy*. Huxley in-tended it as an aid to those interested in mystical religion, a gathering of the thoughts of the masters, largely in their own words. He speaks with that mingling of dogmatism and humility which marks the recent convert, but his aim is to make the ideas available rather than to exhibit his own literary or philosophical powers.

It is in this sense especially that *The Perennial Philosophy* resembles the small book which Huxley completed during one of the intervals when *Time Must Have a Stop* was not going well. *The Art of Seeing* was written and published in 1942. It related the story of the partial cure of the eye disease which in the summer of 1939 made Huxley fear the possible return of blindness. At this time he heard by chance of the method of eye training W. H. Bates had devised, and began to receive therapy from one of Bates's students. The treatment was successful; Huxley's sight improved considerably, though not permanently, for by 1951 he was having difficulty once again, and this continued intermittently, palliated at times by other treatments, until his death.

These later troubles were unforeseen in 1940 when Huxley realized how much the Bates method had helped him, and was anxious that those in a similar predicament should have the same opportunity. The regular oculists refused to accept the Bates method; they preferred mechanical correction of vision with lenses to recovery of vision through eye training. Wide publicity was needed if the method were to be made available to many people, and Huxley gave his time to preparing a book that would set out in clear and simple language the philosophy and practice of the Bates method. Judging from the number of references to *The Art of Seeing* that appear in his letters, he was more pleased with this little book and its success than with that of his most ambitious novels.

What especially attracted Huxley was Bates's assumption that eye disease and defects of vision are not merely physical in origin, and that as far as they are physical they arise usually from failure to allow the eye to function properly. His treatment—or training—was based on a conception of 'the unitary nature of the human organism', with mind and body constantly acting and reacting upon each other. This made him conceive of seeing not as a simple physical operation, but as a combination of sensing, performed by the eyes and the nervous system, and perceiving, performed by the mind and 'related to the individual's accumulated experiences, in other words, to memory'.

Such a view was closely related to Alexander's theories of the interconnection of bodily and mental functions; like Alexander, Bates invented physical exercises but recognized that these were useless without a proper training of the mind in perception and memory. Huxley saw this discipline of remembering 'as an aid to mind-body relaxation, and, through mind-body relaxation, to vision', and he brought the idea of non-attachment to the fruits of our labour even into this context.

> In seeing, as in all other activities of mind and mind-body [he remarked], it is essential, if we are to do our work adequately, that we should cultivate an attitude of confidence combined with indifference–confidence in our capacity to do the job, and indifference to possible failure.

In *The Art of Seeing*, one understandably finds great use of the duality of darkness and light which figures so prominently in Huxley's work; it is at these extremities–he suggests–that the patient may gain most benefit. The shutting and covering of the eyes, reinforced by the injunction to 'imagine black', is one aspect of the treatment; on the other hand, the patient is taught not to fear light, and even to go out into strong sunlight with no dark glasses and to read from pages illuminated by the sun. For the eye is 'an organ of light', and light is 'its element'.

Vision is a word of multiple meanings; the inner eye has its own darkness and light; and the disciplines of mysticism, which all have their physical manifestations, are directed–in that phrase from Blake which Huxley so loved to quote–towards 'cleansing the doors of perception'. The analogy was not lost on Huxley, and he regarded the Bates method not merely as a form of therapy, but also as a link in the chain of interconnected bodily and mental disciplines by which man could gain a healthy body and a mind receptive to intellectual light; both were necessary to embark on the quest of the perennial philosophy.

The Perennial Philosophy had been in Huxley's mind for some time before he completed it in the spring of 1945. He first mentioned the idea during 1942 to Julian as a piece of 'more or less philosophical writing' dedicated to isolating 'the only common element, at once theoretical and practical, speculative and devotional, in the various religions of the world'; in other words, 'non-dogmatic religious mysticism'. Thinking in mid war, he stressed the practical advantages of a religion concerned with 'the eternal present' over the future-oriented religions and quasi-religions (e.g. Communism and Nazism) which always sacrifice what is for what will be. The great advantage of mysticism, he remarked, trimming his argument to a correspondent who was after all a scientist, is that 'it is empirical and does not depend on revelation or history.'

To other correspondents, Huxley was less communicative, stressing the anthological character of the book, reducing his own role to that of a commentator 'sufficiently cautious to avoid long-drawn meta-physical disquisitions and logical arguments', and remarking that forty per cent of the book would be by people in whom he had more confidence than in himself, since they were saints and often geniuses.

Such comments provide a just preview of *The Perennial Philosophy*, whose contents Huxley gathered with the help of the Vedanta Society, of which he was a sceptical member, and of Gerald Heard and other luminaries of Trabuco College; an assiduously dispersed legend asserts that he actually wrote the book at Trabuco College, but there is no evidence of this in his published letters. In any case, he had been familiar for many years with much of the material he used – some of it he had known since his undergraduate days – and even his com-mentary emerged out of an internal dialogue which had been going on for a decade.

The one direction in which Huxley positively undervalued his own contribution is that of style. The writings of mystics are notoriously difficult for non-mystics to follow, partly because of the esoteric tradition which demands that certain truths should be only obliquely stated, and partly because literary eloquence is not a necessary ac-companiment of religious insight; few of the writers Huxley quotes are as clear as William Law or as eloquent as Thomas Traherne, and with the Buddhist and Hindu writers there are unfamiliar ways of expressing religious truths which require either special knowledge or effective paraphrase to be comprehensible. Huxley's commentaries and transitional passages admirably perform the function of relating and explaining where necessary the writings of many different schools of mysticism – Christian, Moslem, Hindu and Buddhist. In the process of writing them he was influenced by the condensed aphoristic form of statement which one finds so often among the mystics, and one might compile out of this volume a small and useful anthology of Huxley's own maxims.

The hundreds of quotations that form the basis of *The Perennial Philosophy* illuminate both the range and the limitations of Huxley's reading. He is especially knowledgeable in the Christian mystics, quoting many and understanding clearly their relationship to the wider Christian tradition. Of the rich contribution of Jewish tradition, however, he displays no knowledge, and among Moslem mystics he quotes only a few of the more celebrated Sufis. He admits that he 'is not competent to discuss the doctrinal differences between Buddhism and Hinduism', and his knowledge of the texts of both religions is obviously less complete than it became in later years; the mystical elements in Jainism and Sikhism he ignores completely. He also appears imperfectly aware of the historical background of Hindu mysticism, since he clearly does not know – or if he does fails to tell – that Shankara, the famous Vedantist, from whom he quotes copiously, may have been an Indian Father Joseph, whose actions negated his spiritual insights; there is a strong and reasonably authenticated tradition in Kerala that Shankara was responsible for the particularly rigid caste system, with its vast dividend in human misery, that flourished until recent years in the states of the Malabar Coast.

History, indeed, is not one of the strengths of The Perennial Philosophy. It might be argued that in a work discussing doctrines of the 'everlasting now' it is not a necessary strength, if it were not for the fact that Huxley makes an attempt to be historical which simply does not go far enough to be useful. For example, he talks briefly and vaguely about the possibility of a kind of proto-mysticism existing among primitive man, but he does not provide any facts or quotations from the considerable literature on shamanism which illuminates the nebulous borderland between mysticism and occultism. He also treats Dionysius the Areopagite as if he marked the beginnings of Christian mysticism, yet Dionysius was only a synthetist of earlier strains. Even more rashly, Huxley asserts that it was mainly through Dionysius that 'medieval Christendom established contact with Neoplatonism and thus, at several removes, with the metaphysical thought and discipline of India'. Direct contact between Alexandria and India in fact existed not later than the 1st century B.C.; by the 2nd century A.D. Christianity had reached the Malabar Coast (where Buddhism then flourished) and the reverse process had taken place, so that something was known among Alexandrian Christians about Buddhism, long before Dionysius wrote. Furthermore, the links between mysticism and the antique mysteries, particularly Orphism, are more than semantic; a mysticus, after all, was originally one initiated into the mysteries. Huxley completely neglects this obvious line of filiation.

Within its limitations, however, *The Perennial Philosophy* is penetrating and informative as a theoretical exposition of mystical religion in its various forms, laying a particular emphasis on the common elements. The nature of God, immanent and transcendental, is considered in mystical terms, and the paths of work, devotion and spiritual knowledge by which man can approach him are charted. The great paradoxes are stated—Grace and Free Will, Good and Evil, Time and Eternity—and given their position in the unifying order. And, with masterly inevitability, having led us through a series of chapters that examines every question the enquirer is likely to raise, from miracles to ritual, from prayer to mortification, Huxley reaches the conclusion that, far from being a vague doctrine of withdrawal, mysticism in fact equips men better to handle the affairs of this world; it enlightens action, relates it to present needs rather than future ambitions and inspires social activity with divine compassion. For, as Huxley ends, it is the mystics who, 'dying to themselves, become capable of perpetual inspiration and so are made the instruments through which divine grace is mediated to those whose unregenerate nature is impervious to the delicate touches of the Spirit'.

There are many aspects of this exposition that invite criticism. Huxley's argument tends often to be strictly analogical. He proceeds thus from the operation of the human mind and body to the operation of the divine Will, and so falls into an anthropomorphism which always remains a shadow in the background of his argument, and which emerges in the peculiar doctrine of the Fall that he enunciates when he attempts to weld evolution on to the perennial philosophy.

His argument is that on the biological level all species but man have reached the terminal point of evolution because at one time they succumbed to the temptation of specialization. This is for them the Fall; they can proceed no farther. Only man, the sole generalizing species, kept open his evolutionary opportunities, and thus biologically was not involved in the Fall. As a result human individuals—and human individuals alone—'now possess the momentous power of choosing either selflessness and union with God, or the intensification of separate selfhood in ways and to a degree, which are entirely beyond the ken of the lower animals'.

It is a provocative idea, but if we accept it Huxley's theory of the unified tradition of the perennial philosophy falls in ruins, since such a view of the Fall is repugnant to Hinduism, Jainism, Buddhism and all the eastern faiths whose concept of evolution extends into the

spiritual realm and, through metempsychosis, conceives the possibility of an advance in a series of existences from species to species
towards enlightenment. The very basis of Mahayanist Buddhism is the
idea that universal compassion, mediated from the spiritual to the
physical realm through the Bodhisattva Avalokiteshvara, aims at the
eventual passage beyond suffering and into the Clear Light of the Void
of all living beings, not of man alone.

One can argue with many other statements which show Huxley in
an unguardedly dogmatic mood. For example, he asserts that according to the perennial philosophy 'the aim and purpose of human
life is the unitive knowledge of God'. I would question, to begin with,
whether this is what Buddhist mystics believe: Buddha himself avoided
all talk of the purpose of human life or of the nature of God, and set
the very pragmatic aim of discovering the nature and causes of
suffering and the way to avoid it. 'I show you sorrow, and the ending
of sorrow,' was the sum of his claims. Huxley's assertion approximates
to the beliefs of many Christian mystics, but it is still subject to a
criticism he does not choose to apply. For though it seems evident
that there is a pattern in the shaping of the universe, and that an intelligence inspires the pattern, there is no reason to assume that the
mystic's experience is a knowledge of that intelligence or that the
purpose of human existence is an ecstasy that may have no meaning
beyond itself. There is a curious presumption in the inverted anthropo-
centrism that lurks in the supposition that the aim and purpose of
human life has any direct relation to God. For surely that is a way of
constraining God to human wills, and hence a form of magic which
differs from other forms in having a spiritual rather than a material
objective.

This leads one to a final point that will have occurred to many who
have encountered teachers who claim to be adepts of mystical cults,
whether European or Asian. It is the paradoxical result of the attempt
by the self to will the self out of existence. Consciously pursued, this
leads to an increased rather than a diminished preoccupation with the
ego, a preoccupation that leads often to the spiritual pride from which
the guru characters in Huxley's novels so palpably suffer, the ineffable
certainty of rectitude which humility merely disguises. At every stage
in the mystical process, is not the will to escape, from desire and the
self, itself a desire initiated by the self? The paradox seems insoluble,
and one is led to ask whether the pure selfless mystic in fact ever
existed. Is not man by nature imperfect, and hence doomed to mere

approximation even in his urge to sainthood? That such doubts developed in Huxley's own mind was shown in the extraordinary essay on Maine de Biran which he wrote four years after the publication of *The Perennial Philosophy*.

CHAPTER ELEVEN

The Diabolic Element

I

It was not without personal knowledge that in 1956 Huxley wrote 'visionary experience is not always blissful. It is sometimes terrible. There is hell as well as heaven.' This, he tells us, happens when the visionary has not reached the unitive knowledge of the divine Ground which is the attainment of the true mystic. So far as we know, Huxley never enjoyed that ultimate beatification, and it is doubtful if he even enjoyed anything that might be called visionary in the spiritual sense before, in 1953, he began to take mescalin; even then his experiences were not markedly different from the epiphanies which many people have been vouchsafed without considering themselves exceptional.

In thinking of Huxley as a writer, we cannot speculate far beyond what he sets down on paper, yet even here it is evident that the pre-occupations of his books go through alternations–covering obviously far longer periods than the experiences of visionaries–in which the light that appears to shine in *The Perennial Philosophy* and in the last pages of *Time Must Have a Stop* recedes, and we are once again in a cave of darkness where the scanty luminescence picks out a baleful countenance like the Holy Face of Lucca. It is the face of negation, of decay, of death; it is the face of time from which Huxley can never escape.

During the years that follow the publication of *The Perennial Philosophy*, his books are melancholy, foreboding, haunted by demons. Shortly after *The Perennial Philosophy* he writes, for the pacifists of the Fellowship of Reconciliation, a short book on the alarming future that the world enters as the war draws to an end: it is published in 1946 as *Science, Liberty and Peace*. The following year his fears of the possibility of civilization being destroyed by nuclear war lead him into writing that grim novella, *Ape and Essence*. By 1951 he completes what is perhaps the last of his major works, that horrifying study of prejudice and superstition, *The Devils of Loudun*. And spanning the period there are the essays which he collected in 1950 under the title of *Themes and Variations*, the first of them written in 1943, the last in the year of publication.

What distinguishes *Themes and Variations* is its tacit admission that sainthood is somewhat more rare and remote than *The Perennial Philosophy* suggested. These essays are mainly studies of men who have passed into the dark night of the soul but have never reached the full light whose glimmerings they perceive at the end of that vast metaphysical tunnel. They are, all of them, writers and artists—Goya and El Greco, Piranesi and the French philosopher Maine de Biran—and one has the sense that in considering their cases Huxley is in part analysing his own inability to escape from time and its realm of darkness.

The principal essay—almost a book in itself since it fills more than half the volume—is 'Variations on a Philosopher', the study of Maine de Biran. Living from 1766 to 1824, Biran served in Louis XVI's life guards, survived the Revolution, defied Napoleon as a member of the Emperor's Corps Legislatif, and eventually gained public office under the Restoration, to die, prematurely aged, in opposition to the ultra-Conservativism of Charles X.

Huxley treats Maine de Biran as one of those whose inclinations turned them towards mysticism, but who never made that escape from the world of time towards which their philosophy directed them. The case of Biran was neither so dramatic nor so reprehensible as that of Father Joseph. There are no indications that his official life led him into committing great harms, and the conflict his diaries record is that between his metaphysical inclinations and his weakness for the vanities of the social world. It was not that he even enjoyed those vanities, for he was diffident in the extreme and his poor health made pleasure more often than not a punishment. But he slavishly followed the round that was prescribed, and in his diary recorded the qualms of conscience he experienced for being so taken up with it. He set out to analyse his motives, and his greatest quality was the remorseless analytical logic which he applied as an introspective psychologist. He sought to shape his philosophy on an actual existence—his own.

There is a great deal of the novelist's art in the way Huxley treats Biran. We are introduced to him first through an imaginary sketch of him—taking the waters at some spa of the Midi—which sets his character;

next we are given enough biography to set him in time and place; then Huxley proceeds to consider his patterns of behaviour, his role in the world, and the inner man whom the behaviour and the role so deceptively present.

Apart from the fascination of the personality revealed in Biran's diary, Huxley was drawn to this obscure philosopher because Biran had reacted against the philosophers of the Enlightenment in the same way as Huxley reacted against the fashionable materialists of his own time. As a connoisseur of the intermittences and discontinuities of human life, he was also intrigued by a man in whom these tendencies existed to the degree of extravagance, and yet who was moved by a single-minded desire to understand himself and to establish in some way his relationship to the universe.

The most depressing lesson which Biran's case reveals is the dependence of the mind on bodily states. Wavering between ill health and a condition of partial well-being, Biran noticed: 'Certain bodily states produce good dispositions of the mind. Sometimes these dispositions have led me towards God; they were not for the body, though they came from the body.' But, to the end of his life, he never acquired the true contemplative's power of shutting out distractions to maintain his mind on a course of meditation. His was a case of the difficulty which people of ill health experience in following the mystical path, and Huxley's own physical disabilities may have increased his interest in this well-documented instance of the philosopher enslaved by his body and his nerves.

The essay on Biran is also a criticism of the inadequacies of introspective psychology as a means of gaining the ends of the perennial philosophy. For if we are concerned only with our own thoughts, we are aware merely of our bodies and our conscious minds; it is from outside that the operations of subconscious urges are likely to be perceived. Moreover, as Huxley points out, Biran's lack of interest in mesmerism, the fashionable form which hypnotism took in the early nineteenth century, showed an unawareness of those states of consciousness in which the mind becomes susceptible to influences from without and hence more open to the intuitions that lead towards the apprehension of mystical truths.

And though, as Huxley remarks, a great deal of human life–including sleep and sickness, sexual experiences and old age–takes us into a kind of timeless limbo if not into eternity itself, the fact is that even the most enlightened cannot live wholly outside history. 'One of the many reasons for the bewildering and tragic character of human existence is the fact that social organization is at once necessary and fatal.' And so the philosopher has to make his obeisance to time and, if he is to see human existence as a whole, to observe—as neither Biran nor Huxley in their respective times could avoid doing—the worlds of society and politics whose operations continue no matter what the actions or inactions of the saints.

But even here, Huxley shows, man is tempted to be unhistorical, to slip mentally from the stream of time, and to see his own period out of the historical perspective that will seem evident to later generations. Biran was unaware of the industrial revolution, and though he prophesied that the result of the political revolutions of his time would be an increase in tyranny, he had no conception of how the development of the machine would breed the cult of efficiency, which gives tyranny an extra-political dimension, nor did he foresee the growth of nationalism which accompanied the decline of Christianity. Here Huxley's concern with the urgencies of his own world breaks through, and into the very centre of 'Variations on a Philosopher' he introduces a plea for decentralization and co-operation so as to reduce the possibilities and the temptations of power. Yet, having just read George Orwell's newly published *1984*, he feels the pessimism of *Brave New World* reinforced, and concludes:

> At the present time, unfortunately, all signs point, not to decentralization and the abolition of man-herders, but rather to a steady increase in the power of the Big Shepherd and his oligarchy of bureaucratic dogs, to a growth in the size, the complexity, the machine-like efficiency and rigidity of social organizations, and to a completer deification of the State, accompanied by a completer reification, or reduction to thing-hood, of individual persons.

Biran, Huxley suggests, was genuinely conscious of the light within him, and yet his chronic sickness led him into dualism, into the Platonic division between the body which is evil and the soul, which is good; the unitive knowledge he never gained. Huxley's portrait of this agonized imperfect man, like his portrait of Father Joseph, carries far more conviction than his fictional reconstructions of saintly gurus of impossible wisdom and virtue.

Of the remaining essays, most in one way or another stress the darkness of the human way. 'Variations on a Baroque Tomb' is a study of the emphasis on the physical presence of death in baroque mortuary sculptures, which Huxley sees as the sign of an age when the belief in progress and man's perfectibility was weak. This recognition of the reality of death, when the social being is shed and man stands alone before the light, Huxley considers praiseworthy, for the consolations of philosophy are earned at the price of experiencing its desolations, and man can know himself only by learning the worst truths about his destiny.

Still, there are times when to know the worst truths can mean to remain in darkness. As Huxley shows in a fine essay on Piranesi's sombre series of engravings, *The Prisons*, here is a case of works that have reference only to what is negative in the depth of human souls, 'to *acedia* and confusion, to nightmare and *angst*, to incomprehension and panic bewilderment'. No spiritual light glimmers through the insane mechanisms of Piranesi's nightmares. Nor is there any sign of that light in the terrible works of Goya, which present the grim metaphors of human destiny familiar to the world's great religions, but reveal none of the consoling ways to the ending of sorrow those religions have also shown.

Even in the works of El Greco, to whom he returns in 'Variations on El Greco', a companion piece to the 'Meditation' written in 1931, he is disturbed by a strange duality. El Greco has studied Dionysius the Areopagite, and appears to have practised some form of meditation. Huxley sees his paintings as genuine attempts to express mystical aspirations. Yet he finds them, 'for all their extraordinary beauty . . . strangely oppressive and disquieting', filled with 'an agitation wholly incompatible with the spiritual life of which he had read in the pages of Dionysius'. He talks of the closeness and density of those El Greco heavens in which one could hardly swing a metaphorical cat, and concludes that in the great Cretan painter 'the divine Spirit is over-ridden by a sub-conscious longing for the consolations of some ineffable uterine state.'

Yet the essay ends with the ironic twist which Huxley liked to give his stories, and one is astonished, after so much discussion of the negative duality of El Greco's paintings, to find him expressing the ultimately paradoxical view that: 'Out of the visceral forms and cramped spaces, imposed upon him by a part of his being beyond his voluntary control, he was able to create a new kind of order and perfection, and, through this order and perfection, to re-affirm the possibility of man's union with the Spirit–a possibility which the raw materials of his pictures had seemed to rule out.' Huxley has already argued so capably for the opposite viewpoint that we are left, at the end, unconvinced. We remain under the impression that, like Maine de Biran, El Greco was unable ever completely to transcend the organic and accept the supremacy of spirit.

Themes and Variations, indeed, is a record of spiritual casualties, of the gulf that may lie between the truths of art and the truths of religion, and of the fragility of that life of the spirit which the mere weakness of the flesh can irremediably imperil. If *The Perennial Philosophy* is a chart of the Way, *Themes and Variations* is a record of its pitfalls.

2

The unity of *Themes and Variations*, with its reflections on the religious elements in certain forms of literature and art, is broken at the end with what seems at first unwarranted abruptness by the completely different character of the final piece, 'The Double Crisis', a long essay published first in the *World Review* in 1948, in which Huxley, ahead of intellectual fashion, argues that the human crisis of our age exists 'on two levels—an upper level of political and economic crisis and a lower level of demographic and ecological crisis'. In 1948 the upper-level crisis received much attention; of the low-level crisis, as Huxley remarked, 'hardly anything is heard in the press, on the radio or at the more important international conferences.' Only in the Sixties, indeed, did this crisis become a matter of universal popular concern in the civilized world. Thus in 'The Double Crisis', as in the futurist speculations of *Brave New World*, Huxley showed an exceptional foresight.

The years between 1945 and 1948 were, indeed, a time when Huxley returned to topical issues, but on a different level from his pacifist activities a decade before. Having once learnt that the writer who enters a political movement is doomed to the intellectual frustration that inevitably accompanies organizational activity, he chose to approach the problems of his time from a detached and philosophic viewpoint. He adopted no specific partisan position, but he remained a pacifist by conviction, and in terms of practical politics he remained near to those anarchists who had eschewed violence and concentrated their efforts on the study of self-governing social mechanisms. He even shared their disinclination to make plans for the future, for the perennial philosophy stressed the value of trying to live in the eternal now, while his studies of history and of contemporary political events had taught him that movements oriented to the paradise-to-come were likely to destroy whatever approximation to paradise existed in the present.

Science, Liberty and Peace, in which he endeavoured to deal realistically with contemporary predicaments, was written under the immediate shadow of the war, in the year 1945. Then, despite the tragedy of Hiroshima, it was hoped that great post-war conferences would construct a more peaceful, just and hopeful world. The early atom bombs had called in question the ends to which the work of scientists had been put, and what concerned Huxley most was to find a way in which their discoveries might be turned to positive uses. He wanted, as he told Victoria Ocampo, to say 'some things that need saying, absurdly simple things such as "the Sabbath is made for man, not man for the Sabbath", things which men of science like to forget because it is such enormous fun enquiring into the processes of nature and designing bigger and better gadgets that they do not wish to realize that human beings are being sacrificed to applied science'.

It was to applied science that he turned his main attention, since, as he said, 'basic research is essentially disinterested'; it is with the way it is used that we must concern ourselves. In simple terms and a functional expository style–rather like that of *The Art of Seeing*–Huxley considered the various ways in which science and technology had assisted capitalists and governments to establish their increasingly pervasive rule over mankind.

Science had contributed to the sheer physical power of the state by creating more efficient war machines, more foolproof systems of coercion; it was now virtually impossible to resist an established government successfully by the use of violence, even if that were morally acceptable. Science had also increased the powers of persuasion through encouraging the popular addiction to newspapers and the radio (television was still in the experimental stages); the spread of free compulsory education, contrary to the expectations of many of its originators, had contributed to the susceptibility of the masses to propaganda. Science and technology favoured the growth of centralized power by encouraging mass production and distribution, and–through the vagaries of technological unemployment–by creating areas of insecurity which made the workers dependent on welfare and therefore even more at the mercy of the state. Even the trade unions had been affected by the trend towards gigantism.

As important as the concrete results of the prostitution of science to political and economic centralization was the change in mental climate produced by the illusion that science held the solution to every problem. In fact, as Huxley points out, the very processes of science, which operates by abstraction, induce a simplification of reality because there are so many aspects of existence which the kind of 'nothing-but' philosophy based merely on science is bound to ignore (among them of course the goals of mystical religion). It was confidence in science that led the Victorians to develop a facile philosophy of progressivism, which Huxley regards as a cardinal heresy. Faith in the future, he argues, is always the enemy to freedom in the present. The cult of progress involves man in *hubris*, the sin of pride which leads him always to expect something for nothing, represented in the present age by his squandering of the world's irreplaceable natural resources. Huxley calls on men to abandon 'the unknowable Utopian future' and to find their ends in 'the timeless eternity of the Inner Light'.

With the cult of progress, men should abandon the religion of nationalism, which not only breeds wars but consolidates the structure of power, since national rivalries allow governments to maintain their control over individuals through conscription, and to use armaments as a means of assuaging industrial unrest. Once power is established, it is rarely abandoned willingly.

> The appetite for power grows with every successive satisfaction of that most alluring and pernicious of all the lusts. Against the temptation to abuse power there is no armour except sanctity.

(Even sanctity, as the career of Gandhi showed, is in fact no real armour.) There is no easy optimism in Huxley's proposals to change this situation. He suggests that *satyagraha* is the only means of physical resistance to governmental power, and that we can largely counter propaganda by abstaining from attending to the mass media. Scientists can play their part by both negative and positive action. Negatively they can refuse to take part in the destructive application of scientific discoveries. Positively they can organize internationally to establish a 'professional policy', administered by 'an international organization of scientific workers'. In practical terms, they can turn their research to establishing the economic foundations of maximum self-government, which means the greatest degree of self-sufficiency in industry and agriculture and a society based on individual small ownership and localized co-operative communities. This involves research into small-scale machinery, into foods, into forms of energy – such as sun and wind – that will make men independent of atomic power (which Huxley regards as a perilous temptation for those who enjoy political power). Anything that involves wide international arrangements he views with distrust, and world government he dismisses as a dubious panacea:

> The Pax Romana was a very uneasy affair, troubled at almost every imperial death by civil strife over the question of succession. So long as the lust for power persists as a human trait – and in persons of a certain physique and temperament this lust is overmasteringly strong – no political arrangement, however well contrived, can guarantee peace.

It is no easy optimism that emanates from *Science, Liberty and Peace*; Huxley obviously realizes how great are the odds against a majority of men or even a minority of scientists attending to his words, and he puts the minimum requirements for a desirable society because he feels they represent the only viable way to real peace, not because he thinks that way will be taken.

3

Like Dostoevsky, whom he resembled in little else, Huxley found damnation as fascinating as sanctity; it was one of the ways in which, to the end of his life, he walked in darkness as well as in light. There was, of course, the essential difference in his mind, that while the saint sought unification with the 'otherness' of God, the damned were the victims of self-generated evil, possessed by devils of their own creation. Damnation was dualism, the denial of the unity of all being, the insistence on the separateness of man from God.

It was towards sanctity that Huxley yearned; it was towards the damned that, in the years after he had written *The Perennial Philosophy*, he found himself irresistibly drawn. During this period, from 1946 to at least 1950, he was gathering material for a novel on the life of Saint Catherine of Siena, the great fourteenth-century Italian mystic; in 1950 he even went to Siena to complete his researches. But the novel was never finished, and we are unlikely to know how much of it Huxley wrote, for the notes and whatever he had written of the manuscript were destroyed in the fire that consumed his Californian home in 1961.

This novel about the life of a saint obviously aroused difficulties of creation which prevented Huxley from completing it, yet during this period he was able to write two very different books about demoniac possession. The reason, I suggest, is that Huxley, who never laid claim to the ultimate beatific vision, felt himself in the last resort incapable of reliving and describing that ecstatic withdrawal into what St. Catherine called 'the inner cell' of her knowledge of God. On the other hand, damnation and possession, because they were extreme expressions of common human flaws, he found all too familiar, all too easy to portray with the bitter pen of dark irony.

Of his two studies of possession, *Ape and Essence* was projected into a malign future, when man had abandoned himself to self-created evil; *The Devils of Loudun* was enacted in a past era in which both sanctification and damnation tended to take on the dramatic quality of the baroque. But in each case, by the adroit use of rhetorical devices, Huxley took care that we should understand clearly that the moral of his story applied as firmly to the present as to any other age. For if the beatific vision belongs to the eternal now, the experience of damnation is constant within time.

Though *Ape and Essence* was the earlier of the two books – written in 1947 and published in 1948 – it was the idea of *The Devils of Loudun* that first occurred to Huxley. His attention had been drawn while he was gathering material for *Grey Eminence* to seventeenth-century accounts of possessed nuns and an innocent priest burnt for sorcery at Loudun. The fate of Urbain Grandier, the priest, had been largely dominated by the caprice of Cardinal Richelieu, and Father Joseph had appeared briefly on the frenzied scene of demon-ridden Loudun. As early as 1942 Huxley decided it would make an excellent companion volume to *Grey Eminence*, a story – as he told one of his publishers – 'of enormous picturesqueness', containing characters who were 'absorbingly interesting'. In wartime California it was impossible to get the necessary documents, and not till 1950 did Huxley return to the subject; that year he went to France, visited the setting of the drama, and conceived it now in terms more characteristic of his later period, as a work 'exhibiting the entire gamut of the religious life from the bestial to the sublime'.

In the meantime the subject of demoniac possession had not been allowed to lie fallow in his mind; the events of World War II and the hideous prospects opened by the first use of the atomic bomb made it seem exceptionally urgent, and, before he wrote his historical study of events in Loudun three centuries ago, Huxley decided to write a futurist and anti-Utopian novella that, like *Brave New World*, could be interpreted alike as a satiric criticism of tendencies in existing society and a sardonic warning of future possibilities.

Ape and Essence, like Huxley's other novelle, differs from the novels in its brevity and thematic simplicity. Nevertheless, it is illuminating to consider it as a remote sequel to *After Many a Summer*. Its setting is California, some generations after the violently destructive nuclear holocaust of the Third World War, and much of it is enacted in a great cemetery like that which Joe Stoyte owned and operated. There is a haunting similarity of theme between the two books, suggested by the title of *Ape and Essence*, adapted from a passage in *Measure for Measure*:

> man, proud man,
> Drest in a little brief authority–
> Most ignorant of what he is most assured,
> His glassy essence–like an angry ape,
> Plays such fantastic tricks before high heaven
> As make the angels weep.

The 'glassy essence' has no Mr. Propter to speak for it in *Ape and Essence*; its presence is implied. But the ape which the fifth Earl of Gonister became is there in abundance; Lord Monboddo's theories of the essential humanity of the orang-outang are turned on their head as man is revealed to be as mischievous as the apes and far more powerful.

Fictional Huxley differed from factual Huxley in his treatment of the animal kingdom. His equation of man's negative nature to the apes is hard to reconcile with the arguments in *The Perennial Philosophy*, where he states categorically that 'moral evil' belongs to man alone. In *Ape and Essence*, however, it is the traditional literary image of the ape as a caricature of human irresponsibility and malignity that Huxley uses. Thus he makes for rhetorical purposes a subtle transference attributing what he elsewhere represents as purely human faults to the animal kingdom, and suggesting that what really distinguishes man is his spiritual capacity in opposition to his psycho-physical 'ape' self.

Perhaps in part because of the urgency of its message, *Ape and Essence* shows a further decline in Huxley's literary creativeness. It misses the directness of narrative, the psychological concentration, that were the virtues of his earlier novelle; it lacks the unity of an imagined world essential to a convincing fantasy. Like many writers after him, Huxley experiments with the application to fiction of film-writing techniques; he is only imperfectly successful, and one is perpetually aware of the contrivance with which the book has been put together. The ease of *Crome Yellow*, the dark inevitability of *Point Counter Point*, have been lost; they will not be recovered. Abdicating as an artist, Huxley has remained a good craftsman, but one of the characteristics that distinguishes craft from art is that one is aware of effort rather than vision.

Ape and Essence comes to us in the guise of a scenario, written by a Californian misanthrope whose Tudor-sounding name – William Tallis – immediately suggests withdrawal from the world of the present. The script is set within a Conradian frame of narration which enables the anonymous discoverer to set the perspective that runs from the present into the future.

It is the day of Gandhi's assassination, 30th January 1948 (a date which shows that the introductory chapter was written after the body of the novella), and 'I' is sitting in the office of the film writer Bob Briggs, hearing of his sexual adventures and misfortunes. The narrator's mind wanders sadly over the perspective of human achievement, seeing even in the geometrical art of Piero della Francesca an analogy to the totalitarian order, seeing in Gandhi another lost saint, not so negatively harmful as Father Joseph, but equally mistaken in the illusion that nationalism and the politics of power can achieve good, and too late discovering his error.

> We killed him because, after having briefly (and fatally) played the political game, he refused any longer to go on dreaming our dream of a national Order, a social and economic Beauty; because he tried to bring us back to the concrete and cosmic facts of real people and the inner Light.

As Bob (prisoner alike of his senses and of romantic illusion) and the narrator walk out through the studios, a truck loaded with film scripts on their way to the incinerator turns a corner sharply, and a few fall off. Out of curiosity the narrator picks them up. One catches his eye with a few lines of free verse.

> *Surely it's obvious.*
> *Doesn't every schoolboy know it?*
> *Ends are ape-chosen; only the means are man's. . . .*

It is a rejected script written by Tallis. The two men drive out to the edge of the desert in search of him, among the tough ascetic vegetation where a sudden epiphanous shifting of distant buttes from darkness into light (like that which occurs at the end of *Those Barren Leaves*) heralds the discovery that Tallis is dead.

It is thus against a background of Hollywood follies perpetrated in a setting of splendid natural beauty that the script of the elusive Tallis is introduced. As we read it we are expected to keep in mind the writer as well as what is written, for this is the view of a man who despises his kind: not, then, a Huxleian saint.

The script begins with a crude caricature of the modern world, in which men are seen as baboons. In *After Many a Summer* the baboons were the captives of the cold, ruthless intellect of Dr. Obispo the scientist, but here it is the intellect that is captive to the ape. A doglike Faraday runs at the heels of a purple-muzzled radio singer; collared Einsteins are servants of baboon armies.

In these preliminaries a fifth of the book passes before we reach the world of 2108 A.D., with which the novel is centrally concerned. Generations ago nuclear wars have swept the world except for New Zealand and Darkest Africa. Now, while the tribal warriors are working their way around the Mediterranean, the New Zealanders, who have regressed to the Victorian world of Huxley's childhood, are exploring the Pacific by sailing ship. A party arrives on the coast of California, and Dr. Alfred Poole, Fellow of the Royal Society of New Zealand and a virgin of thirty-eight, is captured by the survivors of nuclear destruction, who live in the ruins of Los Angeles.

He is the prisoner of a barbarian and parasitic society; the people have mutated, so that most are deformed and have regressed to the seasonal sex life of the beasts; in their condition we find the reign of Circe, that Huxleian witch, ultimately and permanently established. Since they have no industries, they live by primitive agriculture and by plundering the ruined houses and great cemeteries of California's 'Golden Age'. The tribal secular chiefs and a hierarchy of eunuch priests of Belial keep the people in subjection and ignorance, not allowed even to read, and, apart from two annual weeks of indiscriminate orgy, forbidden to indulge in sex. Children born with extreme deformities are sacrificed; 'Hots' who have normal sexual desires are buried alive if they are caught making love out of season; women are regarded as 'unclean vessels'.

This return to a barbarian dark age seems the reverse of the clean, sterile, inanely happy future of *Brave New World*, yet there are many similarities. The monstrous children, distorted by mutation, are as much the end product of scientific process as the stunted Deltas and Epsilons of Huxley's other future. The alternation of orgy and restraint is characteristic of both books, though in *Brave New World* it is secured by conditioning and in *Ape and Essence* by violence. In both societies motherhood is obscene, and marriage non-existent.

The Arch-Vicar of Belial, the most impressive personality in a novella where characters are little developed and psychological penetration is shallow, is the counterpart of Mustapha Mond in *Brave New World*; he is the cynical elder of the early Huxley novels in his most grotesque guise. Sitting in his chapel, he expounds to Dr. Poole the basic theology of the world of the damned over which he presides. As he talks, the annual sacrifice of deformed babies and the flogging of their mothers is going on outside, the crowd whipping itself up to the state of excitement that will culminate in the great annual orgy. Poole watches in horrified fascination as the Arch-Vicar – who terminates the line of Satanists that runs from Coleman through Spandrell and Obispo – presents his interpretation of history as a triumph of the diabolic principle, finally assured in the nineteenth century when the Devil fooled men into believing that Progress and Nationalism were positive goods. From that success came the great wars and revolutions that destroyed civilization and turned the earth into a realm of Belial. That man is diabolically possessed seems to the Arch-Vicar self-evident. How else explain the folly and villainy of history, the fact that man accepted and prepared his own degradation and destruction?

Dr. Poole's old-fashioned science has no answer to offer. Nor is his neo-Victorian respectability proof against the spirit of orgy. Yet during that dionysiac two weeks his sexual awakening leads him for the first time into a real personal tenderness – for Loola, a self-concealing eighteen-year-old Hot with two extra nipples. This is an interesting inversion of *Brave New World*. In that novel a savage comes into civilization, falls in love with one of the women he encounters, gets drawn into the orgiastic pattern, and destroys himself in disgust. Here it is a civilized man who comes among savages, falls in love with one of their women, becomes involved in their orgiastic pattern, but – and here lies the important difference – is neither destroyed nor destroys himself. Instead, when the Arch-Vicar presses him to accept eunuch-hood and power, he flees with Loola across the sierras and deserts to join the community of Hots near Fresno, where the reign of Belial ends. Huxley abides by his own criticism of *Brave New World*. He provides a way out into sanity. But of what sanity consists he does not tell us, and perhaps this is the novella's greatest weakness–to provide merely a gleam of improbable hope in a world which by every device at his command the author has portrayed as totally ruined. Though *Ape and Essence* ends with the fugitives well on their way to safety, and with Poole reading from Shelley's 'Adonais' about 'that Light whose smile kindles the Universe', it abides in one's memory as one of Huxley's darkest books. Its typical scene is the Los Angeles Coliseum at night, the great congregation chanting to Belial in the 'smoky and intermittent light of torches' as the children are sacrificed, while Poole and the Arch-Vicar eat fried pigs' trotters and talk of a world possessed, a world into which, as the death chant changes to the sounds of orgy, Poole looks with fascinated horror. Appropriately, the Arch-Vicar hands his guest a pair of binoculars ('Night-glasses from before the Thing') to see more clearly; indeed, it is a future seen 'through a glass, darkly'.

4

'Every now and then sensible and fundamentally decent people will embark, all of a sudden, on courses of which they themselves are the first to disapprove. In these cases the evil-doer acts as if he were possessed by some entity different from and malignantly hostile to his ordinary self.' Thus Huxley lays out the central theme of *The Devils of Loudun*. It is a study not so much of demonology as of the flaws in human beings that make them appear the victims or partners of diabolical influences. It is, I believe, one of Huxley's most remarkable books–the real termination of his career as a significant literary artist, and nearer than any other of his works to genuine tragedy.

Inexorably, once he himself has set the processes in motion, Urbain Grandier's fate moves through a forest of enmities to that point when, condemned unjustly, excruciatingly tortured and taken to the stake, he shows an exemplary heroism for which his self-indulgent life had prepared no-one; in supreme irony he is made to die as an infidel at that point when he is at last a true Christian. Equally ironically, the woman whose malice and hysteria have assured his death, the Prioress Jeanne des Anges, dies in what the world regards as a state of beatification. In these stories alone, with their Websterian juxtaposition of macabre comedy and harrowing tragedy, there are catharses deep enough to satisfy any devotee of high drama.

But Huxley is still the novelist of the Whole Truth, and that truth is attained in the final movement of the book, after Grandier has gone to his death and the tragedy proper is over. In poetic justice, many of the exorcists of the Prioress and her fellow nuns, and certain other inhabitants of Loudun whose false witness led Grandier to the flames, have died, themselves possessed by the demons of remorse. Afterwards, when the possessions continue, one of Huxley's Whole Truthers appears on the scene in the person of the Jesuit priest, Jean-Joseph Surin. Surin, a highly strung man with a lurid imagination where anything spiritual is involved, has been called in as an exorcist when the members of the other orders have failed. He succeeds eventually but not before he himself has caught the psychic contagion, has acted in the classic manner of one possessed, and has dismissed himself as damned—so damned indeed that he regards it as a sin that his actions are not evil enough to match the condemnation God has laid upon him. Eventually, Surin's possession leaves him, and, in the rigorous practice of spiritual exercises, he attains the sense of mystical fulfilment expressed with an unusual poetic evocativeness in his final work, *Questions sur l'Amour de Dieu*.

There are references in Huxley's letters which suggest that all along Surin had been his real quarry, for here, in Father Joseph's own age, was the example of a man who had gone through the darkest of the soul's nights, and had come at the end into that light of beatitude which the Grey Eminence had lost as if it were a mere *ignis fatuus* in the forest of politics. But on the way to Surin there was fascinating material that could not be neglected: the redemption of Urbain Grandier, that Renaissance clergyman, insolent, sensual, surviving more dangerously than he knew into the puritanical days of the Counter Revolution; the sinister comedy of Sister Jeanne des Anges, that most equivocal of blessed ones, obviously a more congenial subject for a satirist in fiction than Catherine of Siena, whose most interesting life went on in a private world that only her companions in beatitude could possibly conceive and then not in a manner amenable to description.

The Devils of Loudun turned in the writing into a hybrid work which combined virtually all the forms except verse and drama in which Huxley had exercised his literary abilities. It was good social and philosophic history, telling us much in detail of French provincial life in the age of Richelieu and also illuminating the strange confusions of ideas that existed when the age of faith was breaking down into the age of reason. It was biography: a multiple biography in fact whose three subjects illuminate different aspects of the religious life of their time: the ceremonial worldliness of Grandier, the superstition to which

Sister Jeanne gave such histrionic expression, and the contemplative life which Surin sought and after so many vicissitudes carried through to its appropriate conclusion. Some chapters are virtually essays in the history of witchcraft or the psychology of possession, and there is a fascinating appendix, which no student of Huxley's religio-philosophic development should fail to read, on the varieties of surrogate self-transcendence, including those unrecognized but particularly virulent forms of possession which belong to the life of politics.

All this is welded into an imaginative whole by the use of fictional techniques. Huxley is no academic biographer, following and anno-tating meticulously his given source material. Instead, he constructs the form which the story seems to require, fits into it such of the given material as he finds useful and, for the rest, invents as if he were writing a historical novel, taking us into the minds of characters who in the records may appear as little more than names and reconstructing men's motives on the evidence of action that has come down to us in shadowy form. Dozens of characters play out plausible roles, and the tragedy of Grandier, which in its bare facts seems too monstrous for a man outside the age to understand, is presented as a struggle of wills so convincing that one feels drawn into the collective mind of the time, and experi-ences the priest's last agonies as immediately as one experiences the mental agonies of characters in a Tolstoy novel. Certainly, if Huxley failed to incorporate the didactic element convincingly into his last novels, he succeeded admirably, in *The Devils of Loudun* even more than in *Grey Eminence*, in infusing the biographer's didactic craft with a novelist's imagination.

The Devils of Loudun was Huxley's last successful work of literary art, but his primary intent was far from artistic. It was to examine, in terms of an age that believed fervently in damnation, the nature of man's alienation from God. The cases of Urbain Grandier and Sister Jeanne were clear. Both of them had displayed the almost universal human urge to seek transcendence of their mere selves. Grandier, for whom religion was in the beginning a mere form, sought transcendence in sex, pursuing the role of the accomplished seducer with a calculation worthy of Dr. Obispo. Sister Jeanne, like Mary Thriplow and Grace Peddley, was really a 'Bovarist', one of those who seek to live in imitation of some being outside themselves. As little fitted for the spiritual life as Father Grandier, she amused herself and acquired a delicious notoriety by allowing her hysteria to produce those extra-ordinary symptoms which in the seventeenth century were regarded as signs of demoniac possession. But where there were demons it was believed that sorcerers were at work, and Sister Jeanne, with a malice bred of sexual desire and jealousy, accused Father Grandier of having bewitched her and the members of her convent. Many even at that time held Grandier innocent, but years before he had offended a young bishop, and that bishop had become Cardinal Richelieu, dictator of France. By that accident, and by the enemies his amorous exploits had made him in Loudun, Grandier was doomed.

It was the kind of doom that had overtaken Hutton in 'The Gioconda Smile'; Grandier was being punished horribly, but not for the sins he had committed. The experience brought out qualities in the man that he had never shown before: a steadfastness in refusing to confess to what he had not done, even under the question extraordinary; an exemplary courage in the face of pain and death; an access of personal devotion towards Christ. If Grandier did not die a saint in the tradition of the perennial philosophy, he certainly died, by any standards, a devout and at last a practising Christian.

But even when he was following the way of *l'homme moyen sensuel*, Grandier had never been one of the possessed, at least in the deeper sense. For, as Huxley says:

> On such merely carnal sins as gluttony and lust, the body imposes, by its very nature and constitution, certain limits. But however weak the flesh, the spirit is always willing. To the sins of the will and the imagination, kind nature sets no limit.

And it is these sins that lead to possession, whether it is the hysterial possession of the nuns at Loudun, or the more sinister varieties of possession, by hatred, by envy, by fear, by the brutalization of power, that turned Grandier's enemies into judicial murderers. In the end, like so many of the possessed, they died of the frenzy that—Huxley would argue—sprang from the fact that they had chosen separation—from God and thence from their fellow men—rather than seeking the way of unity. For Sister Jeanne no such unequivocal fate impends. After her devils depart, she parades around France with a chemise which she claims is impregnated with miraculous Holy Oil and Bovarizes in the role of a second Santa Teresa. On her death, her head is placed in a reliquary in the Ursuline Convent, and, unrecognized by the Church, she becomes the object of one of those ambiguous popular cults that centre on reputed saints who retain a whiff of the brimstone.

Grandier and Sister Jeanne were ordinary people thrown into a prominence that in an age which did not believe in sorcery they would never have achieved. Grandier transcended his unworthy self through suffering; Sister Jeanne remained a fool to the end. Surin, on the other hand, was the kind of character who delighted Huxley—a true saint and a genuine contemplative, intelligent and highly literate, but in some ways so humanly stupid that he was capable of a hundred pathetic follies, superstitious and neurotic to the point of paralysing hysteria, 'psychic' in the popular sense of being acutely aware of supernatural evil, and intensely conscious of the negative impulses that lurked under the surface of his consciousness awaiting the call to emerge.

> At one and the same moment he was aware of God and of Satan, he knew beyond all doubt that he was eternally united with the divine Ground of all being, and yet was convinced that he was already and irrevocably damned.

Here was a real-life saint, a good deal more complicated than Saint Catherine of Siena, and infinitely more interesting than the tedious home-made saints—Miller, Propter, Rontini—of Huxley's own rather defective inventiveness. Surin was even more appealing than Maine de Biran, because the role which fate had picked for him was more fantastic. He was a startling example of the fool who, persisting in his folly—and there can have been few follies greater than the grim comedy of credulity that made him convinced of damnation—in the end becomes wise and hears the trumpets sounding him into the city of silence. For a long period Surin was treated by his fellow Jesuits as a madman, and the therapeutic methods of the seventeenth century —described by Huxley in another of his interpolated essays—were so inhuman that he showed no signs of recovery until one priest more humane and more intuitively understanding of neurosis took him under his care and nursed him back towards sanity.

In the end—with such skill and feeling does Huxley treat his story— one becomes so involved in the agonies of Surin that it is with a shadow of Huxley's own empathy that one follows his final upward way towards the light. But there is a disquieting afterthought, for one realizes that, in spite of all Huxley has said in *The Perennial Philosophy* about the healthy body and the healthy mind that are necessary for mystic sainthood, in spite of the almost muscular-Christian healthiness of Miller and Propter, the only saint he convincingly presents to us is clearly a man sick in body and unbalanced in mind. Huxley's fascination with the morbid seems here to have carried him beyond his own argument. Why in such a man as Surin, one wonders, should his intuitions of beatitude be accepted as objectively more real than his sense of certain damnation? Why, as the radical Buddhist mystics would have asked (a point Huxley always forgets when he includes them among his perennial philosophers), should this kind of experience of eternity be seen as more significant than Grandier's experience of time? Such questions, of the importance to be attached to experience that can only be subjectively apprehended, recur with growing frequency as we move into Huxley's final years.

CHAPTER TWELVE

Shadows in the Void

I

Huxley approached his last decade under the returning shadows of the past. In 1951 he suffered an attack of iritis, and was confined to a dark room; he would never again be free from eye trouble. And in an agony that lasted for more than three years another nightmare of his childhood was re-enacted; in 1952 Maria, like his mother, was attacked by cancer and the treatments merely postponed an end for which both she and Aldous prepared themselves; she died in March 1955, with Huxley beside her, trying to ease her way into the light of eternity.

Through these misfortunes Huxley showed a rare stoicism. The loss of Maria, to whom he had been more attached than to any other person since the death of Trevenen, affected him deeply. But his philosophy taught him not to dwell in sorrow in the past, and a year after her death, in the spring of 1956, he married an Italian musician, Laura Archera; she was twenty years younger than he. The wedding took place at the Drive-in Wedding Chapel in Yuma, Arizona.

During these years, ill luck followed Huxley like that 'grim shape' from Wordsworth's *Prelude* which had always fascinated him, 'with purpose of its own/And measured motion like a living thing'. His son's marriage, which at first seemed happy, ended in divorce. Efforts to earn what he called 'real dough' came to nothing; he spent many months on a stage version of his novella, *The Genius and the Goddess*, only to achieve box-office failure; a script he wrote for a musical of *Brave New World*–he hoped Stravinsky would compose the score– did not even reach the stage. When his house burnt down in 1961, the tangible records of his past were destroyed–his letters, note-books and manuscripts, all except the unfinished typescript of his last novel, *Island*, which he rescued with a curious disregard for anything else. 'You are looking at a man without a past,' he said to one of his friends, and to Robert Hutchins, who had offered hospitality until he could find a new home, he remarked:

> It is odd to be starting from scratch at my age. .... I am evidently intended to learn, a little in advance of the final denudation, that you can't take it with you.

All these misfortunes he accepted with a serenity which did not leave him when he in turn was attacked by the disease that killed his mother and his wife. The cancer of the tongue from which he died manifested itself first in 1960; as in Maria's case early hopes of successful treatment proved in vain; an operation in 1962 failed to halt the progress of the disease, and he finally died in November 1963, showing an exemplary calm through all the stages of his decline. His death fitted the pattern of his final years, when, as Julian Huxley and others have witnessed, he showed an exceptional gentleness and understanding in his relations with others.

Huxley would have been the last to lay any claim to sanctity, and there were aspects of his life, such as his anxiety for theatrical success, which showed that he never attained complete non-attachment, just as his mystical experience never moved beyond the lesser ecstasies. Huxley remained, despite his wishes, an intellectual to the last, as sceptical of his own experiences as he was of the dogmas of others, yet, with that blind spot of faith which most intellectuals possess at some point of their field of vision, willingly accepting not merely the accounts other mystics gave of their experiences (which were obviously subjectively true) but also their rationalizations of them (which were not necessarily objectively correct). Yet, precisely because the beliefs he now treasured were linked with no rigid system of dogma, and because it is impossible to concentrate indefinitely on something higher than oneself for a long period without absorbing its qualities, he was probably a morally better as well as a happier man in that last decade than in the years when he was conscious merely of living in a meaningless universe without even enough desperate faith in man to adopt the dramatic and defiant stance of a Malraux or a Camus.

But, as Huxley himself said in the essay on Gesualdo ('Variations on a Musical Theme') which he wrote in 1956, 'between an artist's work and his personal behaviour there is no very obvious correspondence. The work may be sublime, the behaviour anything from silly to insane or criminal. Conversely the behaviour may be blameless and the work uninteresting or downright bad.' He goes on to remark that there is no connection between any other kind of merit and artistic merit, and that 'talent is a gratuitous grace.'

The remarks apply to Huxley himself, as an artist. His late fiction reflects the virtues of charity and understanding by which he sought to rule his personal behaviour. No former friends are pilloried; no hurt relatives have cause to protest the dragging of skeletons out of family cupboards. But, while nothing Huxley ever wrote could be dismissed as merely 'uninteresting' or 'downright bad' (there was always enough intelligent discussion to preserve interest and enough craftsmanship to avoid complete failure), neither *The Genius and the Goddess*, which appeared in 1955, nor *Island*, which appeared seven years later, can really count as an example of the art of fiction, even in the limited Huxleian application of the fiction of ideas. Every other aspect of these works is cavalierly sub-ordinated to the didactic intent; character and action are sketched in with cartoon crudeness, and the subtleties of mood and tone hardly survive under the battering floods of talk. The grace of artistic talent appears to have been withdrawn, or perhaps, more exactly, to have atrophied in the shadow of more compelling interests.

For the interesting fact is that his power of aesthetic appreciation remains, though rarely used. In Huxley's last collection of essays, *Adonis and the Alphabet*, there are only two examples of true criticism, but both are excellent in his characteristic biographical-psychological manner. 'Doodles in a Dictionary' is one of the most sensitive appreciations ever written of Henri de Toulouse-Lautrec, while the essay on Gesualdo evokes with sombre eloquence both the agonized personality of that murderer, masochist and musical genius, and his setting of Renaissance Italy in which the transition between medieval and modern music took place. Significantly, however, Huxley does not write in this volume on literature, though he does write on the imprisoning of thought by language. One is astonished, in fact, to realize that thirty years have passed since the introduction to Lawrence's *Letters* and that during this time Huxley has published no formal essays on literary art, though, to be sure, his well-stocked mind was always throwing up passing references in his novels and elsewhere to books and their writers. Only at the very end of his life did he return to the consideration of the art he himself had practised, when he wrote *Literature and Science* in the early months of 1963 and completed on his deathbed the essay on 'Shakespeare and Religion'. One has the impression—and there are enough oblique remarks to confirm it—that

Huxley came to regard literature as a lesser art: that he felt that words, and especially words presented in an alphabetic as distinct from a pictographic language, emphasized the separateness of things and tended to increase man's knowledge but to diminish his understanding whereas in painting it was easier for an artist to see things as they are, shining in their own essential nature, and to render them according to their proper rhythms. Needless to say, this meant that he rejected abstraction in art as much as in science, for to him the ultimate purpose of art–as he remarked in 'Doodles in a Dictionary'–was to convey 'the underlying rhythm of the mysterious spirit that manifests itself in every aspect of our beautiful, frightful, unutterably odd and adorable universe',[1] and that aim could not be achieved by the separation from the natural world which abstraction involves.

2

Huxley's diminution as a novelist was linked with the lessening of his interest in one among the three elements into which our natures, in his view, were divided. It is impossible to remain a good writer of fiction unless one is passionately and dominantly interested in the humanity of men. The early Huxley was so interested, and it was the dynamic balance between his desire to illuminate human psychology and his desire to embody ideas in fiction that produced the good novels up to *Eyeless in Gaza*. A kind of cynical misanthropy even then contributed its sardonic tone to his view of existence, but it was different from the view of the later Huxley that the human element in man's makeup was especially dangerous, and capable of infinite moral evil, because of the human craving for separateness, which meant a failure to live in harmony with the nature of things. Most human beings, he states in *The Perennial Philosophy*, are in a chronically improper relation 'to God, Nature and some at least of their fellows'.

> The results of these wrong relationships are manifest on the social level as wars, revolutions, exploitation and disorder; on the natural level, as waste and exhaustion of irreplaceable resources; on the biological level, as blindness to divine Reality and complete ignorance of the reason and purpose of human existence.

[1] I quote from the ending to the essay as published in *Tomorrow and Tomorrow and Tomorrow*. Owing to the varying demands of editors in New York and London, an abbreviated and impoverished ending appears in the English version in *Adonis and the Alphabet*.

The organic world proceeds by its natural and predictable rhythms, and the spiritual life exists as an emanation of the inspiring intelligence of the universe. But it is man as a self, free from the imperatives of instinct yet lacking experiential knowledge of the divine, who is the unpredictable, destructive element in the harmony of the world.

The solution, Huxley contends, cannot be found on a purely human level. Righteousness, without 'total selflessness and God-centredness', merely makes Pharisees. And, while one can propagandize for pacifism and devise the kind of decentralist society that will give the slightest opportunity for the power urge to take root, this in itself is not enough, since it leaves out of account man's relation to Nature and his relation to God, on which depend not merely the spiritual life of the individual, but also the physical survival of the race.

In *Island*, the Utopian novel he had kept in his mind since 1940, and on which he began serious work in 1956, we shall see Huxley attempting to bring the organic, the human and the spiritual together in a harmonious way of life. And all his work during the decade from 1952 to 1962, even where it is not a deliberate preparation for *Island*, in fact leads towards that novel. On the one side are the political essays inspired by a sense of the urgency of crises produced by over-population, environmental destruction and depletion of vital resources. On the other side is the quest for spiritual understanding that leads him to dabble in parapsychology and to experiment with psychedelic drugs. Out of the former side of his activity came *Adonis and the Alphabet* and *Brave New World Revisited*. The latter produced the two brief volumes on experiences with hallucinogenic drugs, *The Doors of Perception* and *Heaven and Hell*.

One's immediate thought on reading *Adonis and the Alphabet* is that, even if Huxley the artist died after *Eyeless in Gaza*, Huxley the prose craftsman remained as much alive as ever. The discussion is brilliant; the style is vigorous and economical; and the insistence that the perennial philosophy provides the only way out of our troubles, while it is rarely absent, is equally rarely obtrusive.

Almost all these essays were written with a double purpose. With his production of books declining, and the film studios providing such unsure largesse, Huxley was obliged to return to the regular journalism he had practised in the 1930's, and from the end of 1954 to early 1957 he contributed a series of articles to *Esquire*, the best of which, with a few unpublished pieces, and a couple of essays written *con amore* for *Vedanta and the West*, were collected in *Adonis and the*

Alphabet. Many of them are occasional pieces, starting off from books Huxley had read or places he had visited, and the collection has no formal unity, though there is the same kind of loose unity of intent which existed earlier in *Do What You Will.*

The essays are mostly written in a discursive form. Huxley would take a book, a detail of travel, a historical incident, and use it as the point of departure for a series of loosely related reflections on which the mind would soar into the realms of generalization. 'Faith, Taste and History' begins with the Huxleys driving through Nevada in driving gusts of untimely snow, and finally coming into Utah, to the great Mormon capital beside the glittering lake of salt. At the sight of the vast but abysmally ugly temple of Salt Lake City, built by faith-inspired men in the days when ox wagons were still the principal means of transport in the west, Huxley goes into a meditation on the relationship between faith and taste, which leads him to a consideration of church architecture, and to the conclusion that religious enthusiasm and the traditions of high art are less closely linked than we like to believe. The Mormons and many other nineteenth-century American religious sects believed just as strongly as medieval man, but, because there was no living American tradition of architecture, there were no splendid cathedrals like those of thirteenth-century France. Inside the temple, Bach is played on the great organ built from trees cut in the Rockies a century ago, and Huxley speculates on the music the original Mormons played, and realizes that even between the arts there are no certain links. The Victorian age was a period of passable taste in music and bad taste in the visual arts. Indeed, to talk of 'ages' in intellectual or artistic terms is largely a fiction, since, though we all live in the same objective time, we do not all live within the same *Zeitgeist*; it may even happen that within the same person there are several selves living each according to a different *Zeitgeist.* And Huxley ends the essay by returning us from the general to the particular and serving up an old Mormon who lives mentally in the age of Brother Juniper, so naïve are his thoughts of heaven, and a couple of tourists whose primitive reactions would have seemed fitting in the caves of Neanderthal man.

In such an essay there is none of the indiscipline of mere free association, yet the movement of thought is flexible, and the interaction of the particular and the general is preserved in a way that not only attracts the attention of the reader, and thus is rhetorically successful, but also exemplifies in practice Huxley's philosophic view, that in human matters we must never lose sight of the concrete in an excess of abstract thought, any more than we should allow our concern for the particular to lead us into the impasse of specialization.

Specialization is certainly not Huxley's weakness, for in these late essays he is as much the polymath as in any of his earlier writings. The opening ceremony at a fish cannery provokes a series of reflections on the effect of climatic changes on the habits of fish, and of these in turn on the prosperity of maritime nations–a reminder of how far we are dependent on our natural environment. An abandoned silo in the California desert leads him into the calamitous history of the socialist community of Ozymandias which briefly flourished there, and thence to a series of reflections on the reason why some communities fail and some succeed. The communities that succeeded, he believes, were those which had some kind of ritual which acted therapeutically on group differences and individual neuroses, and one community, that of Oneida, interests him so much that in an appendix to the book he returns to consider the solution to the problem of sex by the practice of Male Continence which was introduced by the leader, John Humphrey Noyes. This essay, 'The Desert', shows Huxley immersed in the Utopian preoccupations that led to *Island*, while an essay inspired by Mother's Day leads to ancient Levantine fertility goddesses, and is clearly related to *The Genius and the Goddess* with its special treatment of the 'eternal feminine'.

Education, as always, is a leading preoccupation with Huxley, and the two opening essays of *Adonis and the Alphabet*, 'Education of an Amphibian' and 'Knowledge and Understanding', are concerned with the prime problem, which, as Huxley sees it, is to harmonize the many selves and not-selves that man contains, a task that can be performed satisfactorily only if the ego learns to let go, and if the conscious mind allows itself to accept the guidance of the unconscious, as it does, of course, in any creative process. Mere knowledge is not enough. The failure of universal education to improve the condition of man is evidence of that.

> Today everybody *can* read and write, and we find ourselves living in a world where war is incessant, liberty on the decline, democracy in peril, a world moreover where most of the beneficiaries of universal education read only the tabloids, the comics and murder mysteries.

What has to be discovered is a way in which human beings can enjoy the best of what Huxley calls, with personally evocative imagery, 'the small, bright world of personal consciousness and the vast mysterious world of the unconscious' which can achieve things impossible for the unaided ego. This requires a liberation from the tyranny of words and conditioned reflexes, the re-establishment of 'direct, unmediated contact with experience', and the establishment of a state of mind in which understanding, a spiritual quality that cannot be acquired by deliberate intent, may come to us.

But, important as education may be, it cannot alone avert the human and natural catastrophe which will ensue if the growing population of the world, with all it means in the mounting depletion of natural resources, is not stabilized. One essay, 'Tomorrow and Tomorrow and Tomorrow' (which gave its title to the American edition of *Adonis and the Alphabet*), is a survey of recent studies by men of science in the 1950's on the kind of future humanity can expect. Their views are little more optimistic than those of the more strident prophets of the 1970's, and Huxley himself, while he cannot give up his faith in the power of life to continue, is not at this point especially sanguine regarding the physical prospects of the human species. As for the political prospects, he foresees scientific dictators using parapsychology and every other means of conditioning the human mind in the psychological revolution to end all revolutions.

We have had religious revolutions, we have had political, industrial, economic and nationalistic revolutions. All of them, as our descendants will discover, were but ripples in an ocean of conservatism—trivial by comparison with the psychological revolution towards which we are now so rapidly moving. *That* will really be a revolution. When it is over, the human race will give no more trouble. ('Miracle in Lebanon')

It is this final revolution that is the subject of *Brave New World Revisited*, whose conclusion regarding the future of man as a free being is hardly less pessimistic. The mood of this book, most of whose material appeared originally as a special supplement to *Newsday*, is one of urgent warning. *Brave New World* itself looked with a dispassionate eye on a future that might take place centuries ahead. But by 1958 Huxley sees the situation completely changed; conditions unforeseen in 1931 have immensely accelerated the tendency towards universal totalitarianism.

The main danger is the biological one—the drastic lowering of the death rate in the poorer countries, which has brought a rise in population that proceeds by geometric rather than arithmetic progression.

Rising population means in turn that any increase in agricultural productivity is cancelled before it can have beneficial effects; the resultant situation of permanent biological crisis encourages the other great enemy to human freedom, over-organization, already too far advanced in the industrial nations.

As a result of these pressures, Huxley sees the possibility of a totalitarian world in twenty years' time, which brings one to 1978, six years before Orwell's doomsday. And, while he admits that in 1948 the brutal world of *1984* 'seemed dreadfully convincing', Huxley in 1958 believes that because of recent developments in psychological techniques a world like that portrayed in *Brave New World* is after all more likely. For persuasion is more effective than force, and rulers now have in their hands all the basic techniques for the creation of a foolproof system of mental conditioning. Moreover, while in the Thirties when he wrote *Brave New World* men were acutely concerned for their liberties, in 1958 'even the desire for this freedom seems to be on the wane'. What Huxley did not take into account was the volatilization of opinion that came with the appearance of television and the civil rights campaigns of the early 1960's, which between them resulted in an apparent thaw of the conformity rampant in the McCarthy era. Whether in the long run this will make any difference is another question. The young of today seem just as suggestible in their own way as those of the 1950's, and their vaunted counter-culture appears on examination to be merely a counter-conformity. Huxley's placing of *Brave New World* in time may, like Orwell's, be pessimistic, but unless the political crises caused throughout the world by demographic changes are quickly solved there seems no alternative to a totalitarian world that will mean the end to civilization as we have known it in the western world since the Renaissance; the great civilization of China has already succumbed, and ours shows every sign of following.

What Huxley presents in *Brave New World Revisited* is no longer a working model of an anti-Utopia, but a series of essays examining various techniques of persuasion and suggestion already being developed in the 1950's. He argues that these alone, once they have been perfected, would be enough to end freedom for ever.

And indeed, when one remembers how successfully a majority of Germans were conditioned by the Nazis for more than a decade, with the crudest of propaganda methods, and when one witnesses the speed with which the most absurd of modern cults spread across the world on the wings of television, it seems likely that a planned effort of the rulers in any modern country, accompanied by the legalization of hallucinogenics and the widespread use of modern detection devices, could produce in less than a generation the kind of docility of which every past dictator has dreamed in vain. Add the more esoteric techniques of subconscious persuasion, both in the waking and sleeping states, and there seems no reason why man should not be for ever enslaved. No reason, except that man is an embodied but free spirit, whose tendency to rebel in the long run, as the witness of Russia shows, seems irrepressible while the species itself is left unchanged. It is only the kind of pre-natal conditioning envisioned in *Brave New World* itself, in which the beings produced from bottles are so changed that they are no longer *Homo sapiens*, that will permanently keep men down. The changeover from mere suggestion and persuasion to complete biological conditioning would doubtless be the most difficult transition for the World Controllers of a hypothetical future to effect. But, once it were carried out, hope would end. For, as Huxley remarks: 'Under a scientific dictator education will really work–with the result that most men and women will grow up to love their servitude and will never dream of revolution. There seems to be no good reason why a thoroughly scientific dictatorship should ever be overthrown.'

Yet even if, as Huxley fears, 'the forces that now menace freedom are too strong to be resisted for very long', he argues that we must still do what we can to resist them, since he believes that 'without freedom, human beings cannot become fully human', by which, of course, he means spiritually enlightened. But the means he can offer are far from impressive. As a pacifist he does not suggest violence, which in any case is self-defeating in a battle for freedom, as every revolution has shown. Education to resist persuasion, the fight against over-population, the attempt to establish a communitarian alternative to the over-organization of a centralized society: they are no more than the programme he advocated more than a decade before in *Science, Liberty and Peace*, and he presents them without any illusions about the ease with which they may be implemented. For, fundamentally, he doubts if the people–even the young–really want freedom.

3

Because of the limitations of mere words, even in their most extended connotations, Huxley sought the spiritual world not only in the books of the mystics, but also by associating with other seekers of like mind, and by practising the disciplines that might lead towards enlightenment. His friendships with Gerald Heard, Alan Watts and Christopher Isherwood, who were following similar quests, was supplemented by a loose association with the Vedandists, though, apart from them, he avoided the esoteric cults that flourished in California. He took a growing interest in parapsychology, corresponding at length with J. B. Rhine, and forming a friendship, which lasted the remainder of his life, with the American medium Eileen Garrett. He became a fervent defender of hypnosis, and he was one of the first to experiment in the 1950's with the psychedelic drugs.

This is an aspect of Huxley's later life which it would be easy, given the drug cult that has proliferated in the years since he died, to present sensationally. But Huxley embarked on this course neither to gain sensation for himself nor to provoke it in others. In his encyclopaedic reading, even before he turned towards mysticism, he had realized the importance in certain non-Christian religions of visionary experiences induced by the taking of drugs. He had also heard, since coming to the United States, circumstantial reports of the use of the cactus known as peyote in the ceremonials of a semi-pagan Indian church in New Mexico. He realized that the ways to enlightenment were many; that prayer and meditation in themselves were only techniques, and that there could be other techniques–mortification was one of them– which might more effectively break down the resistances of the ego and serve to 'cleanse the doors of perception'. From all the accounts he had heard certain drugs might also fulfil this function, and when he did experiment first with mescalin and then with LSD, it was partly in the hope that this might bring him nearer to the enlightenment he desired for himself, but partly also because he was a seeker after knowledge.

Huxley never exaggerated the importance of his experiment or of its outcome. The two books he did write on the subject were modest in size and tone alike. He never claimed that in drugs lay the universal panacea, that man would be saved by the 'chemical revolution', as some of his more flamboyant successors have done. Indeed, having published his two small works, he deliberately avoided becoming involved in public controversy on the subject. In 1956 a friend of mine, a television producer, invited Huxley to visit Vancouver and make a film on mescalin. Huxley accepted and then withdrew; later, when his letters were published, I was interested to read his reasons, which fitted both the genuinely scientific side of his interest in drugs, and his natural inclination to avoid the sensational.

Mescalin, it seems to me, and the odder aspects of mind are matters to be written about for a small public, not discussed on TV in the presence of a vast audience of baptists, methodists and nothing-but men plus an immense lunatic fringe, eager to tell you about *my* revelation and to get hold of the dope on its own account. One gets plenty of lunatic fringe even after the publication of a two and a half dollar book; after a gratuitous broadcast, it would be overwhelming.

Under the supervision of Dr. Humphrey Osmond, the recipient of this letter and a Canadian pioneer in the study of the effects of psychedelic drugs on schizophrenia, Huxley first took mescalin in May 1953. Later he experimented with LSD. He continued at intervals to take both drugs until the end of his life, and he remained deeply interested in any experiments that went on in this field.

As late as *The Devils of Loudun* in 1952, listing drugs among the 'toxic short cuts to self-transcendence', Huxley had said: 'In every case, of course, what seems a god is actually a devil, what seems a liberation is in fact an enslavement. The self-transcendence is invariably downward into the less than human, the lower than personal.' Later in the same book he returns to the perils of drug-taking: 'This is a descending road and most of those who take it will come to a state of degradation, where periods of sub-human ecstasy alternate with periods of conscious selfhood so wretched that any escape, even if it be into the slow suicide of drug addiction, will seem preferable to being a person.'

The change in his attitude came about partly because he had learnt that peyote, and the synthetic drug mescalin which reproduced its properties, were not addictive and did not appear to pose any grave threat to bodily or mental health. Perhaps after all, he felt, this was the euphoric drug without unpleasant consequences on which he had speculated in *Music at Night*. And the fact that peyote played a part in the rituals of primitive mystics in New Mexico gave it a fascination which, in his search for an elusive enlightenment, he appears to have found irresistible. Hypnosis, autohypnosis and systematic meditation had all apparently failed to produce the results he desired; now he turned to drugs in the hope that 'I might so change my ordinary mode of consciousness as to be able to know, from the inside, what the visionary, the medium, even the mystic were talking about.'

It is difficult to determine how much Huxley did in fact learn from his experiments; certainly *The Doors of Perception* reveals little more than the poverty of his natural equipment for metaphysical explorations. He describes in some detail his reactions to that first experiment with mescalin. What he had expected were visions in the mind's eye; to see the drab inner world of the poor visualizer he was, 'transformed into something completely unlike itself'. This did not happen; he visualized as poorly under mescalin as without it. For him mescalin produced neither hallucinations nor visions. 'The great change was in the realm of objective fact. What happened to my subjective universe was relatively unimportant.'

What he in fact perceived was a transfiguration of the world outside, so that everything seemed to shine with the 'Inner Light' of its own 'Suchness', and through these miraculously intensified colours, these forms preternaturally significant of themselves, he gained a joyful sense of 'the glory and wonder of pure existence'.

One is left, after reading *The Doors of Perception*, with the impression that Huxley's experiences may have been little different from those which others have enjoyed repeatedly without the stimulation of drugs. For a long period during my late adolescence and even into my early twenties I had the ability, almost at will, to see landscapes, buildings and natural objects with the kind of transfiguring irradiation which Huxley's description would exactly fit, reaching at times an ecstatic intensity, and even now, in my fifties, there are occasions, when I am in an unfamiliar country, on which the mood and the light can combine to produce a similar experience, though now it is involuntary, while thirty years ago it would often be voluntary.

This is the kind of grace that comes to many people who have no inclination to interpret it religiously or to regard it as a stage on the way to mystical experience. It is the seed of much painting and most poetry, as Huxley freely acknowledges in both *The Doors of Perception* and *Heaven and Hell*, and it is probably necessary for any deeply felt pantheistic belief. Huxley greeted it with so much delight because he had experienced nothing like it since the days of his childhood before the curtain of blindness fell.

Reading these two little books, one is led to believe that the form Huxley's experience took was intimately linked with his physical disabilities. It is *vision* in the literal sense that he is telling us about: something he sees with his physical eyes, those sick and inadequate organs, but more intensely than ever before. His inner vision is in no way involved; his other senses only slightly. Whatever he learns from the experience is in fact tied to the senses and mainly to one sense. There is never the suggestion of some disembodied faculty, some spiritual organ such as the real mystics suggest as the means by which they perceive the Clear Light of the Void.

That the experience of taking psychedelic drugs is not the whole way to enlightenment Huxley is ready to admit; the taker becomes so involved in his experiences that he is no longer concerned about other human beings, and so the moral element in the path to enlightenment, that compassion for which the Bodhisattvas rejected *nirvana*, is absent. Thus the spiritual gain from taking mescalin is only partial, and Huxley sees its value as a means of supplementing 'systematic reasoning' with at least a degree of direct perception 'of the inner and outer worlds into which we have been born'. It is, he is ready to admit, no more than a 'gratuitous grace', but it may help on the path to enlightenment, the goal which he describes with summary clarity at the end of *The Doors of Perception*.

To be enlightened is to be aware, always, of total reality in its immanent otherness–to be aware of it and yet to remain in a condition to survive as an animal, to think and feel as a human being, to resort whenever expedient to systematic reasoning. Our goal is to discover that we have always been where we ought to be.

One senses, reading this and other passages in *The Doors of Perception*, that one of the effects of Huxley's taking mescalin and later LSD was, through the enhanced perception it gave him of the natural world, to propel him towards the pantheistic end of the spectrum of perennial philosophy. This feeling is largely supported by the discussion in *Heaven and Hell* of the symbolic importance of landscapes in Taoist mysticism, and the generally visionary character of landscape painting. If one cannot attain the Clear Light of the Void, the next best thing is obviously a world preternaturally illumined, and that brings one very near to pantheism.

4

At times a writer is his own most acute critic; no one has better demonstrated the flaws of *Island* than Huxley himself when he said to a chance correspondent: 'The weakness of the book consists in a disbalance between fable and exposition. The story had too much weight, in the way of ideas and reflections, to carry.'

What Huxley attempted in this final novel was to recapitulate
reconcile the contradictions of a lifetime. Conceived in 1940, medit
for sixteen years before the writing began in 1956, and compl
with difficulty after five years of work, it was meant as a Sum
Philosophica, a final statement on the nature and meaning of
presented in the fictional form which Huxley had always used for
deeper statement of his beliefs. It was incompletely successful,
merely because the load of 'ideas and reflections' was too heavy; ev
Huxley novel had been constructed to carry such burdens. Its fail
was due rather to the inadaptability of a fictional technique, develo
for the ironic criticism of men and societies, to the much more diffi
task of extolling the virtues of an ideal community.

Island was intended as an exemplary novel in the same way as
Genius and the Goddess was an exemplary story, and these two
works of Huxleian fiction are intimately related, since both wro
with a theme that had again moved into the centre of Huxley's vis
–the theme of death. In *Antic Hay*, *Those Barren Leaves* and *P
Counter Point*, the gratuitous and meaningless horror of death
emphasized. *Time Must Have a Stop*, written when Huxley
beginning to accept the belief that the human self may not die v
the body, moves forward to the point where death is presented,
as a fall into nothingness, but as a dividing path along which one
make the choice whether to find one's way into the illimitable sp
of the clear-lit void, or to return through reincarnation into
darkness of life. *The Genius and the Goddess* and *Island* concentrate
the process of dying itself. We can see it as a horror and an injus
to fight against; we can accept it as the end of a process of shedd
attachments. The first view can, by that process of inversion whic
so familiar a feature of human mental developments, lead to the otl
its apparent opposite.

It is to the exploration of this process that *The Genius and the God
is partly if not entirely devoted. In form it is a rather simple re
whose action is narrated to the anonymous reporter by the physi
hero, Rivers; none of Huxley's works reveals quite so boldly
paucity of his powers of visualization, for Rivers spends as much ti
in shallow and bumptious philosophizing as he does in evoking
happenings of which he tells.

As suggested by Huxley's original title, *Through the Wrong End
Telescope*, the real point, which completes as well as denying the m
action of *The Genius and the Goddess*, is not kept for an ironic tv

he end as in the classic story, but is hidden quietly in the beginning,
:n Rivers talks of his dead wife, Helen. 'If you want to live at
ry moment as it presents itself, you've got to die to every moment.
it's the most important thing I learned from Helen. . . . Helen even
1aged to make the best of life while she was dying.' And he
tinues:

)ying's an art and at our age we ought to be learning it. It helps to
ave seen someone who really knew how. Helen knew how to die
ecause she knew how to live–to live now and here and for the
reater glory of God. And that necessarily entails dying to there and
nen and tomorrow and one's own miserable little self. In the process
f living as one ought to live, Helen had been dying by daily instal-
1ents. When the final reckoning came, there was practically nothing
) pay.

other words, non-attachment *in* life makes us non-attached *to* life.
ers's words were written some months before Maria Huxley died,
she was already approaching her end with clear knowledge and
mplary calm, and, while Helen is not a portrait of Maria, there is
doubt that Huxley's involvement in Maria's fate had helped to
n the view of death that Helen embodied. Long ago his mother
rebelled against death and so increased its horror; Maria accepted
nd neutralized it.

t is against Helen's death that Rivers tells of the other death–and
er life–that led him to Helen. This story–of Henry Maartens the
ious physicist and his wife Katy and Rivers as a young man–forms
main substance of the novella. Maartens is a personification of the
itations of science; a genius in advanced physics, he has forgotten
w to solve a simple problem out of Euclid. He is the specialist
ried to absurdity, an exemplar of the inutility of science divorced
m the realities of human life; he can only make contact with that
through the magnificent body and understanding mind of Katy,
young wife, a grown-up version of those strapping young American
uties Huxley had admired on the California beaches when he first
ched America. If Henry is the intellect in need of the flesh, Katy is
suality personified, a veritable fertility goddess who possesses a
ychic' regenerative power over and above the gifts of the flesh.
t it is a power that can be sapped, and is renewed only through
sual enjoyment, which leads her to seduce Rivers, who–in all the
our of his fundamentalism–burns for her with a fiery combination
passion and chastity.

Their affair is not suspected by Henry, but it is by Katy's adolescent daughter Ruth, who has conceived a Swinburnian passion of her own for Rivers, and the whole slight plot struggles to its gory end through a blizzard of moralistic analysis as Katy and Ruth, who have been passionately disputing over Rivers, are both killed when their car runs into a truck. Katy, who had never interested herself in the things of the spirit, is treated by fate with grotesque brutality–'destroyed . . . with every refinement of physical outrage–an eye put out by a splinter of glass, the nose and lips and chin almost obliterated, rubbed out on the bloody macadam of the road . . .'. All this, Rivers believed, was part of the predestination to which Katy's nature had condemned her; it was also an item in his own 'psychological Predestination'. While Henry Maartens soon finds himself another equally dispensable wife, Rivers is haunted at night by the dream and in waking by the vision of Katy destroyed. He fears madness, decides on suicide, and then meets Helen, who rescues him.

It is an oddly Victorian moral tale, even down to using the Calvinist terms of Rivers's childhood, Predestination and Grace, to signify the essentially Buddhist point the story is really making: desire leads us to suffering, and through meaningless death back into the chain of suffering; non-attachment releases us not merely from the things to which we have been attached, but also from anything more than a physical involvement in bodily decay and extinction. In its intent, it seems far from Huxley's earlier and better works of fiction, yet there are resounding echoes from the past: the mutability of personality in which Katy Maartens resembles Grace Peddley; the renewed presentation of sexuality as a destructive element; the portrayal of apparently gratuitous physical horror, once used to suggest the absurdity of all existence, now used in a more restricted way to characterize the destructive meaninglessness of life without enlightenment.

It is hard for any believer, even one who follows the undogmatic course of the perennial philosophy, to avoid the simplicities of a crypto-Manichean view of the world, a division into the elect and the damned, into the forces of Good and Evil. In whatever parallel to Christian categories one might use for a mystical religion, Henry and Katy seem irrevocably among the Goats; Rivers and Helen by election Sheep. And one of the striking features of *Island* is a similar duality: on the philosophical level between true and false religious and social philosophies; on the territorial level between the island kingdom of Pala with its Utopian system based on freedom, well-being and enlightenment, and the neighbouring realm of Rendang with its militarist system based on tyranny, poverty and error; between the characters who project evil and those who project good; and finally, within the Gulliver-like visitor from outside, Will Farnaby, between his unregenerate and unhappy past and the influence of a successful experiment in inspired and balanced living.

In *Island* Huxley is trying to achieve several not entirely compatible ends. The novel is a final statement of philosophy, in which he attempts to neutralize the criticism often made of *The Perennial Philosophy*, that it presented a path towards the truth which could be followed only by a temperamentally limited minority; in *Island* the means are there for every man to find his way towards enlightenment. It is a Utopian fable which portrays an ideally good rather than a badly ideal society, and, by inversion, turns to good purposes many negative aspects of *Brave New World*. It is an attempt to reconsider, in the calm of age, some of the problems, such as sex and death, which had seemed insoluble in youth. It is the last of Huxley's stories of conversion, as we watch Will Farnaby turning from a cynic scarred by the Essential Horror of existence into a seeker after enlightenment. Finally, it is an ironic farewell to Huxley's past; there are many deliberate and playful echoes from the earlier novels, and personal ghosts are laid at last.

Such a multiplicity of aims involved Huxley in an almost impossible task. He was trying to unite two different forms of fiction, the introspective novel of recollection and self-analysis, leading to conversion, and the objective narrative intended to portray and explain, in history and time present, the Utopian society of Pala. The almost inevitable failure to reconcile these aims in structural form detracts from *Island*'s success as a unified vision. The old world of misery represented by Farnaby's past and the old world of villainy represented by the fifth column of Rendang within Pala are far more convincing than the brave new world which this time we are invited to approve. It is the contrast between Tragedy and, if not the Whole Truth in this case, at least the Pleasant Truth, too bland in its sufficiency to be credible or even interesting, and expounded at tedious length by Palanese of all ages in dialogues which have neither the wit nor the Peacockian disputatiousness of the earlier novels of ideas. One longs for an occasional flash of the sardonic humour of Scogan or Cardan; one finds it only in the sinister Voltairian Mr. Bahu, and he happens to be the Ambassador of Rendang and therefore one of the enemy.

Yet, under the creaking expository dialogue and the stilted mechanism of visits to educational and experimental institutions, one discovers within *Island* the blueprint of a way of life which is a good deal more sensible than the action of the novel suggests, Pala is a tropical island – its physical form derived from Huxley's memories of his visit to the Indonesian Archipelago in 1925 – in which, by the accident of a Scottish doctor having been hired by an enlightened Raja in the early nineteenth century, oriental philosophy and western science have mingled, enriching and purifying each other, until both are dedicated to the service of man. The Palanese, whose religion is Mahayanist Buddhism influenced by Tantrist practices, believe in the full acceptance of life.

> If you're a Tantric [one of them says] you don't renounce the world or deny its value; you don't try to escape into a Nirvana apart from life, as the monks of the Southern School do. No, you accept the world, and you make use of it; you make use of everything you do, of everything that happens to you, of all the things you see and hear and taste and touch, as so many means to your liberation from the prison of yourself.

Seen in this light, so many things that in Huxley's past novels (and especially in *Brave New World*) had appeared negative, become means towards enlightenment. Mental conditioning is used to weaken aggressiveness. Drugs provide Everyman with the transfigured vision that is the first step towards the Clear Light of the Void. Sex is turned into a means to communal harmony by the Palanese practice of a form of male continence called *maithuna*, which gives them the joy of sex without its sadness. And death loses its sting, not by being turned into a drugged slipping away out of consciousness, as in *Brave New World*, but by being lived out in awareness of itself and of the light beyond it.

Yet, in spite of Huxley's emphasis on the spiritual implications of Palanese life, the impression that lingers in the mind is that of a very physical Eden, in which men and women live joyfully on the organic level, have learnt to harmonize their volatile human impulses, and use their spiritual alertness mainly to regulate other levels of their existence. One radical change has been forced on Huxley by the decision to portray a complete society susceptible to mystical illumination. He has had to turn the perennial philosophy, that creed of solitary seekers, into a cult, a veritable church, with priests, ceremonies of initiation, and congregational occasions when the taking of the sacred drug – the *moksha*-medicine–becomes a kind of eucharist and when God personified as Siva is worshipped and receives offerings.

On the political level, Pala has carried out all the reforms Huxley suggested in *Adonis and the Alphabet*, *Brave New World Revisited* and, farther back, in *Ends and Means*. There is population control, erosion has been checked, the resources of the land have been conserved, industry is small-scale and localized, nobody is much richer than anybody else, education is based on the ideas of Huxley's favourite unorthodox teachers, Sheldon and Alexander, there is no army, and politics is decentralized. But it is hard, even in the best system, for power not to keep a foothold, and this is the tragic flaw in Pala. The new order was introduced in the nineteenth century by Raja's fiat, and successive Rajas have continued to develop Pala as a Utopian state, retaining a power in practice unused but in theory absolute. The dormant danger is reactivated because the last Raja had married a princess of Rendang, a sinister Priscilla Wimbush who takes up theosophy and detests the life of Pala, with its sexual freedom and its mockery of the gods; she influences her son, the present Raja, so that when he comes of age he adopts the militarist philosophy of neighbouring Rendang and becomes the puppet of Rendang's dictator.

The situation is complicated by oil intrigues in which Will Farnaby, as agent of Lord Aldehyde, betrays the Palanese by arranging a deal which encourages the Rani and Murugan, the young Raja, to stage a coup with the troops of Rendang, The pacifist Palanese give in without struggle: 'the work of a hundred years destroyed in a single night'. It is Will's final betrayal, and ironically it comes at the point when he has become convinced, by argument and experience, of the rightness of the Palanese experiment.

It is Will's Odyssey that links *Island* with the earlier Huxley novels, and which also embodies the author's own reconciliation with his past. For Will brings with him to this island of the blessed all the curses with which life has burdened him as it burdened earlier Huxley characters. He remembers his aunt Mary–who acted as a surrogate mother to him–dying in agony and anger of cancer, as Gumbril's mother–and Huxley's mother–had done. He holds in his mind the betrayal of his wife Molly, a monument of Virtue like Marjorie Carling whom Walter Bidlake betrayed, and the guilt of her death–like that of Katy Maartens–in a car accident. Like so many of the earlier Huxley heroes, he has become enslaved through his own sensuality to a Circean mistress. Sickness, death and sex horrify him as manifestations of meaningless evil, yet in his career of journalist he pursues them all obsessively into the unhappiest parts of the world.

Yet in Pala he sees the very things that have seemed horrors in his own life deprived of their evil. He watches while Lakshmi, the wife of his host, dies in the serene light of awareness of the same sickness that had so repulsively killed his aunt Mary. He sees sex turned into a means of guiltless joy. By psychological and chemical therapy the Palanese rid him of his obsessions. And, though he witnesses the destruction, largely through his own work, of the society he has learnt to love, he is able to reflect: 'And yet the fact remained–the fact of the ending of sorrow as well as the fact of sorrow.'

Despite its tragic ending, *Island* is the happiest of Huxley's books, and the most compassionate. One feels that Huxley has come to terms with a great many things, partly through advancing age and partly through maturing philosophy: with death, with sex, even with the limitations of his own insight and experience. Yet reconciliation and the end of suffering, as Huxley himself had often remarked, are not the subjects of great literature–certainly not of great fiction, which depends on human beings revealed by the chiaroscuro of deep and conflicting emotions. *Island* itself exemplifies this fact. The Palanese are beautiful, well-adjusted people, yet, as individuals, they are un-memorable; their faces merge quickly, like their bad poems, into bland anonymity. It is the unhappy and even the evil characters who remain in one's mind: Will Farnaby in his long and tortured past, Molly his dead wife and Babs his mistress, and the grotesque destructive trio of the Rani, Mr. Bahu and Murugan.

Yet, though Huxley recognized at least in part the flaws which others detected in his last novel, he still thought it 'important', and was distressed when critics condemned it on literary grounds. It was the content in this 'pragmatic dream'– as he once called it– that seemed significant to him–the sketch of the kind of world we might have if we were not involved in seeking power and making wars. Rome was burning, and those who persisted in judging his books on aesthetic grounds seemed like Nero in the poem he had written nearly forty years before, declaring to Sporus:

> Christ died; the artist lives for all . . .
> And while the music plays, God lives.

For Huxley the artist had died in the prophet; the celestial light, that living emptiness, had repelled the strange and fascinating creatures of the human darkness. The austerity of the aspiring mystic had destroyed the austerity of the novelist; dedicated to the spiritual elimination of the self, *Island* was an act of literary self-indulgence, a spare fable turned into an unwieldy manifesto.

To gain one kind of vision means often to lose another. The Clear Light of the Void can, as Huxley sometimes said, be a blinding light; like every other light, it casts its shadows.

Aldous Huxley: A Selective Bibliography

There is no complete and up-to-date bibliography of Aldous Huxley. The best that exists is *Aldous Huxley: A Bibliography 1916-1959* by Claire John Eschelbach and Joyce Lee Shober, with a brief foreword by Huxley himself; it was published in 1961 by the University of California Press. There are few omissions, and virtually all Huxley's books, stories, essays, poems and reviews up to 1959 are fully noted, together with a good selection of the books, articles and reviews devoted to him by other writers. Huxley's many contributions to the ephemeral pages of newspapers are, for the most part, identified merely by the date and name of the paper, without–unfortunately– the title of the article.

Below I list, as a convenience for readers, Huxley's works in volume form, and the books that have been devoted entirely or mainly to him.

I. BOOKS BY ALDOUS HUXLEY

The Burning Wheel. Oxford, Blackwell, 1916.
Jonah. Oxford, Holywell Press, 1917.
The Defeat of Youth and Other Poems. Oxford, Blackwell, 1918.
Limbo. London, Chatto & Windus, 1920. New York, Doran, 1920.
Leda. London, Chatto & Windus, 1920. New York, Doran, 1920.
Crome Yellow. London, Chatto & Windus, 1921. New York, Doran, 1922.
On the Margin: Notes and Essays. London, Chatto & Windus, 1923. New York, Doran, 1923.
Antic Hay. London, Chatto & Windus, 1923. New York, Doran, 1923.
Little Mexican and Other Stories. London, Chatto & Windus, 1924. New York, Doran, 1924.
Those Barren Leaves. London, Chatto & Windus, 1925. New York, Doran, 1925.

Along the Road: Notes and Essays of a Tourist. London, Chatto & Windus, 1925. New York, Doran, 1925.

Two or Three Graces, and Other Stories. London, Chatto & Windus, 1926. New York, Doran, 1926.

Jesting Pilate: The Diary of a Journey. London, Chatto & Windus, 1926. New York, Doran, 1926. (In the American edition the subtitle is changed to *An Intellectual Holiday.*)

Essays New and Old. London, Chatto & Windus, 1926. (A limited edition of 650 copies.) New York, Doran, 1926.

Proper Studies. London, Chatto & Windus, 1927. Garden City, Doubleday Doran, 1928.

Point Counter Point. London, Chatto & Windus, 1928. New York, Literary Guild of America, 1928. Garden City, Doubleday Doran, 1928.

Arabia Infelix and Other Poems. London, Chatto & Windus, 1929. New York, The Fountain Press, 1929.

Do What You Will: Essays. London, Chatto & Windus, 1929. Garden City, Doubleday Doran, 1929.

Brief Candles: Stories. London, Chatto & Windus, 1930. Garden City, Doubleday Doran, 1930.

Vulgarity in Literature: Digressions from a Theme. London, Chatto & Windus, 1930. (This essay never appeared separately in the United States but in 1933 was included in *Retrospect,* q.v.)

The World of Light: A Comedy in Three Acts. London, Chatto & Windus, 1931. Garden City, Doubleday Doran, 1931.

The Cicadas, and Other Poems. London, Chatto & Windus, 1931. Garden City, Doubleday Doran, 1931.

Music at Night, and other Essays. London, Chatto & Windus, 1931. Garden City, Doubleday Doran, 1931.

T. H. Huxley as a Man of Letters. London, Macmillan, 1932.

Rotunda: A Selection from the Works of Aldous Huxley. London, Chatto & Windus, 1932.

The Letters of D. H. Lawrence, edited and with an introduction by Aldous Huxley. London, Heinemann, 1932. New York, Viking, 1932.

Brave New World. London, Chatto & Windus, 1932. Garden City, Doubleday Doran, 1932.

Texts and Pretexts: An Anthology with Commentaries. London, Chatto & Windus, 1932. New York, Harper, 1933.

Retrospect: An Omnibus of Aldous Huxley's Books. Garden City, Doubleday Doran, 1933.

Beyond the Mexique Bay. London, Chatto & Windus, 1934. New York, Harper, 1934.

What Are You Going to Do About It? The Case for Constructive Pacifism. London, Chatto & Windus, 1936. New York, Harper, 1937.

Eyeless in Gaza. London, Chatto & Windus, 1936. New York, Harper, 1936.

The Olive Tree and Other Essays. London, Chatto & Windus, 1936. New York, Harper, 1937.

An Encyclopedia of Pacifism, edited by Aldous Huxley. London, Chatto & Windus (under the auspices of the Peace Pledge Union), 1937. New York, Harper, 1937.

Ends and Means: An Enquiry into the Nature of Ideals and into the Methods Employed for their Realization. London, Chatto & Windus, 1937. New York, Harper, 1937.

After Many a Summer. London, Chatto & Windus, 1939. New York, Harper, 1939.

Grey Eminence: A Study in Religion and Politics. London, Chatto & Windus, 1941. New York, Harper, 1941.

The Art of Seeing. London, Chatto & Windus, 1943. New York, Harper, 1942.

Time Must Have a Stop. London, Chatto & Windus, 1945. New York, Harper, 1944.

The Perennial Philosophy. New York, Harper, 1945. London, Chatto & Windus, 1946.

Verses and a Comedy. London, Chatto & Windus, 1946.

Science, Liberty and Peace. New York, Harper, 1946. New York, Fellowship Publications, 1946. London, Chatto & Windus, 1947.

The World of Aldous Huxley. An Omnibus of his Fiction and Non-Fiction over Three Decades, edited and with an introduction by Charles J. Rolo. New York, Harper, 1947.

The Gioconda Smile: A Play. London, Chatto & Windus, 1948. New York, Harper, 1948. (Under the title of *Mortal Coils*.)

Ape and Essence. London, Chatto & Windus, 1949. New York, Harper, 1948.

Themes and Variations. London, Chatto & Windus, 1950. New York, Harper, 1950.

The Devils of Loudun. London, Chatto & Windus, 1952. New York. Harper, 1952.

The Doors of Perception. London, Chatto & Windus, 1954. New York, Harper, 1954.

The Genius and the Goddess. London, Chatto & Windus, 1955. New York, Harper, 1955.

Heaven and Hell. London, Chatto & Windus, 1956. New York, Harper, 1956.

Adonis and the Alphabet, and Other Essays. London, Chatto & Windus, 1956.

Tomorrow and Tomorrow and Tomorrow, and Other Essays. (The same text as the above.) New York, Harper, 1956.

Collected Short Stories. London, Chatto & Windus, 1957. New York, Harper, 1957.

Brave New World Revisited. London, Chatto & Windus, 1958. New York, Harper, 1958.

Collected Essays. New York, Harper, 1959.

On Art and Artists, edited and introduced by Morris Philipson. New York, Meridian Books, 1960.

Island. London, Chatto & Windus, 1962. New York, Harper, 1962.

Literature and Science. London, Chatto & Windus, 1963. New York, Harper, 1963.

Letters of Aldous Huxley, edited by Grover Smith. London, Chatto & Windus, 1969. New York, Harper, 1969.

2. Books about Aldous Huxley

Henderson, Alexander. *Aldous Huxley.* London, Chatto & Windus, 1935. New York, Harper, 1936.

Shelvankar, Krishnarao S. *Ends Are Means: A Critique of Social Values.* London, Drummond, 1938.

Brooke, Jocelyn. *Aldous Huxley.* London, Longmans, Green, 1954.

Atkins, John. *Aldous Huxley: A Literary Study.* London, Calder, 1956. New York, Roy Publishers, 1957.

Hines, Bede. *The Social World of Aldous Huxley.* Loretto, Pa., The Seraphic Press, 1957.

Huxley, Julian, ed. *Aldous Huxley: A Memorial Volume.* London, Chatto & Windus, 1965. New York, Harper, 1966.

Huxley, Laura Archera. *This Timeless Moment: A Personal View of Aldous Huxley.* London, Chatto & Windus, 1968. New York, Farrar, Straus & Giroux, 1968.

Clark, Ronald W. *The Huxleys.* New York, McGraw Hill, 1968.

Bowering, Peter. *Aldous Huxley: A Study of the Major Novels.* London, Athlone Press, 1968. New York, Oxford, 1969.

Meckier, Jerome. *Aldous Huxley: Satire and Structure*. London, Chatto & Windus, 1969. New York, Barnes & Noble, 1969.

Holmes, Charles M. *Aldous Huxley and the Way to Reality*. Bloomington, University of Indiana Press, 1970.

Brander, Laurence. *Aldous Huxley: A Critical Study*. London, Hart-Davis, 1970. Lewisburg, Pa., Bucknell University Press, 1970.

Index